THE ROMANS

THE ROMANS

THEIR LIFE AND CUSTOMS

E. Guhl and W. Koner

SENATE

The Romans – Their Life and Customs

This edition published in 1994 by Senate, an imprint of Studio
Editions Ltd, Princess House, 50 Eastcastle Street,
London W1N 7AP, England

ISBN 1 85958 055 6
Printed and bound in Guernsey by The Guernsey Press Co Ltd

PUBLISHER'S NOTE
This book was previously published as part of a larger volume entitled
The Greeks and Romans – Their Life and Customs. Senate has now pub-
lished *The Greeks – Their Life and Customs* and *The Romans – Their
Life and Customs* as separate companion volumes. As a consequence,
the page numbering for *The Romans* begins at page 297.

CONTENTS.

———

THE ROMANS.

61. THE design of the Greek temple, in its highest perfection,
was, as we have seen, a gradual development of the dwelling-
house. This simple, necessary, and logical growth of artistic
perfection would be looked for in vain in Roman sacred architecture. The numerous indigenous and foreign elements observable
in the general development of that nation have produced a
variety of forms in their sacred edifices which makes the
methodical evolution of a purely artistic principle, like that of
Greek architecture, impossible. It is true that all the forms of
the Greek temple described by us also occur among the Romans;
at the same time essential differences occur, owing to the above-
mentioned mixture of indigenous and Greek elements in the
national life of the Romans. In speaking of the architecture of
the Roman temple we therefore shall have to consider three
points—viz., firstly, the requirements of the original Italian
religion; secondly, the introduction of Greek forms; and, lastly,
the reciprocal influence of Roman taste and culture on the forms
borrowed from the Greeks, and the modification of the latter
resulting therefrom.

Concerning the religious ideas of the old Italian tribes, we
have to bear in mind that their notions of the Deity did not
approach the human type as nearly as did those of the more
artistic Greeks. The rational and reflecting Romans considered
the gods as the rulers of human affairs and the prototypes of
human virtues. Even the names of the old Italian deities were
identical with those of the particular phases of moral and
physical life protected by them; hence the symbolism and want
of individuality of type in Roman mythology. The notion of the
god as an idealized man into which the Greeks had developed

the original symbolism of their religion was absent from the Roman mind. Roman deities, therefore, were not in want of a protecting dwelling.

Nevertheless, statues of gods and houses for them occur amongst the Romans at a very early period, originating partly in the universal tendency of primitive nations in that direction, partly in the influence of Greek on Italian culture, which dates back to farthest antiquity. But whenever these houses are of purely Italian origin, their form differs essentially from that of the Greek temple. For to the desire of giving protection to the deity another purpose of no less, perhaps even greater, importance was added.

For, instead of humanising their gods, the Romans were intent upon pointing out, in the strongest manner, the divine influence on human affairs. Hence their anxiety to know the will of the god so as to regulate their actions accordingly. This knowledge, however, they did not derive from the utterance of a god-inspired person, as was the case in Greek oracles; the practical mind of the Romans was directed entirely upon obtaining from the gods a decisive Yes or No with regard to a particular action or resolution. Hence the development of augural science, which, by certain signs in the sky, as the flight of birds or the flashes of lightning, determined the positive or negative decision of the divine will. The observation and explanation of these signs most likely belonged originally to the head of the family, in whom centred the authority with regard to both religious and legal questions. As social and political relations grew more complicated, and the prediction of the future itself took the form of a science, the function of an augur seems to have devolved, first upon the king, afterwards on students of the science, who took the official name of augurs, and formed one of the most important priestly colleges amongst the Romans. Individuals were allowed, and representatives of the State compelled, to consult the augurs on all important occasions.

For the observations of these augurs a space in the temple had to be assigned, and protected against the intrusions of the profane. The Romans derived the origin of the science from the Etruscans, in whose theology, it is true, the limitation of the *templum* was determined in its minutest details; it seems, how-

ever, certain that the science itself was common to all old Italian
tribes. The observatory of the augurs was originally a square
piece of ground, enclosed in the simplest and, at the same time,
most appropriate manner. The generic term for such a space was
templum, from an old Italian root related to the Greek word
τέμνειν (to cut off, to border), whence τέμενος, the Greek analogue
of *templum*. In order to enable the augurs to decide the favourable
or unfavourable character of the auspices, the
space alluded to, and, in accordance with it,
the sky, was, by a line drawn from east to
west (Fig. 323, *e, f*), divided into a day and
night side; a second line drawn through it
in a right angle to the first, from north to
south (*g, h*), marked the sides of the increasing and decreasing day, or of morning and
evening. The former line (*e, f*) was called

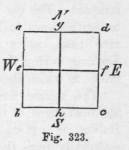

Fig. 323.

decumanus, the latter (*g, h*) *cardo*. The whole space was thus
divided into four equal rectangular regions. The augur stood
in the point of section (*decussis*) of these lines, the regions
taking their different denominations according to the lines.
The cardo divided the space into a right or western half (*a, g, h, b*),
called *pars dextra*, or *exortiva*, and into an eastern one (*g, d, c, h*),
called *pars sinistra*. The former comprised the third and fourth
(0 to 180°), the latter the first and second (180° to 360°), chief
regions; that is, the range of sight of the augur, when turned
towards the south, comprised the south-east on the left and the
south-west on the right. The decumanus, on the other hand,
divided the space into a northern half (*a, e, f, d*), *pars postica*,
lying at the back of the augur, and a southern half (*e, b, c, f*),
pars antica, lying in front of him; that is, the augur looking
towards the east had the north-east on his left and the south-east
on his right. Signs appearing on the left were always considered
as lucky, those on the right as the reverse. This division of the
templum into four chief regions was the common one in the
times of Cicero and Pliny, the older rule being observed no more.
The older division of the temple into sixteen regions originated
with the Etruscans; it implied a close observation of the con-
stellations. This division is of the utmost importance for the
investigation of Roman temples, which, according to Nissen's

clever researches, are by no means all built in the same direction.* The axis of the temple was directed towards the point of the horizon in which the sun rose on the day of the foundation-stone being laid, which coincided with the native day or chief feast of the god to whom the temple was dedicated. This point changes in Italy during the course of the year by 65°, in consequence of which the Italian temples lie in almost all directions of the compass. The old Etruscan rule of building temples from north to south seems to have been adhered to by the Romans only in rare cases, as is proved by Nissen's investigations. As the Romans during their prayer always turned towards the east, the image to which their prayer was directed had to look westwards.

The square form of the templum necessitated an almost identical shape of the temple-enclosure. In this respect the old-Italian, or as it was called by the Romans Tuscan, temple differs essentially from the Greek, the latter being an oblong with a depth almost twice as long as its frontage; in the Tuscan temple the proportion of depth to frontage was 6 : 5. No examples of

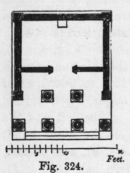

Fig. 324.

the Tuscan temple remain, it having been supplanted by the forms of Greek architecture; but with the assistance of Vitruvius's description (iv. 7) we are able to gain a tolerably clear notion of its appearance. Fig. 324 shows the plan of an Etruscan temple according to Hirt's conjectures. It strikes us at once that inside the cellæ, which occupy about one-half of the whole area, no columns are to be seen. The pronaos has four columns in front, the two corner ones of which correspond with the antæ-pillars. Two other columns are placed between these pillars. Peculiar to the Tuscan style is the slender smooth column seven diameters in height and tapering by one quarter. It has a base divided into two parts, viz., a circular plinth and a torus, of equal height, and a capital consisting of three parts, of equal height. This older form of the column occurs frequently in the decorative semi-columns of later Roman architecture.

62. The design of larger temples was much more varied. The style seems to have attained its climax in the temple of the

* Nissen, "Das Templum." Berlin, 1869.

Capitoline deities, which, according to Roman tradition, Tarquinius Priscus intended for a national sanctuary of the Roman people. He chose for the purpose the highest summit of the Capitoline Hill, which, however, was found insufficient both with regard to size and level surface, and therefore had to be extended and propped by means of enormous substructures. In this manner an all but square area 800 feet in circumference was formed for the reception of the temple, either on the western (present site of the Chiesa Araceli) or eastern (present site of the Palazzo Caffarelli) summit of the hill. The undertaking however, both with regard to working power and expense, was so enormous that Tarquinius Priscus did not even begin the temple itself, which was brought nearer its completion only by Tarquinius Superbus, after (according to some writers) Servius Tullius had made efforts in the same direction. To the Republic was reserved the honour of completing the national sanctuary. M. Horatius Pulvillus, who was consul together with P. Valerius Poplicola in the third year of the Republic, is said to have inaugurated the temple. It stood in its original form for 413 years, when it was totally destroyed by fire.

It was rebuilt by Sulla, essentially unaltered with regard to the original measures and proportions, although modified as to architectural details, as appears from Tacitus's expression: *"iisdem rursus vestigiis situm est"* ("Hist.," iii. 72).* The description, therefore, of the later temple by Dionysios of Halikarnassos (iv., pp. 251, 260) applies to some extent to the original Tarquinian structure. Fig. 325 gives the

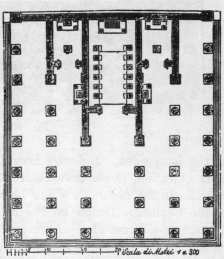

Fig. 325.

plan, Fig. 326 the view, of the temple according to L. Canina's

---

* It was again burnt down during the Vitellian riots, and rebuilt by Vespasian. After this new structure had also been destroyed by fire it was rebuilt, and inaugurated for the fourth time, by Domitian.

conjectural designs. In Fig. 325 we recognise the above-mentioned divisions of the temple into a front and a back half, the former
of which, turned towards the south, is enclosed by columns without
a wall, while the latter contains under a common roof the three
cellæ of the Capitoline deities to whom the temple was dedicated. The centre cella belonged to Jupiter, the two smaller ones
to left and right being assigned to Minerva and Juno respectively.
By diminishing the dimensions of these two latter cellæ, Canina
has succeeded in making his reconstruction to some extent tally
with that part of Dionysios's description according to which the
temple had three rows of columns in front and only two on each

Fig. 326.

of the long sides. Differing from Dionysios, and not quite free
from objection, is Canina's conjecture of there being only six
columns in the façade, to which he was led by the representation
of the Capitoline temple on Roman coins, where it undoubtedly
appears as a hexastylos. At any rate the illustrations offered by
us will give the reader a correct general notion of this and other
temples with three cellæ. For Fig. 326, old Roman and Etruscan
monuments have been consulted to determine not only the columns
and their proportions, but also the beams and their ornamentation
with triglyphs and metopæ. The statues on the gable were, according to Etruscan custom, of burnt clay.

63. So much about the original Roman or Tuscan style of architecture which, as we said before, was founded on the requirements of old Italian worships. The detailed rules given by Vitruvius for the Tuscan order of columns remind one of Greek forms, and may serve to prove Greek influence on this as on other branches of earliest Italian development—an influence which will appear still more distinctly in our remarks about old Italian graves and wall-structures.

In following the further history of Roman civilisation one observes this influence becoming stronger and stronger. During the times of the kings, to which the development of Tuscan architecture belongs, the relations of the two nations were of the simplest kind; a conscious imitation of Greek customs cannot be thought of, least of all in Latium, the poverty and simplicity of whose inhabitants prevented a deeper-going influence in that direction. This, however, was different in Etruria, the political security and greater wealth of which made it more susceptible to the charms of Greek culture. Hence the notion common amongst the Romans, although considerably shaken by modern science, of the Etruscans having introduced Greek culture to them.

After the expulsion of the kings the influence of Greek on Italian manners begins to increase. The time when first the Roman people were enabled to model more fully their political and legal institutions coincided with the highest climax of Greek culture with regard to political, military, and artistic phases of development. No wonder, therefore, that over the whole Italian peninsula a new civilisation, akin to the Greek model, and fashioned after it, began to gain strength more and more. Etruria began to abound with Greek works of art, and even to rival those great models; Apulia had, from the first, followed Greek examples; in Lucania and Campania Greek language and Greek characters of writing prevailed to a great extent—the surest sign of mental affinity. Rome, which always must claim our chief attention, was, by its constitutional struggles and the warlike spirit of its inhabitants, prevented from receiving with a collected mind the germs of Greek civilisation. Nevertheless, the world-conquering power of this civilisation could not wholly be evaded, and we can look for no more striking proof of the civilizing mission of the Hellenes than in the fact of the Romans becoming more and more subjected to their genius, notwith-standing these unfavourable circumstances.

This influence is recognisable in political no less than in legal and commercial matters. After the conquest of Campania, in the fifth century of the city, the knowledge of Greek institutions, formerly limited to individual statesmen and lawgivers, became diffused amongst wider circles. But, besides this strong and ever-increasing intrusion of Greek uses and (but too frequently) abuses, we have to consider another point of affinity which, from the very beginning of this new epoch, became more and more important, particularly as far as sacred architecture is concerned.

We are alluding to the old religious connections between Greece and Rome, which remained unobliterated in the conscious-ness of the two nations—the signs, as it were, of a common origin, and which led to continued intercourse. The want of personality in the old Italian myths was thus supplied from the rich stores of Greek mythological lore, and the worships of certain gods were, by public authority, transferred from Greece to Rome. This enlargement of the religious horizon is not without political signi-ficance. At first the priestly office was entirely monopolized by the patricians; but, with the growing power of the plebeian element, the introduction of new objects of public worship became necessary. The kings already tried to mediate between plebeians and nobles by erecting a centre of national worship, and the frequent intro-duction, in the following centuries, of Greek deities by government was, in a manner, a continuation of this attempt at conciliating these classes.*

The adoption of Greek architectural forms was, therefore, due to religious causes, previous even to the entering of æsthetical considerations into the question. During the last century of the Republic the attachment to the old indigenous form of worship was more and more supplanted by the influence of modern Greek civilisation. This admixture of Greek mythology and, but too often, Greek scepticism soon tended to abolish the deep religious

* The temple of the Capitoline deities must be considered as this centre of *national* worship (Ambrosch, "Stud.," i. 196), independent of patrician exclusiveness. Similar transformations of the Roman religion seem to have been attempted by the earlier Tarquinians. Tarquinius Priscus is said to have erected the first images of gods, and, after him, Servius Tullius ordered the statue of the Aventine Diana to be fashioned after the model of the Artemis of Ephesos, known to the Romans through the Greeks of Massilia.

feeling characteristic of the old Romans. The religious indifference of the upper classes grew into a decided aversion to religion itself, and soon complaints began to be raised of the temples standing empty and being allowed to go to ruin. Augustus restored as many as eighty-two temples, most of them undoubtedly according to the principles of Greek taste, which at that time prevailed in all artistic and poetical creations of the Romans.

Such were the different phases of the influence of Greek on Roman sacred architecture, which gradually led to the entire transformation of the old Italian temple. Indeed, all the different forms of the Greek temple are met with amongst the sacred edifices of the Romans.

The simplest form of the *templum in antis* (see § 5) occurred, according to Vitruvius (III., 1), in a temple of the Three Fortunes, outside the Porta Collina: the prostylos (see § 7) was very frequent. To this we shall have to return (§ 65). Even of the amphiprostylos (see § 8), which was rare amongst the Greeks themselves, and of which Vitruvius mentions no example either in Greece or Rome, we have at least one specimen in the temple on the Forum of Velleja (compare § 82). Of the peripteros (see § 9) Vitruvius mentions two examples, viz., the temple of Jupiter in the Hall of Metellus, and that of Virtus and Honos, also in Rome, which the architect Mutius had built for Marius. The form of the pseudo-dipteros, of which only one specimen exists in Greece (see § 10), was frequently used by Roman architects, as we shall see hereafter. Vitruvius mentions one specimen of the dipteros (see § 12), viz. the temple of Quirinus, erected by Augustus on the Quirinal. It had double colonnades of seventy-six columns, and was counted amongst the most splendid edifices of Rome. Of this temple no traces remain. We, therefore, shall specify the influence of Greek on Augustan architecture by some remains of a Greco-Roman temple at Athens. We are speaking of the beautiful columns standing south-east of the Akropolis, 60 feet in height, and partly still showing their architraves. They belonged to the temple of the Olympian Zeus, the building of which was begun by Pisistratos, but not continued till the reign of Antiochus Epiphanes. On the latter occasion we hear of a Roman knight, Cossutius, acting as architect. The temple was finished by the art-loving Emperor Adrian. Vitruvius, in the preface of his seventh book, says that Cossutius built the walls and the double colonnade, and also covered the beams. The additions of Adrian must therefore have consisted either of the ultimate completion of the last-mentioned parts, or of the decorative arrangements of the interior. Fig. 327 shows the plan of the

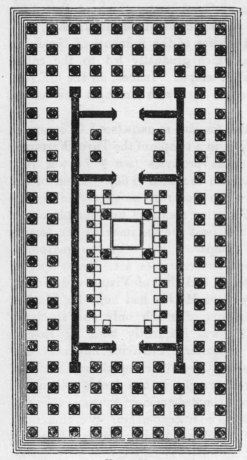

temple. It was a dipteros 173 feet broad by 359 long. Livy (XLI., 20) justly designates it as unique. It had ten columns on the narrow and twenty on the long sides; on the narrow sides it had three rows of columns instead of the two usually found in the dipteros, as may still be seen from the remains. Of the two other orders of the temple, the pseudo-dipteros (§ 13) and the hypæthros (§ 11), there were, according to Vitruvius, no specimens in Rome. The temple of Venus and Roma, however, to which we shall have to return (§ 66), undoubtedly showed the essential characteristics of the pseudo-dipteros; and Vitruvius's own description (III., 2) proves that the just-mentioned temple of Jupiter Olympius was, like the Parthenon in its vicinity, a hypæthros.

Fig. 327.

64. The forms of Greek architecture thus adopted by the Romans were considerably modified by them. These modifications were of a twofold kind. They either originated in the reaction of the Italian on the Greek temple, in which case the

design and local division of the building were affected; or they
were caused by entirely new modes of construction being applied
either to the purely Greek or Greco-Roman temple. In that case
the whole character of the edifice was altered.

Before, however, entering into these more important modifications, we must mention a few minor changes, chiefly with
regard to the order of columns. All the Greek orders of columns
described by us were also used by Roman architects. As examples
of the Doric order, we name the temples of Quirinus at Rome
and of Hercules at Cori: not to mention several other specimens

of the Doric style col-
lected by Canina, "Arch-
itettura Romana," Tav.
67. The graceful forms
of Greek architecture
have, however, been fre-
quently misunderstood;
and have, in consequence,
lost their original purity
and harmonious propor-
tions. The Tuscan order,
frequently used by the
Romans, is itself nearly
related to the Doric style.
It must be explained from
the adoption and partial
modification of the Greek
original by the Etruscans,
from whom it again was
borrowed by the Romans,
the latter developing the
forms thus received into
a system of their own.
The statements of Vitru-
vius, together with some
archaic specimens found
on Etruscan graves (for

Fig. 328.

instance, the fragments of columns of the Cucumella of Vulci), and
other examples of this style in later Roman buildings, enable us

to form a distinct notion of this old-Etruscan order of columns.
It must suffice to refer the reader to the façade of the Capitoline
temple (Fig. 326), which displays the Tuscan order with the
modifications alluded to.

The Ionic order of columns, likewise, is found in Roman
edifices; for instance, in a small temple of Tivoli (see Fig. 330),
and in the still standing temple of Fortuna Virilis in Rome ; also
in that of Saturn in the Roman Forum. The second stories of
both the Coliseum (§ 85) and the theatre of Marcellus are
adorned with Ionic semi-columns; a few specimens of this style
have been found at Pompeii. Almost all these specimens show
more or less important deviations from the pure Greek form.
Particularly, the graceful sweep of the curvatures and the spiral
lines of the volutes have been lost—an observation which also
applies to the large Ionic temples of Asia Minor (see Figs. 9 and
10). A characteristic example of the Roman form of the Ionic
capital occurs in Desgodetz's description of the temple of Fortuna
Virilis in Rome (Pl. III.).

While the Ionic and Doric orders were thus deteriorated by
Roman architects, the Korinthian column, and especially the
Korinthian capital, received a richer and more splendid development at their hands. The peculiarities of this style seem to have
been congenial to the Roman mind; it is, indeed, particularly
adapted to an architecture which derives its effects more from the
grandeur of massive structure than from the harmonious proportions of architectural lines. The capitals are formed by two or
three rows of delicate acanthus-leaves, from between which
appear volutes, flowers, or the forms of men and animals, the
richer development of the beams being in harmony with this
splendid style of ornamentation. This order has been most
frequently applied by the Romans, the greater number of whose
edifices are, indeed, built in the Korinthian style. We have met
with it already in the temple of the Olympian Zeus at Athens,
and shall find it again in almost all the monuments we shall have
to mention. One of the finest specimens of the style is the
Pantheon (see Figs. 342 to 344), a column of which, with the
beam resting on it, is shown in Fig. 328. In later times, the style
became overloaded, and by the addition of Ionic volutes the so-
called "composite capital" was arrived at, of which Desgodetz

(V., 17) and Cameron ("Baths of the Romans," Pl. 30) show examples (compare, also, the triumphal arch of Titus, Fig. 448).

65. The requirements of the old Italian religion led naturally to the adoption of that more or less modified form of the Greek temple which was most suited to its peculiar rites; this form was the prostylos. The Tuscan temple, the frontage of which consisted only of colonnades, so as not to obstruct the view of the sky, was itself a prostylos. At the same time the prostylos could, by means of a simple enlargement, be easily adapted to the demands of Italian worship. This enlargement was effected by adding one or more rows of columns to the one which in the Greek temple formed the portico of the building. In this manner the front part, surrounded only by columns (*pars antica*, § 61), became of almost equal size with the back part (*postica*), occupied by the cella. The door of the cella, therefore, where the augur used to stand, was exactly, or at least

Fig. 329.

very nearly, in the centre of the temple. This form of the prostylos with a far-protruding portico occurs so frequently that it may be called that of *the* Roman temple *par excellence*. As such, it is distinguished from both the Tuscan and purely Greek temples, the elements of which it amalgamates to artistic unity.

The simple form of the prostylos, protruding in front by one column only, is also frequently found amongst Roman edifices, more frequently, indeed, than in Greece, where it was used very rarely. Vitruvius, for instance, mentions no specimen of it in Greece, but two in Rome, viz., the temple of Faunus and that of Jupiter in the Island of the Tiber. Figs. 329 and 330 show the design and view of a small half-ruined prostylos at Tivoli, near the well-known round temple (see Fig. 340 *et seq.*). It is preserved up to the height of the capitals; the wall of the cella is adorned with Ionic half-columns, and therefore appears in the form of

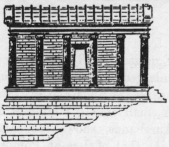

Fig. 330.

a pseudo-dipteros (§ 10), frequently applied by the Romans. On each of the long sides, between the two pairs of centre columns, (counting those of the portico) we see a small window growing narrower towards the top, and adorned with an elegant cornice. According to Canina, from whom our woodcuts are taken, the temple was built towards the end of the republican era, and dedicated most likely to the Sibylla Tiburtina or Albunea.

The first and most natural enlargement was effected by the addition of another column to the projecting one which carried the portico. This form also occurs frequently. Besides the above-mentioned temple of Fortuna Virilis (at present S. Maria

Fig. 331.

Egiziaca) in Rome, the temple of Isis at Pompeii shows this enlarged form of the portico. The all but square size of this temple reminds one of Vitruvius's rules for the Tuscan temple. A small oblong temple at Palmyra, most likely from the time of Aurelianus, shows the same form of the enlarged prostylos. Like that of Isis at Pompeii, it has four columns in the façade, which, together with the two on each side, form the pronaos, almost equal in size to the cella.

The design is more interesting where the portico projects by three columns. This arrangement is shown in the beautiful temple of Antoninus and Faustina, the portico of which is carried by six columns in front and three on each side, each of the columns consisting of one piece of green-veined marble. The walls of the cella, also preserved, consist of the stone called commonly travertine.

Fig. 331 shows an unusually well preserved temple of the same order at Nismes (the old Nemausus), in southern France. It belongs to the best period of Roman architecture, and was erected, according to an inscription on it, by Augustus, in honour of the sons of the faithful Agrippa, Caius and Lucius, adopted by the emperor. The temple, known as *Maison quarrée*, consists of a cella (pseudo - dipteros) adorned with Korinthian half-columns, and a portico formed by six columns in front and three on each side. The beams, in perfect preservation, resting on the wall and the columns, show a frieze with beautiful bas-relief ornaments. The old pediments with their beautiful cornices are also preserved. The interior of the temple is at present used as a museum, in which the numerous antiquities found in and near Nismes are kept.

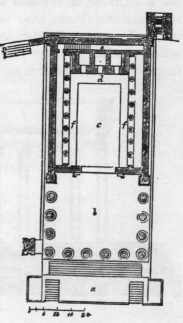

Fig. 332.

A further development of the same principle of Roman architecture appears in the large temple of Jupiter at Pompeii, which at the same time may be considered as one of the finest examples of this style. Fig. 332 (scale 24 Par. feet) shows the plan, Fig. 333 a restored section, of the building. The protrusion of the portico is increased by a further column, six columns standing in front and four on each side. In front of the portico (*b*) lies a platform, with steps leading up to it (*a*), by means of which the whole front part was made equal in length to the back part, in accordance with Vitruvius's rules for the Tuscan temple. The position of the temple from north to south also accords with these rules. Through the door which lay exactly in the centre of the building one entered the cella, on both sides of which there were galleries of eight Ionic columns each (*f f*). In front of the back wall of the cella lay a kind of substructure containing three small cellæ (*d*). The Ionic columns (as appears from Fig. 333) seem to have carried a gallery of Korinthian columns, up to which led a staircase in the back wall of the cella (Fig. 332, *e*). The substructure (*d*) may have supported a statue, the head of which, in the character of Jupiter, has been discovered there. The three cellæ most likely served to keep documents and treasures, as was frequently the case in temples. The walls of the cella were richly

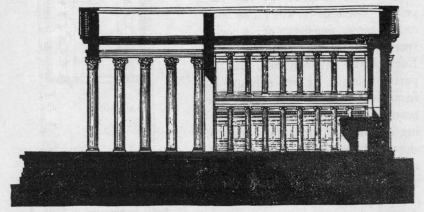

Fig. 333.

painted, as were also the columns of the portico, consisting of lava. The floor of the temple was adorned with mosaic. The temple itself lay in the most beautiful part of the Forum. A tasteful and clever reconstruction of both it and the Forum is found in Gandy's "Pompeiana" (Pl. 51).

In connection with these specimens of the Roman prostylos we mention the temple of Concordia in Rome, differing in design from all other similar buildings. It was built in consequence of a vow made by Camillus after he had spoken in the senate in favour of the claims of the plebeians to the consular dignity. It was intended as a symbol of the restored concord between patricians and plebeians. It lay at the northern end of the Forum

Romanum, close to the enormous foundations of the Tabularium
(see § 81). The remains found on the spot do, however, not
belong to the older temple of Concordia, but to the splendid
temple built by Tiberius on its site. Only the large substructure

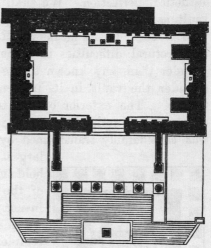

Fig. 334.

of the temple, to which led a
flight of steps from the Forum,
may be recognised by some
remnants of masonry, which,
together with the Capitoline
plan of the city, enable us to
define the original situation of
the building. The entire building (see plan, Fig. 334) formed
an all but regular square
stretching from north to south,
one half of which (*postica*)
was occupied by the transverse cella, while the other half
(*antica*) consisted of the substructure and the portico, pro-
jecting by six columns. The cella was used at the same time
as the meeting-hall of the senate, and therefore was known at
first by the name of *senaculum*, in later imperial times by that
of *curia*. (The same was the case with the cella of the above-
mentioned temple of Jupiter at Pompeii.) To judge by the few
preserved pieces of the architrave, with the cornice, and by the
slabs of painted marble which formed the floor, the beauty and
purity of the style of this temple must have been unsurpassed in
Rome. According to ancient writers, the interior, most likely
the senate-hall, contained twelve statues of gods by the hands of
the greatest masters.

66. The third modification of the Roman temple above referred
to was caused by the introduction of a mode of construction seldom
used by the Greeks, and never on a large scale. It enabled
Roman architects to cover the cellæ of the temples in an imposing
monumental manner. We are speaking of the vault, by the bold
and consistent development of which Roman architecture differs
essentially from the art of the Greeks. We cannot here discuss
whether and when the art of vaulting became known to the

Greeks, or whether it was invented by the Italians. Suffice it to
say, that vaulted buildings occur at a very early period amongst
the Etruscans and other Italian tribes; but that it was left to the
Romans to carry this important principle to its technical and
æsthetical perfection. We shall have frequently to speak of the
vault, as applied to canals, bridges, aqueducts, gates, and triumphal arches. By its means the Romans were enabled to get over
architectural difficulties in a manner differing from, and much
grander than, any known to the Greeks. At present, we must
consider the vault in its influence on the development of the
temple.   The exterior of the temple never displays vaults or
arches in any noticeable manner; the interior, on the other hand,
was considerably transformed by the new principle, even the

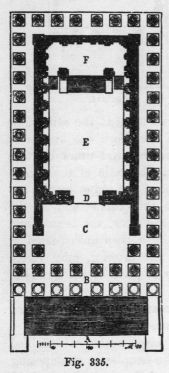

largest cellæ now being spanned by
bold and richly decorated vaults, instead
of the flat *lacunaria*-ceiling formerly
in use. As an example of this style
we mention the smaller of the two
temples at Heliopolis, in Syria, to
the larger of which, the so-called
Temple of the Sun, we shall return
(§ 68). Fig. 335 shows the plan (scale
80 feet English measure), Fig. 336
the view, of a prostylos of the above-
described kind, which, in addition, has
been surrounded by a colonnade. Excepting the front row of columns of the
façade, it has been perfectly preserved.
A flight of steps (A) leads to the colonnade (B), through which one enters
into the pronaos (C), the ceiling of
which consists of a transverse barrel-vault. A splendid door (D), on
each side of which a staircase has been
let into the wall, opens into the inner
cella. It is divided into two parts;

Fig. 335.

the first of which, lying on a level with the pronaos, is spanned
by a bold barrel-vault richly adorned with *laquearia*. The
side walls are adorned with beautiful Korinthian half-columns

enclosing niches. Opposite the entrance lies a raised space (F), up to which seem to have led steps. It was separated from the space in front of it by two columns, and most likely

Fig. 336.

contained the statue of the temple. In the inside of the raised platform is a space evidently destined for the reception of sacred implements and other valuable objects. The style of the archi-

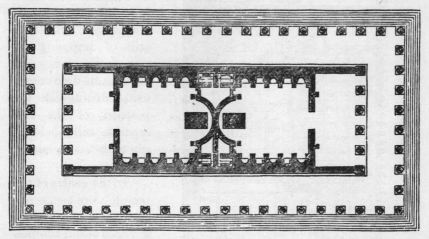

Fig. 337.

tecture is splendid, as was usual under the Emperor Caracalla, who seems to have finished the building begun most likely by his father Severus.

Fig. 338.

The temple of Venus and Roma in Rome shows the same principle of vaulting, although belonging to an earlier period. It is, at the same time, one of the few specimens of a double temple in Roman architecture. It stood between the Forum Romanum and the Coliseum, rising on a strong substructure. It was begun by Adrian, a lover of art, and himself an amateur architect, and most likely finished by Antoninus Pius. It belonged to the most splendid monuments of Rome, and its ruins are still of imposing aspect. These remains at the same time enable us to distinguish the position of the two separate cellæ belonging to the above-named goddesses.

In the centre of the temple were two semicircular niches touching each other, adorned with beautiful semicupolas, and containing the statues of Venus and Roma. One of them was turned towards the west, the other towards the east. Fig. 337

shows the plan of the temple. It must be described as a pseudo-dipteros dekastylos, having ten columns in the façades. The distance of the colonnade from the wall was sufficient to leave space for another omitted row of columns (compare § 13). Each of the long sides had twenty columns. The entrances to the two divisions of the cella lay towards east and west respectively; the entrance to them was through pronaoi, formed by the prolongations of the cella-walls, and by four columns placed between the *antæ* of these walls. The two cellæ were covered by richly adorned barrel-vaults (see Fig. 338), which were in beautiful harmony with the semi-cupolas over the two niches. The side walls contained niches with half-columns enclosing them, additional splendour being produced by coloured tablets of marble. The outside consisted entirely of Prokonnesian marble. Steps led from the Forum to the terrace (500 feet long by 309 wide) on which the temple stood. Some remains of these steps are still in existence. The two long sides had no steps. Fragments of shafts of columns made of grey granite have been found near the edges of the substructure. They tend to prove the existence of a colonnade round the building. The temple itself lay on a separate platform inside the colonnade, by six or seven steps above the level of the substructure

67. In the examples of vaulted temples hitherto cited a so-called barrel-vault was joined immediately to the quadrangular shape of the cella or the pronaos. Another no less important kind of the vault is the cupola applied to circular buildings. The Romans used it frequently, sometimes with great effect.* We have mentioned the round temple in Greek architecture (§ 14), without, however, being able to cite examples of this style, barring, perhaps, the monument of Lysikrates at Athens (Fig. 152) and the conjectural design of the Philippeum of Olympia (Fig. 36). In Rome these buildings were both more frequent and more developed than amongst the Greeks; they indeed form a considerable fraction of Roman edifices. According to Servius (see

* Adler ("Das Pantheon zu Rom," 31. "Programm zum Winckelmannsfest der archæolog. Ges. zu Berlin, 1871, p. 16 *et seq.*), contends that the cupola was an old Oriental, not a Roman, invention. In Alexander's time it attained its climax in Western Asia and Lower Egypt, whence it came to the Romans, who brought it to its highest perfection in the cupola of the Pantheon.

" Æn.," IX., 408), they were dedicated chiefly to the goddesses Vesta and Diana, also to Hercules and Mercury. Vitruvius (IV., 7) mentions two kinds of this temple, one of which he calls monopteros, the other peripteros. The monopteros consists of a number of columns, arranged in a circular form, standing on a base with steps (*stylobat*), and carrying the beams, also circular in shape, and, by means of them, the vaulted cupola, made either of stone or wood. These temples, in the centre of which the statue of the deity was placed, had therefore no separate cella; which want was perhaps supplied by railings between the single columns, as appears from a bas-relief. No specimens of this style are preserved. To judge by a coin of Augustus, the temple of Mars Ultor (not to be mistaken for the splendid temple of later origin) in the Capitol, built by that emperor, was a monopteros,

which form also appears on another coin representing an open temple containing the statue of Vesta (Fig. 339). On the top of the cupola is a flower-like ornament quite in accordance with Vitruvius's statement, who (IV., 7) prescribes a certain measure for this flower (*flos*). The inaccuracy of such representations, however, prevents us from deciding with certainty whether our illustration is not perhaps intended to represent the Roman temple of Vesta still in existence, although that belongs to the second form of round temples.

Fig. 339.

The temples of the second kind also rest on a circular base;

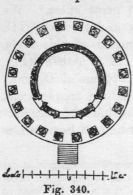

but here the separate columns encircle a round cella, which is covered by a cupola resting on the colonnade. This arrangement is specified by the above-mentioned temple of Vesta, more commonly called the temple of Hercules Victor. It has been transformed into a Christian church (S. Maria in Cosmedin), to which circumstance it owes its preservation. The celebrated temple of Vesta, which now has entirely disappeared, lay at the foot of the Palatine, near the church S. Maria Liberatrice, a little way from the Via Sacra.

Fig. 340.

The ruins of another temple, ascribed to Vesta with more certainty, are found at Tivoli. Its original appearance can distinctly be recognised. It is one of the finest specimens of the class of round temples called by Vitruvius peripteroi. Fig. 340 shows the design, Fig. 341 the view, both after Valladier's drawings of the remains, to which Canina has added the missing parts. The cella is formed by a circular chamber (see Fig. 340), whose wall contains a handsome door and two elegant windows.

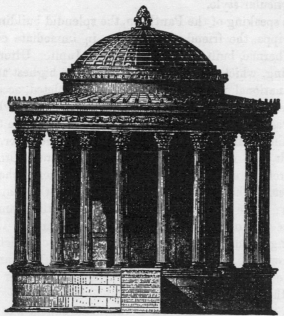

Fig. 341.

The cella is surrounded by twenty Korinthian columns, carrying richly ornamented beams (see Fig. 341). The upper part of the cella-wall, surrounded by a graceful cornice, rises above these beams, the conclusion being made by the cupola, crowned by an ornament. The whole structure stands on a base, also surrounded by a slight cornice, up to which base leads a narrow flight of steps in accordance with Vitruvius's rule. The building must be considered as one of the finest specimens of late republican architecture.*

* Weiss in his "Costümkunde" (Part I., p. 1169) suggests that the round temple may have been a reminiscence of the circular huts of the old-Italian populations.

Hirt has called attention to the remarkable circumstance of Vitruvius limiting his description to these two kinds of the round temple without mentioning a third class, in which the circular body of the building (in that case generally of larger dimensions) is not enclosed by columns at all, but only shows a projecting portico like the other Roman temples (prostyloi). This omission on the part of Vitruvius is all the more remarkable, as in his time already Roman architecture had achieved its highest success in that particular style.

We are speaking of the Pantheon, the splendid building erected by M. Agrippa, the friend of Augustus, in immediate connection with the Thermæ, built and dedicated to Jupiter Ultor by him. This building, which embodied, as it were, the highest aspirations of Roman national pride and power, was completed, according to the original inscription preserved on it, B.C. 25, in which year Agrippa was consul for the third time. According to the statement of Pliny ("Hist. Nat.," 36, 24, 1), which, however, has been disputed, it was originally dedicated to Jupiter Ultor, whose statue, therefore, undoubtedly stood in the chief niche opposite the entrance. The other six niches contained the statues of as many gods; those of the chief deities of the Julian family, Mars and Venus, and of the greatest son of that family, the divine Cæsar, being the only ones amongst the number of which we have certain knowledge. Was it that the statues of Mars and Venus showed the attributes of the other principal gods, or that the statues of the latter stood in the small chapels (*ædiculæ*) between the niches, or that the unequalled enormous cupola was supposed to represent heaven, that is, the house of all the gods? Certain it is that, together with the old appellation, the new name of the Pantheon, *i.e.*, temple of all the gods, was soon applied to the building. This latter name has been unanimously adopted by posterity, and has even originated the Christian destination of the edifice as church of all the martyrs (S. Maria ad Martyres). Without entering into the consecutive changes the building has undergone in the course of time, we will now attempt a description of its principal features. The temple consists of two parts, the round edifice and the portico (see plan, Fig. 342). The former was 132 feet in diameter, exclusive of the thickness of the wall, which amounts to 19 feet. The wall is perfectly circular, and

contains eight apertures, one of which serves as entrance, while
the others form, in a certain order, either semicircular or quadrangular niches; the former are covered by semi-cupolas, the
latter by barrel-vaults. Only the niche opposite the entrance is,
at the present time, uninterrupted, and open up to its full height,
thus corresponding with the formation of the entrance (compare
section, Fig. 344); in front of each of the others, two columns
have been erected, the beams of which close the opening of the
semicircular vault. To this chief portion of the building is
attached the splendid portico which, in the manner of the above-

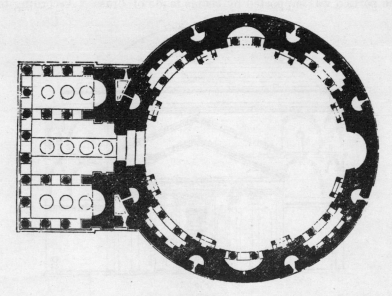

Fig. 342.

mentioned temples, projects by three columns, besides a massive
wall-structure. The frontage shows eight columns. As a rule,
the whole space of the pronaos was without columns; contrary to
this rule we here see it divided into three naves by means of two
pairs of columns. The centre nave, which was also the widest
led to the entrance-door, each of the two others being terminated
by an enormous niche. Not to mention æsthetical considerations,
these columns were required as props of the roof covering this
vast space (the portico is about 100 feet long).

The columns of the portico (one of the capitals is shown, Fig.

328) carried beams, on the frieze of which the following inscription in large letters has been placed : M·AGRIPPA·L·F·COS·
TERTIUM·FECIT.   Another inscription below this one, in
smaller characters, states the building to have been restored
by Septimius Severus and Caracalla.   The beams carry a large
pediment, originally adorned with groups of statues representing
Jupiter's victories over the Gigantes.   Behind and above this
gable rises a second one of the same proportions, serving as an
ornament of the projecting wall which connects the round
building with the portico (see also plan, Fig. 344).   The roof of
the portico was supported by beams made of brass.   According to

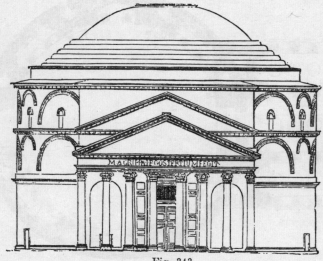

Fig. 343.

the drawing of Serlio, these beams were not massive, but consisted
of brass plates riveted together into square pipes—a principle
frequently applied by modern engineers on a larger scale in
building bridges, &c.   Unfortunately, the material of the roof,
barring some of the large rivets, has been used by Pope Urban
VIII. for guns and various ornaments of doubtful taste in
St. Peter's Cathedral.   The large columns carrying the ugly
tabernacle on the grave of St. Peter are one of the results of this
barbarous spoliation.   The old door, also made of brass, which
leads from the portico into the interior has, on the contrary, been
preserved.   The outer appearance of the round building is simple

and dignified. It most likely was originally covered with stucco and terra-cotta ornaments, of which, however, little remains at present; but the simple bricks, particularly in the upper stripes, where the insertion of the vault becomes visible, look, perhaps, quite as beautiful as the original coating. The whole cylinder of masonry is divided into three stripes by means of cornices, which break the heaviness of the outline, the divisions of the inner space corresponding to those of the outer surface (see Figs. 343 and 344). The first of these stripes is about 40 feet high, and rests on a base of Travertine freestone. It consists of simple horizontal slabs of stone, broken only by doors which lead to chambers built in the thickness of the wall between the niches (see plan, Fig. 342). It corresponds to the columns forming the first story of the interior, the two cornices, in and outside, being on a level. The second stripe, about 30 feet in height, answers to the second story of the interior, where the semicircular arches of the niches are situated. The horizontal stone layers outside are accordingly broken by large double arches, destined to balance the vaults in the interior. They alternate with smaller arches, thus forming a decoration of the exterior at once dignified and in harmony with the general design of the building. The two cornices in and outside are again on a level. The third stripe corresponds to the cupola, the tension of which is equal to 140 feet. The outer masonry reaches up to about a third of its height, from which point the cupola proper begins to rise in seven mighty steps.

The height of the dome is equal to the diameter of the cylindrical building, which adds to the sober and harmonious impression of the whole building. The lower of the above-mentioned interior stories is adorned with columns and pilasters, the latter of which enclosed the niches. Eight of these columns, over thirty-two feet in height, are monoliths of *giallo antico*—a yellow kind of marble beautifully veined, and belonging to the most valuable materials used by ancient architects. Six other columns are made of a kind of marble known as *pavonazzetto;* by an ingenious mode of colouring these columns are made to harmonize with those consisting of the rarer material. Above the first lies a second lower story, the architectural arrangements of which may be recognised from Adler's ingenious attempt at reconstruction (see Fig. 344). Its original decoration consisted of tablets of coloured marble, the effect being similar to that of a sequence of narrow pilasters. This original decoration has later been changed for another. Above the chief cornice which crowns this story, and at the same time terminates the circular walls, rises the cupola, divided into five stripes, each of which contains twenty-five "caskets" beautifully worked and in excellent perspective. In the centre at the top is an opening, forty feet in diameter, through which the light enters the building. Near this opening a fragment has been preserved of the bronze ornamentation which once seems to have covered the whole cupola. Even without these

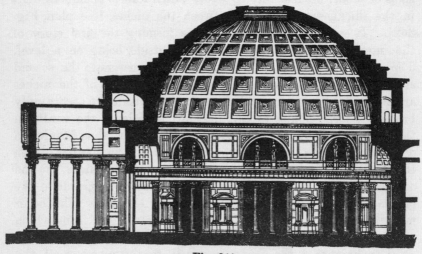

Fig. 344.

elegant decorations the building still excites the spectator's admiration as one of the masterpieces of Roman genius.

68. The temple-enclosures of the Romans were, as a rule, still more splendid than the periboloi of the Greeks. Although few in number, the remaining specimens of these surrounding courts are sufficient to give us a distinct idea of the whole arrangement. The original purpose of these courts was to seclude the sanctuary from the profane bustle of the world, for which purpose the enclosure of the space immediately in front of the temple was sufficient. Several enclosures of this kind have been preserved at Pompeii. In front of a prostylos with a colonnade projecting by two columns, commonly designated as the temple of Æsculapius,

is situated a simple court enclosed on two sides by a bare wall, only the third side fronting the temple being adorned with a portico of two columns. Another still smaller sanctuary, without columns, at Pompeii, formerly described as the temple of Mercury, at present as that of Quirinus, shows an entrance-court the walls of which on two sides are adorned with pilasters, the third consisting of a portico of four columns. Through the latter one enters the court of the temple, in the background of which, on a broad base, rises the cella containing the statue of the god; in the centre of the court stands an altar remarkable for its relief-ornamentation

In other cases the courts were richly decorated and of larger dimensions, surrounding the temple on all sides. This seems to

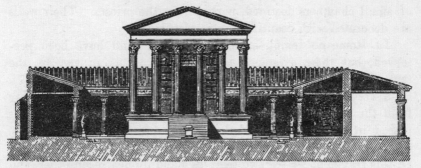

Fig. 345.

have been the case in almost all the larger and in most of the smaller temples wherever the locality would permit it. In Pompeii we again refer to the above-mentioned temple of Isis, which is built in a regular space surrounded by walls. The court is surrounded by a colonnade; in the centre of it lies the cella with the pronaos. A similar arrangement, on a larger scale, we see in the so-called temple of Venus, occupying the western side of the Forum of Pompeii. It is a peripteros surrounded by twenty-eight splendid Korinthian columns, with a portico of considerable projection in front. The temple is enclosed by a covered court adorned with columns; the colonnades on the narrower sides consisting of nine, those on the broader sides of seventeen, detached Korinthian columns. The wall on the right is joined on the outside by a

similar colonnade (Fig. 345 *a*) of Doric columns, which belongs to
the surroundings of the forum.   The remnants of both the temple
and the court are in a state of tolerable preservation.   Mazois has
attempted a trustworthy conjectural design of the original building (see Fig. 345).   The temple rises in beautiful proportions
over the surrounding colonnades.   Both with regard to elegance
of proportions and splendour of decorations it ranks amongst the
finest buildings of Pompeii.   In front of the steps leading to the
base stands the small altar, occupying the centre of the foreground.
The surface of the inner walls of the cella is divided into several
parts separated by pilasters of stucco.   They are of a light-yellow
colour, while those of the peribolos are richly adorned in the
manner of perspective room-decorations—only rarely met with in
temples.   The back wall of the peribolos is joined by a number
of small chambers destined, perhaps, for the priests.   Their walls
are decorated with beautiful figure-pictures.

In Rome no temple-enclosures of this kind have been preserved, but their existence in ancient times is proved by the
temple of Venus and Roma described by us (Figs. 336 and 337).
Of a very early structure of a similar kind, we have knowledge
from the plan of the city of Rome, which, made of marble, was
placed in the temple of Romulus, and the fragments of which are
now let into the walls of the staircase of the Capitoline Museum.
In this fragment we see two temples standing near each other, and
enclosed at a moderate distance by a single oblong colonnade.[*]
This colonnade was built most likely of common material by Q.
Cæcilius Metellus ; Augustus reconstructed it on a larger scale in
marble in the name of his sister Octavia.   In front of the two
temples stood, as appears from the Capitoline fragment, groups of
twenty-five horsemen, the work of Lysippus, which had been
brought as spoil from Macedon by Metellus.   In the reign of
Titus (A.D. 70) both temples were burnt down in a fire which
destroyed a great part of Rome.   They were rebuilt, according to
an inscription found on them, by the emperor L. Septimius Severus
(A.D. 203).   Both temples were dedicated to Jupiter and Juno.
Remains of the portico leading to the court are found in the

---

[*] See F. Reber, " Die Ruinen Roms und der Campagna."   Leipsic, 1863, p. 210
et seq.   P. 211 contains a view of the portico of Octavia ; p. 213, the fragment of the
Capitoline plan referring to it.

Piazza di Pescaria ; some columns of the temple of Juno belong to a private house in the Via di S. Angelo di Pescaria.

The largest temple-enclosure amongst the monuments known to us belonged to the temple of the Sun at Palmyra, the mighty city of the desert, situated on the frontier of the Roman and Parthian empires. In it the most gorgeous specimens of almost all classes of Roman architecture are found. The open colonnade, for instance, more than 4,000 feet long, consisting of four rows of Korinthian columns, had not its equal in Rome, no more than the just-mentioned temple-enclosure. The latter occupies a square nearly 3,000 feet in circumference. The outer wall, of considerable height, is broken on three sides by windows cut into it at regular intervals between the pilasters, which adorn the wall both in front and at the back. The fourth side has no windows, but instead of them a high entrance-portal in the centre, which may be considered as one of the most splendid specimens of Roman architecture under the Emperor Aurelianus. The court which one enters through this portal is of proportionate size and splendour. Each of the sides (over 100 feet in length) is adorned with colonnades ; those on three sides being double (*i.e.* formed by two rows of columns), that on the side of the entrance single. The whole area of the court is covered with slabs of marble, and it contains, on both sides of the entrance, two large regular hollows, most likely used as ponds. Opposite the entrance, facing it with its long side, lies the temple, a dipteros about 110 feet wide by 200 long; the entrance to it lies on the long side of the cella, opposite the portal of the enclosure-wall. This is a deviation from the ordinary design of temples; another irregularity consisting in the windows which are broken into the walls of the cella. The inner sides of each of the two narrow walls of the cella contain a quadrangular niche destined to receive the statue of a god. This fact accords with the statement of Aurelian having placed here the statues of Helios and Belus. The same emperor restored the older temple in a manner the splendour of which is frequently praised by ancient writers, and still is apparent from the remains.

Less in size, but not in splendour or individual peculiarities, were the courts of the temple of the Sun in Heliopolis, the modern Balbek. One of the chief temples of that city we have mentioned in § 66 (see Figs. 335 and 336). The other one, larger than the first, and most likely devoted to Jupiter, as god of the sun, was a peripteros with ten columns in front, and nineteen on each of the long sides. Its width was 160 feet; its length, exclusive of the steps, about 300 feet. The cella of the temple has been destroyed beyond restoration; only the beautiful Korinthian columns of the colonnade (about 7 feet in bottom diameter) may still be recognised. The courts in front of the temple, and the entrance-portal belonging to them, are comparatively well preserved. The latter (see plan, Fig. 346; scale 200 feet) consists of a portico of twelve columns, up to which led a broad flight of steps, the entrance into the first court being formed by three magnificent gates. The court itself shows the unusual

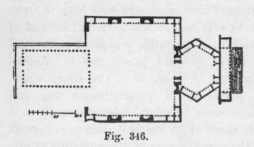

Fig. 346.

shape of a hexagon. Opposite the entrance lies the chief portal, leading to the second court. The four remaining sides show halls, opening towards the court through colonnades; the niches in the walls of these halls, with their beautifully vaulted ceilings, may still be recognised from the ruins. The second court, square in shape, was designed in a similar manner, each of three of its sides (400 feet in length) containing open halls (*exedræ*) alternating with semicircular niches. The walls of the halls are adorned with niches, most likely containing statues. On the fourth side, opposite the splendid portal with three gates above mentioned, rises the façade of the temple, concerning the arrangement of which we have spoken before.

So much about the enclosures and courts of temples. Frequently these temples were also erected in public squares, to which arrangement we shall have to return in speaking of the Fora of Rome and Pompeii (see § 82). The grand impression of a temple is frequently increased by the artificial base on which it stands. We have spoken of such a base in reference to the Capitoline sanctuary (§ 62). The foundations of the court of the temple of Venus and Roma were, as we have seen, on the largest scale. Similar preparatory works were necessary for the base of the just-mentioned temple of Heliopolis. Large walls of freestone had been erected for the purpose on three sides, consisting of stones of thirty or even of sixty feet in length. In a temple erected on rising ground, the base itself could be architecturally developed; terraces, frequently of imposing proportions, often led up to the temple. As an instance, we add the temple of Fortuna of Præneste, at Palestrina, conjecturally re-designed by Canina (Fig. 347). According to this design, the mountain, on the slope of which the old town of Præneste lay, was converted into terraces up to half its height, which were propped by mighty basements of different kinds and ages. The midmost terraces, for instance, show front walls of Cyclopic-Pelasgic workmanship (see § 17),

Fig. 347.

and are therefore dated by Canina back to the time in which the similarly constructed walls of Præneste itself were built. This structure was afterwards enlarged towards both top and bottom, these later parts accordingly showing regular freestone architecture. Other parts again show the so-called *opus incertum* (see § 69), and, also, the regular brick-architecture of imperial times. The modern town of Palestrina has been built amongst these ruins, which latter have been an object of continued research ever since the sixteenth century (we mention only the important works on the subject by Pirro Ligorio and Pietro da Cortona). In comparing the remains with the statements of ancient writers, we find that the temple of moderate dimensions lay about half way up the mountain resting on the above-mentioned terraces, which again were architecturally adorned in various ways. The bottom story, if we may use that expression, was formed by a grand archway carried by pillars; it extended to a considerable length, running parallel with the highway which passes the mountains on that side. On both sides of it two large covered cisterns have been discovered. From here, stairs led up to a terrace of large size, on which two other large tanks were situated—an arrangement met with also in the court of the temple of the Sun at Palmyra. From here stairs led up to a second terrace, in the centre of which remains of a gorgeous building have been discovered. It consisted of two large halls connected by means of a colonnade; in one of the halls a celebrated mosaic floor has been discovered. Pietro da Cortona transferred it to the palace of the Barberini family, built on the ruins of this structure, where it still remains. Double flights of steps led up to a third and a fourth terrace; on the fifth terrace stood an archway running along the front edge; on the sixth we see a large square court surrounded by colonnades (peristylos), joined by another similar court of semicircular shape. From this a flight of steps, semicircular in design, led up to the temple of Fortuna itself, of which, however, nothing now remains.

69. We now have to consider the wall—the most primitive form of protective architecture. A great similarity exists between the first attempts of this kind in Greece and Italy, which proves the relationship and analogous development of the two nations. The oldest Italian town-walls known to us consist of large stones, in the cutting and placing on each other of which we notice the same different modes of proceeding as in the Pelasgic walls (compare Figs. 53 to 56). We therefore need not repeat our previous remarks, and only add, that not only towns, but also other places, were enclosed with walls for purposes of safety or religious worship. Wall-enclosures of this kind are frequently found on heights in various parts of Italy; it is indeed probable that one of the chief centres of Rome, the Capitoline hill, was enclosed originally for the purpose of defence rather than of habitation. In this manner it became, like the akropolis of

a Greek city, the centre point round which the first dwelling-houses of the city were grouped.

When a town was to be founded systematically, as frequently was the case with a colonising nation like the Romans, certain religious ceremonies had to be observed. A bull and a cow were harnessed to a plough in order to encircle the place destined for the city with a furrow. For the gates, the number of which was also determined by holy traditions, a space was left by lifting up the plough. The ploughed-up earth had to lie towards the town, the furrow itself towards the country, this arrangement being in a manner suggestive of the wall and moat of Italian and Roman cities. Where the locality permitted it, the space for the town was designed as a square, an instance of which was the old *Roma quadrata* on the Palatine Hill: this arrangement recalls the form of the templum (see § 61 *et seq.*), the centre of the town being, like that of the temple, considered as holy, and marked as such by the deposition of gifts and offerings.

The walls of the Romans were generally made of bricks. Recently, however, some remains of the oldest fortifications of Rome have been dis- covered which are built of freestone in the Greek manner. On the Aventine Hill, for instance, may be traced for a considerable distance the line of a free- stone wall, which undoubt- edly belongs to the so- called fortifications of Ser-

Fig. 348.

vius. It lies on the top of a large earth-wall (*agger*), which is expressly mentioned amongst those fortifications, and it contains, like the walls of the Greeks, projections for the purpose of defence; the arches placed at intervals for the sake of increasing the firmness of the layers of stones are thoroughly Italian in cha- racter. Of a similar kind are the substruction-walls which have been recently found on the Palatine Hill, forming, most likely, the original fortification of that hill (see Fig. 348).

In later times, as we mentioned before, brick was used in fortifications. Vitruvius states, that first of all masses of earth were heaped up, and the erection thus gained was enclosed on both sides with strong brick walls. In these walls, as well as in

Fig. 349.

those made of massive stone, different modes of structure were in use, by means of which the appearance of the walls was considerably modified. Either the whole wall consisted of a mixture of mortar and unbaked bricks (called *opus incertum* by Vitruvius), or the outer surface of the wall was faced with regular bricks of equal size. In this case, also, two modes of construction became possible, the stones being either triangular in shape and arranged in horizontal layers (Fig. 349), or being cut into

Fig. 350.

quadrangular prisms which were pressed into the soft mortar, so that the joints crossed each other in a net-like manner (*opus reticulatum*). Fig. 350 illustrates the latter mode of structure, which also appears, for instance, in the walls of a conduit of the Alsietine aqueduct. The inside of these walls consists of irregular bricks joined together by mortar (*opus incertum*), while the outer surface consists of reticulated brickwork coated over with stucco. Sometimes the reticular and horizontal principles appear combined, in which case the reticular surfaces are interrupted by narrower pieces of horizontal layers. This is the case, for instance, in several parts of the Roman town walls.

We quote two instances of town walls, in illustration of the principles hitherto insisted upon, viz., the walls of Pompeii and the so-called Aurelian fortification of Rome. In the former the wall consists, according to Vitruvius's rule, of an irregularly heaped mass of stones, faced both in front and at the back with

flag stones (scarp and counterscarp), to which additional firmness
is added by means of buttresses. The upper surface of the wall
is, towards the outside, protected by battlements four feet in
height, into which, at intervals of nine feet, embrasures have
been cut; they project towards the inside by three feet, thus
yielding a safe position to the besieged.

Towards the town side the wall is considerably raised, reaching a height of
forty-two feet from the level of the
ground. Broad but rather steep steps
lead from the town up to the wall.
Square towers communicated with the
top of the wall by means of (generally
round-arched) gates.

In our second example (Fig. 352),
the Aurelian fortification of Rome,
the wall towards the inside is propped by strong buttresses connected
with each other by means of round arches. The top of the
wall here, also, is protected by battlements. A sort of gallery
is formed by these arches, in the single divisions of which
semicircular niches are cut into the thickness of the wall

Fig. 351.

Fig. 352.

which communicate with the outside by means of narrow shot-
holes, thus yielding a strong position both for attack and defence
(another arrangement of the wall is illustrated by Fig. 359).
Here also turrets are placed at certain intervals, such as we have

met with before at Pompeii (Fig. 341) and in Greece (compare § 19,
Figs. 70—77). Upon the whole, Roman towers differ little from
the Greek but for the vault, which adds to their strength. Fig. 353
(scale, 18 feet) shows a section of a turret at Pompeii, rising in
three stories to a height of about forty feet. The ceiling between
the two lower stories inclines slightly
towards the outside, which is also the
case with the openings above referred
to. The steps necessary for communication lie in the back part of the turret,
which is slightly raised. The topmost
chamber communicates with the circuit
of the wall by means of a vaulted gate
(compare Fig. 351). The upper platform also inclines outward so as to let
the rain run off, stone eaves being
added for the same purpose, as is also
the case with the circuits of the wall.
Battlements protect the platform.

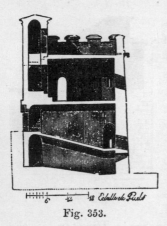

Fig. 353.

A few words ought to be added about fortified camps, so
important in Roman warfare. They were erected at considerable
distances from each other, to protect the frontier from the
barbarians, sometimes connected with each other by long lines
of wall with intervening smaller fortifications. They, of course,
required large garrisons. The remains of a large fortified camp
are still visible in the Taunus Mountains, about an hour's walk
from Homburg vor der Höhe, and 250 paces from the large
Roman line of defence commonly called the *Pfahlgraben.* The
present name of the camp is *Saalburg;* it is most likely identical
with the Arctaunon (Arxtauni) mentioned by Ptolemæus. It
was built by Drusus in the year 11 (B.C.), and re-erected by his
son Germanicus after its partial destruction by the Germans
(A.D. 9). Continued, but not yet finished, excavations have made
it possible to discern the whole plan of the camp (see Fig. 354,
after the designs of Archivrath Habel). The shape of the fortification was quadrangular, being 700 feet long by 450 wide.
The outer wall, consisting of irregular blocks of stone, had a
thickness of 5 feet, slightly increased on the north side, which
was most exposed to the attacks of the enemy. The four angles

are rounded. The original height of the wall cannot be determined with certainty; in some parts the remaining portions rise to six feet from the ground. Outside of this wall lies a double moat; inside of it we see a second higher line of wall, about 7 feet wide, which, in our plan, is marked by a double line of dots. Behind this wall lies a road 30 feet wide, the *via angularis* (E) (marked by a single dotted line in our plan), destined for the reception of larger bodies of troops. The other arrangements of the camp perfectly tally with the descriptions of ancient writers. On the front side, between two towers projecting inside, lies the chief gate, *porta prætoria* (A), with which corresponds, on the opposite side, the *porta decumana* (D). On the two long sides we have the *porta principalis dextra*, also protected by towers (B), and the *porta principalis sinistra* (C). In the centre of the camp, where the connecting lines between the opposite gates meet, stands the dwelling of the commander, the *prætorium* (F).

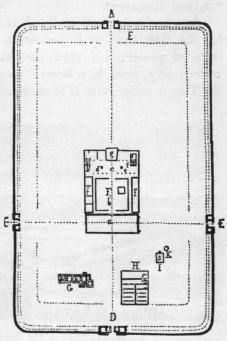

Fig. 354.

Erected without much care and in a hurry, it still shows several compartments, partly for the private use of the general, partly for military purposes. There is no entrance on the side of the *porta prætoria*, in the place of which we see a square tower (*g*); on the opposite side the building terminates in an oblong room (*a*), the three outlying sides of which contain three doors exactly opposite the three gates in the corresponding walls of the camp. Near G and H remains of buildings have been discovered, most likely those of dwelling-houses. The narrow intervals between the cross walls of H seem to indicate the existence of a heating apparatus. I marks a small sanctuary, K a well. The prætorium was reserved for the staff and the *corps d'élite ;* the rest of the army lived, according to the rules of *castrametatio,* in the open spaces between the prætorium and the wall of the camp. Light huts, made of earth or wood, were most likely constructed for the purpose, the German climate being too cold to permit living in tents for long. Stone foundations of the soldiers' dwellings have not been discovered.

Another camp, at Gamzigrad in Servia, carefully investigated for the first time by F. Kanitz, is much larger and in a better state of preservation than the one just described. It dates, undoubtedly, from late Roman times. It was erected to protect the Timon valley, and is of enormous dimensions. It formed an

Fig. 355.

irregular square (Fig. 355), the narrow sides having a length of 1,461 and 1,351 feet respectively, while the two long sides show the enormous measures of 1,908 and 1,896 feet. Round towers, 180 feet in diameter, and with walls 24 feet thick, stand at the four corners, a number of smaller round towers projecting almost circularly from the wall at irregular intervals. At a distance of about 108 feet from this wall the remains of a second row of towers have been discovered also, most likely connected with each other by walls. The substructure of a square building of 84 by 132 feet occupies the centre of the fortification. Unfortunately no excavations have taken place, by means of which the name of this camp might, perhaps, be discovered.

70. The Roman gates differ from the Greek ones more than
is the case with towers or walls. It is true that their position in
the wall remained essentially unaltered; that is, they were
inserted mostly in the parts most protected by nature, and further
strengthened by projections of the wall, built in such a manner
as to afford a point of attack on the left side of the besieging
enemy. As we have seen before, the gates were flanked by towers
(compare also our description of the castle of Salona, § 76, Fig.
392).

All these points the Roman gates have in common with the
Greek. The chief difference consists in the principle of vaulting
applied to the Roman structures. By means of this principle,
applied also to subterraneous canals, the Romans were able to
cover wide spaces without difficulty. We quote a few examples
of Roman gates, classed according to the number of their
openings.

The simplest form naturally consists of one arch, either flanked
by projections and cut into the thickness of the wall, or else
repeated on the opposite sides of a tower. A beautiful specimen
of the first kind is the
gate of Perusia, where a
second decorative arch is
added above the actual
opening. An example of
the second kind we see in
the gate of Volterra, which
shows all the simplicity of
the old Italian arch. The
gate of Pompeii, leading
to Nola, is of later date;
its simple arch does not
lie in the wall but at the
end of a small passage,
which touches the wall at
an obtuse angle, thus compelling the besiegers to

Fig. 356.

expose themselves to the attack of those standing on the side walls
of this passage. Later still, and evidently erected with a view to
decoration as well as to safety, is one of the gates of the above-

mentioned villa of Diocletianus, at Salona, called *porta aurea*, most
likely owing to its splendid ornamentation (see § 78). Like the
other gates of this building, it is flanked by towers, and contains
one opening only. The latter shows a round arch, closed at the
bottom by a straight ledge of stone (see Fig. 356). The surface
of the wall is decorated in the late Roman style, with small
columns on bases, enclosing niches. A cornice, partly destroyed,
adds to the beauty of the gate even in its present condition.

Fig. 357.

Gates with two openings are of rarer occurrence. As an
example we quote one of the oldest and most beautiful gates of
Rome, at present called Porta Maggiore, the original aspect of
which is shown Fig. 357.* The design is very complicated,
owing to various considerations; but it shows, at the same time,
the artistic skill of the Romans in getting over architectural
difficulties. Two high arched portals afford an opening to two
Roman highways, the Via Labicana and Via Prænestina, which
here met at a pointed angle. These portals are enclosed by
two mighty piers, the upper parts of which are broken by
smaller arches and decorated with two semi-columns each, on the
latter of which rest beams and pediments. The centre pier

---

* Compare the gate of Messene (Fig. 67), the opening of which seems to have
been divided into two halves by a pillar.

shows, below the just-mentioned opening, another small round-arched gate. The arches served at the same time to carry two aqueducts. Just above them lies an "attic," which, however, does not contain water; but above this we see two other "attics:" the lower one forms the conduit of the Aqua Claudia, the upper one that of the Anio Nova. Three large inscriptions cover the three attics. The first states that the Emperor Claudius built the aqueduct called Aqua Claudia, by which the waters of the two wells called Cæruleus and Curtius, lying near the forty-fifth

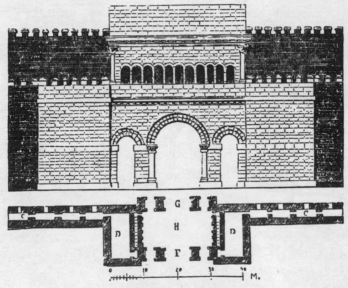

Fig. 358 and 359.

milestone, were conducted into Rome. The second inscription says that the same emperor conducted the Anio Nova to Rome from a distance of sixty-two Roman miles. The third inscription mentions Vespasian and Titus as the restorers of the gigantic building of Claudius.

More frequent than two, are three gate-openings, of which the centre one is usually wider and higher than the two others: the former being destined for horses and carriages, the latter for foot-passengers. The two purposes of defence and traffic are beautifully combined in a gate belonging to the fortifications of Aosta.

built by Augustus (see view, Fig. 358, and plan, Fig. 359). The wall to which the gate belongs differs essentially from those of Pompeii, the interval between the lower and outer (Fig. 359, *a*), and the higher and inner, wall-facings (B) being not filled up with earth, but left empty. The connection between the two wall-facings is effected by means of arches. This interval is thus transformed into a number of small vaulted chambers (C) which

Fig. 360.

open towards the town, and thus somewhat resemble the inner divisions of the Aurelian walls. Two towers (D D), enclosing the outer gate (F), project from this double wall. The gate shows the just-mentioned division into three openings, all of which could be closed by strong portcullis. After this gate follows an open space (H), called by Vegetius *propugnaculum*, because here the besiegers that might have advanced so far could be attacked from the platforms of the low towers. On the opposite side of this space lies the inner gate (G), the three openings of which were closed by doors studded with iron. The architecture is dignified and even severe in style, and this work of Augustus may be counted amongst the finest of its class.

A similar though less fortified structure we see in one of the gates of Pompeii, called, from the direction of the road passing through it, the Herculanean gate (see the outer view of it, Fig. 360, from the conjectural designs of Mazois). On the left it is protected by a projection of the wall; it has one centre and two side entrances, the latter for foot-passengers. The inward side of the gate shows the same arrangement. The narrow space lying between the two chief portals was uncovered, thus forming a kind of *propugnaculum*, similar to that of the gate of Aosta. The side entrances are vaulted in their full length; they were each connected with the uncovered space in the centre by means of two arches, through which the necessary light is conveyed into the long and narrow passages. The large portals could, at one time, be closed by portcullis which, however, at the time of the destruction, seem to have been no more in use. The side entrances contained doors, as indicated by the still-preserved hinges. The whole structure consists of pieces of tufa and mortar, coated with stucco. The remains show how carefully the surface was smoothed. The whole gate was 16·80 metres deep by 14 wide. The width of the centre passage is 4·70 metres, that of each side passage 1·30.

71. The structures of utility, to which we have now to turn, differ from those of the Greeks by their greater variety of purpose, and of the means used to accomplish this purpose. It is here that the practical sense of the Romans shows to greatest advantage.

The Romans soon discovered the political importance of roads, and showed great energy and consistency in carrying out their ideas, differing in this from the Greeks. With the latter, religious purposes formed an important consideration in the building of roads; the Romans only considered the necessities of the State. Artistic road-building commenced as soon as the Roman dominion began to extend beyond its original limits. Conquered provinces had to be connected with the heart of the State, *i.e.* the city of Rome. The roads thus became a means of political, commercial, and intellectual interchange between Rome and the provinces.

The chief and first purpose, however, was of a military kind; large masses of troops had to be conveyed with ease to distant provinces. In this way originated the first artistic road, the Via Appia, and its continuation to Arminum, the Via Flaminia: the subjection of the Boii, on the Po, led to the construction of the Via Æmilia; while that of the Gallic and Germanic nations caused the grand system of roads in the Alps and the countries on the Rhine and Danube. The gradual extension of the Roman territory may be followed in the history of road-building. These large political considerations, of course, were out of the question amongst the numerous and, to a great extent, isolated states of Greece. This difference of purpose between the two nations also influenced their modes of constructing roads. The Greeks built their roads according to the nature of the locality, or even to old traditional routes of travellers, heedless of occasional detours. The Romans, on the contrary, true to the indomitable energy of their character, follow the *one* plan of building as nearly as possible in a straight line. The nature of the ground is almost totally disregarded; where mountains intervene they are broken

Fig. 361.

through; hollows are made level by means of dams; deep valleys or rapid streams are spanned by bridges, the bold design of which still excite the admiration of modern engineers, far superior though they are to the Romans in technical, scientific, and mechanical resources.

Of tunnels through mountains we mention the so-called " Grotto of the Posilippo," near Naples, which is still daily passed through by thousands (Fig. 361). It is cut through a promontory between Naples and Baiæ, being in length 2,654 Neap. palms by 24 wide. The height inside varies from 26 to 74 palms. At the two ends there are arches of 94 and 98 palms respectively, tending to increase the firmness of the structure. The tunnel is bored through the solid rock.

Other difficulties had to be overcome in marshy places. The soil here had to be made firm and its level raised by means of a dam. The Via Appia, for instance, was thus conducted through the Pontine marshes. In other places, again, the road had to be carried on along precipices on walled substructures or viaducts.

This is the case in that part of the Via Appia which descends from Albano to the valley of Ariccia ; just below the village of Ariccia it runs for a considerable distance on an embankment faced with freestone. Fig. 362

Fig. 362.

shows this part of the road with massive balustrades and seats on both sides of it. Vaulted openings in the basement evidently served as outlets for the mountain streams.

As to the technical arrangements of the roads, such as pavement, gutters, &c., full information is derived from Hirt's work, " Die Lehre von den Gebäuden bei den Griechen und Römern," which we have followed in many points. The roads were either strewn with sand and gravel (*glarea viam sternere*) or paved with

Fig. 363.　　　　　Fig. 364.　　　　　Fig. 365.

solid stones. In the latter case generally polygonal blocks of some hard stone, generally basalt, are chosen for the roadway, the surface being made as smooth as possible (*silice sternere viam*) as is shown by the part of the Via Appia in Fig. 363. In case there were raised pavements for foot-passengers, they were generally made of the softer common tufa (*lapide sternere*). The middle of the road was generally raised a little, so as to make the rain-water flow off; small outlets for the water, such as we mentioned in speaking of the wall (see Fig. 353), also occur on roads. Figs. 364 and 365 illustrate the draining-apparatus of the Via Appia, where an arched passage under the road serves as an outlet for the water, perhaps also as a means of communication. Fig. 364 shows the front view ; Fig. 365 the sections. The road-way itself is about 18 feet wide ; it has a massive stone balustrade on each side.

The streets of Pompeii were of similar construction, drains being frequently found below them ; the pavements for foot-passengers to both sides are generally raised a little, posts, connected by kerb-stones, being placed at certain intervals to prevent the intrusion of horses or vehicles. At intervals of 1,000 paces, milestones (*milliaria*) were placed on the highways, with the distances from the larger towns written on them. Frequently seats for exhausted travellers were placed near these milestones.

72. In their construction of bridges the Romans differ widely from the Greeks, owing to the use of the arch in Roman architecture. The viaducts and bridges of the Romans are amongst the

Fig. 366.

most remarkable monuments of antiquity. At the ninth milestone from Rome, on the road to Gabii, is a viaduct across a broad valley, which only during the rainy season of the year is partly flooded. Nevertheless, the viaduct is built on as many as seven arches. It is 285 feet long, and consists of blocks of "peperin" and red tufa. Owing to the softness of the material the pillars are very stout, and the intervals spanned by the arches small. From the simple and solid structure of the work (which is now called Ponte di Nona, and still in use), Hirt believes it to belong to the time of Caius Gracchus, who, while a tribune (124—121 B.C.), constructed a great many roads, and of whom Plutarch distinctly remarks (C. Gracchus, c. III.) that he considered not only usefulness but also beauty and elegance (χάριν καὶ κάλλος).

Where a stream had to be crossed, the arch naturally became

of still greater importance. Bridges, moreover, seem to have been regarded almost like religious monuments. In the early history of the city of Rome, so closely connected with the Tiber, the bridges across that river were of such religious import that the care of them was assigned to a fraternity of priests (*pontifices, i.e.* bridge-makers), of which the highest college of priests in Rome was a further development. The name *Pontifex Maximus* remained attached to the office of high priest, and is at present that of the pope.

Although of great importance, the arch was not indispensable in Roman bridge-architecture. Not to speak of temporary bridges of boats, we mention permanent wooden bridges, such as the Pons Sublicius, the oldest bridge in Rome, and the bridge that Cæsar threw across the Rhine. In other bridges woodwork and masonry occur combined, as, for instance, in the splendid bridge built across the Danube by Trajan. It rested on twenty strong stone pillars, standing at distances of 170 feet, and connected with each other by wooden arches instead of stone vaultings. A representation of this bridge is seen on the column of Trajan.

Arched structures made of stone marked the highest perfection of the art, combining, as they did, firmness of structure with the capability of spanning wide spaces without impeding (owing to the height of the arches) the navigation on the river. Without entering into details we will, in the following pages, quote a few examples of bridges, classing them according to the number of their principal arches. The bridge near Volci, across the river Fiora

Fig. 367.

(Fig. 367), shows one chief arch, with two smaller ones on the banks of the river. This bridge also serves to carry an aqueduct across the river (compare § 74).

Fig. 368 shows a still-existing Roman bridge with two principal arches, generally known as the Ponte de' Quattro Capi,

owing to the two heads of *Janus Quadrifrons* on stelai placed on
the balustrade above the *têtes-du-pont*. According to the inscriptions it was built in 62 B.C. by L. Fabricius, at that time *curator
viarum*. Its condition was, in 21 B.C., examined and testified as
safe by the consuls Q. Lepidus and M. Lollius. It connects the
city with the island of the Tiber, and consists of two arches
extending in graceful lines from a strong pillar in the centre of
the river to its two banks. On the base of the pillar, between the

Fig. 368.

two chief arches, the masonry is interrupted by a third arch,
which gives an appearance of grace to the whole structure. The
side of the pillar turned towards the current of the stream is
made into a sharp edge. Two other smaller arches, nearer the
banks, add to the firmness of the structure, being filled up with
earth.

One of the first Roman bridges is the Pons Ælius, built across

Fig. 369.

the Tiber by the Emperor Hadrian. It opened the access to
the tomb erected by him on the right bank of the river (compare
§ 78). The bed of the river was crossed by three semicircular
arches, joined to right and left by four smaller vaultings. It is in
a state of excellent preservation, and well known by the name of
Ponte S. Angelo. On its restoration at a later date one of the
arches has been filled up, and is hidden by the extended embank-

ment. Fig. 369 shows the original design of the bridge; Fig. 370 its present aspect at low water, which shows the massive structure of the foundations and piers.

73. Of still greater magnificence and boldness of construction than the bridges were the harbours, canals, and similar structures. Hirt ("Lehre von den Gebäuden," p. 367) justly remarks, "that even the splendour of Nero's golden house dwindles into nothing compared with the harbour of Ostia, the drainage works of the Fucinine Lake, and the two large aqueducts, Aqua Claudia and Anio Nova, all built by Claudius. In their waterworks the ancients seem to have surpassed themselves." Of the harbours of the Greeks, partly of considerable dimensions, we have spoken

Fig. 370.

before (§ 20) : in comparing them with those of the Romans we find the same difference as between the roads of the two nations; that is, the Greeks adapt their structures to the conditions of the soil, while the Romans, without neglecting local advantages, as a rule, force Nature to their powerful will. In Greece, harbours generally consisted of natural bays enlarged and fortified by dams and similar structures : the Romans built their harbours where no such natural opportunities offered themselves. It is true that their coasts, compared with Greece, were wanting in bays and promontories. Instead of these, therefore, the Romans built dams and walls far into the sea, to obtain safe anchorage for their ships; nay, entire artificial islands were produced in the sea so as to protect equally artificial harbours from the waves. This was the case, for instance, in the harbour of Centumcellæ (the modern Civita Vecchia), built by Trajan. Of the gradual progress of this structure we are told by the younger Pliny (§ 31) : two enormous

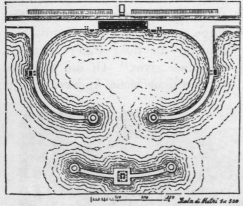

Fig. 371.

piers were being built, of which that to the left was finished first; at the same time an artificial island in front of them was in progress of construction. Enormous loads of blocks of stone were brought in flat vessels, and thrown into the sea in proper places. In this manner a powerful stone wall was formed under the water, which, at the time when Pliny wrote, already protruded from the surface of the sea. (See the plan of the harbour, Fig. 371, according to Canina's design.)

Similar structures, although on a different plan, had been attempted at a much earlier period. When the harbour of Ostia (built at the mouth of the Tiber by Ancus Martius, and already covered with sand about the end of the Republic) was being restored, we hear of an artificial island of this kind. It formed a breakwater in front of the large piers of the harbour, and carried a lighthouse almost equal in size to the celebrated Pharus in the harbour of Alexandria. Instead of rough stones, the Emperor Claudius, who took a particular pride in buildings of this kind, used chalk, mortar, and Puzzuolan clay. Of these materials three enormous pillars were built and sunk into the sea together with the colossal ship on which they stood.* The clay received an indestructible firmness by the accession of the salt water, and in this manner the foundation of the island was formed. As to

---

* This was the same vessel in which, under Caligula, the obelisk of the Vatican had been brought to Italy. By the Romans it was believed to be the largest vessel that ever sailed on the ocean.

the rest, this harbour resembled that at Centumcellæ. Like the
latter, it consisted of an outer harbour built into the sea by
Claudius, and of a large basin afterwards dug into the shore
by command of the Emperor Trajan. The basin was enclosed by
freestone walls, and communicated with the outer harbour by
artificial canals, as also with the open sea by means of the Tiber,
the stream of which was well regulated and embanked. Fig. 372
(scale 1,000 metres) shows Canina's design, made according to the
existing remnants of the harbour. The ruins of the harbour of

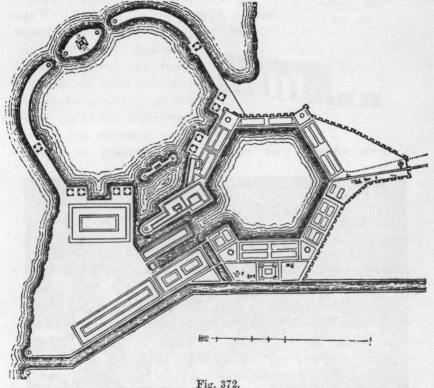

Fig. 372.

Claudius now lie one miglia inland, owing to the deposits of the sea.
Our design also indicates the storehouses for grains and other
merchandise by which the inner hexagonal basin was surrounded. A coin struck during the fifth consulate of Trajan
(A.D. 103) gives a distinct view of this harbour and the buildings
surrounding it. As to the arrangements of such storehouses we

may perhaps derive some knowledge from the remains of a building
discovered by Piranesi near the Emporium in Rome, on the left bank

of the Tiber (see Fig. 374). It rose from
the river to the city in terraces in accordance with the natural conditions of the
ground. The ceilings of the store-rooms
were vaulted ; graceful arches in the
enclosing walls effected an easy communication with the street.

Fig. 374 shows the view of a harbour
from a Pompeian wall-painting. Walls
crowned by towers serve as a means of

Fig. 373.

protection. Storehouses surround the basin, connected
with the shore by means of
a bridge. On an island connected with one of the jetties
we see a temple and a dwell-

Fig. 374.

ing-house adorned with columns, both standing on artificial

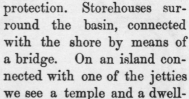

Fig. 375.

terraces, to which lead steps. Groups of trees add to the pictur-
esqueness of the whole. The most remarkable feature is the jetty,

to the right of the harbour, projecting far into the sea, and containing a number of arcades destined for the keeping out of mud or for the reception of smaller vessels.

74. We now have to consider the drainage works of the Romans—less imposing, but no less useful, than their harbours. We mention particularly the drainings of the Pontine marshes, the meadows of the Po, &c., where, by means of canals, ditches, and drains of various kinds, damp, boggy stretches of country have been transformed into arable land. A still more remarkable example of a complicated system of drainage is the city of Rome itself. Lying on several hills, with a river flowing through it, the lower parts of the city naturally were liable to the formation of unhealthy swamps. To remove this nuisance, a system of subterraneous canals was built, whose grand and skilful design still excites our admiration; they serve their purpose, after about 2,500 years, in the most perfect manner. The fundamental idea was to collect the water by means of a system of smaller canals into one large sewer, which conducted it, together with the refuse of the city, to the river. This chief canal, known as Cloaca Maxima, is still preserved for a distance of nearly 1,000 feet. It served, and still serves, to conduct the waters from the Capitoline and Palatine hills, collecting in the Velabrum, into the Tiber (see its open-

Fig. 376.

ing towards the river, Fig. 376). A barrel-vault of tufa, with arches of travertine inserted into it at intervals of 10 feet, covers the canal, which is about 20 feet wide. Its original height was 12 feet, now reduced to 6-7 feet by the mud and dust which have collected in its bed, in spite of frequent clearings out. The commencement of cloaca-buildings in general, and that of the Cloaca Maxima in particular, is generally ascribed to the three last kings; several additions to the latter were necessitated by the increasing size of the city. Frequent clearings out of the canal were required, owing to the gathering of mud;

some of them, carried on at great expense, are mentioned by contemporary writers. One of the late extensions is ascribed to M. Agrippa, the friend of Augustus. He seems to have constructed a new system of canals underneath the Campus Martius, one of which still passes under the floor of the Pantheon.

Of no less importance were the structures serving as outlets of lakes, either to prevent inundations or to regain arable land from the water. Such outlets, *emissaria*, also are mentioned at a very early period. They were either open or covered, and served to conduct the superfluous water from the lake to lower ground. The greatest difficulty naturally consisted in cutting the canals through solid mountains, or in conducting them in subterraneous tunnels. This was, for instance, the case with the drainage of the Albanian Lake, which Livy (V. 15 *et seq.*) connects with the story of the conquest of Veii by M. Furius Camillus (396 B.C.). The waterworks are still in use at the present day. From the high level of the lake, which lay in the crater of the old Albanian volcano, the water was let off by means of a shaft cut through the mountain for a distance of several thousand feet. According to the precept of the Delphic oracle, it was not led into the sea, but divided over the neighbouring fields, which thus were made fertile, the periodical inundations being at the same time prevented.

In a similar manner, but by an open canal, the drainage of the Veline Lake, in the country of the Sabii, was effected, after the conquest of those parts by Curius Dentatus (290 B.C.). By this means the country round Reate was converted into one of the most fertile regions of Italy. These works also are still in use.

The largest structure of this kind were the drainage works of the Lacus Fucinas, in the country of the Marsi, which had been desired for a long time by the inhabitants, owing to the dangerous inundations, and were planned by Cæsar, but not executed till the reign of Claudius. Here the whole basin of the lake was to be laid dry, and thus gained for agricultural purposes. This was effected by means of a shaft cut through the living rock from the lake down to the river Liris (at present called Garigliano), which discharged the water into the Mediterranean, near Minturnæ. According to ancient authors, the shaft was

3,000 *passus* long by 14 high and 9 wide.   Fig. 377, *a c*, gives
the section of the shaft in its full length, the line *a b* marking the

Fig. 377.

horizon so as to show the strong incline of the shaft.   The vertical
and oblique lines indicate shafts and galleries leading from the
surface to the canal ; the former destined for carrying off the
rubbish, the latter for the descent of the workmen, thirty thousand
of whom were occupied for eleven years in constructing the canal.

From the emissaria we turn to the *aquæductus*, destined to
conduct the water necessary for human use from distant places.
The care and skill bestowed on their construction and preservation
was equal, if not superior, to that required by the first-mentioned
canals.

The first thing required after the discovery of a spring in a
high place was to collect the water in a sheltered spot.   This led
to the erection of fountain-houses, specimens of which, in Greece,
we have before described (see Figs. 90 and 91).   In Italy also
some archaic buildings of this kind are extant, as, for instance,
the fountain-house discovered at Tusculum, and made known in
his description of Tusculum by Canina.   It consists of an oblong
chamber divided into several compartments, the ceiling being
constructed by the overlaying of stones on the old Greek system,
afterwards supplied amongst the Romans by the vault.   The
manner of conducting the water to the cities was, of course,
modified by the nature of the soil, as well as by the material
at hand.   One way was to conduct it underground in pipes (*tubi*,
fistulæ) or subterraneous canals.   The pipes were generally made
of lead or clay ; in some towns some of these have been preserved
with the municipal stamp on them.   The canals were, like the
emissaria, either cut into the rock or, where the soil was soft,
dug into the earth and walled in.   In either case shafts or other
openings placed at certain intervals served as communications
of the water with the fresh air.   Such openings were also

contrived where the canal, owing to the nature of the soil, was sunk below its ordinary level. A hollow extension of this kind was called *venter*, and above it a perpendicular shaft was laid as far as, or beyond, the surface of the earth, from which in the latter case it protruded like a chimney. In this shaft the water rose again to its ordinary level, by means of which it not only communicated with the open air, but also received additional pressure. The expenses of these aqueducts, so far as they were used for public purposes, were borne by the municipal governments; the private use of the water for houses, land, or the carrying on of a trade was subjected to a tax.

Where the aqueducts lay aboveground, it was usual to place them on the tops of walls (see Fig. 378). In that case the

Fig. 378.

water-channels usually were made of freestone or brick, and covered, in the former case, with slabs of stone, in the latter with vaults. In either case the interior of their walls received a water-tight coating, consisting of chalk and fragments of bricks, instead of the more common sand. The same coating was used in canals cut through the rock.

An uninterrupted wall would have been a great obstacle to the traffic, for which reason here also the all-important vaulting principle was applied. By means of intervening arches the wall of the aqueduct was divided into pillars at intervals, sufficiently large to leave space for the passage of roads, or even of rivers, without endangering the firmness of the structure. As an example we cite the arches of different dimensions across the Fiora Valley, near Volci, which carry both a road and an aqueduct (see p. 345, Fig. 367).

The Porta Maggiore in Rome (see p. 338, Fig. 357) ought also to be mentioned again as being part of two of the most celebrated Roman aqueducts. We have stated above how across the arches of this gate the waters of the Aqua Claudia and of the Anio Nova were conducted into the city in two different channels. Both aqueducts were begun by Caligula (A.D. 38), and finished fourteen years later by Claudius. The former, comparable by the excellency of its water to the celebrated Aqua Marcia,* began

---

* Called since its restoration by Pius IX., 21st June, 1870, Aqua Pia.

near the thirty-fifth milestone of the Via Sublacensis, in the Sabine Mountains, and was fed by two plentiful springs, besides receiving part of the Aqua Marcia. Owing to some turns necessitated by local conditions the length of the aqueduct was extended to forty-five miles, thirty-five of which were taken up by subterraneous canals, the remaining ten by open-air structures. The Anio Nova was fed, as its name indicates, by the river Anio, the word *nova* being added to distinguish it from an older aqueduct, Anio Vetus. It commenced at the sixty-second milestone of the same road, and received its water not immediately from the river, but from a basin into which it was led for the purpose of purification; near the thirty-eighth milestone a spring of still purer water, the Rivus Herculaneus, joined the aqueduct. Its whole length amounts to sixty-two Roman miles, partly above, partly under ground. About six miles from the city the two aqueducts join, and are carried on to the end by a common structure of arches, in some places 109 feet high; the channel of the Anio Nova, lying above that of the Aqua Claudia, was considered to be the highest aqueduct in Rome.

Some provincial aqueducts reach a still greater height. One of them is found near Nemausus (Nismes), in southern Gaul, whose beautiful temple we have mentioned before. The magnificent aqueduct, which crosses a valley, is in a good state of preservation. Its highest portion, known as *Pont du Gard*, rises in two stories to a height of nearly 150 feet. A row of smaller arcades is added on the top of the chief structure. The arcades are wide-arched, and convey the impression of a bold, graceful construction. Of a similar kind were the aqueducts of Segovia and Tarragona in Spain. The former is 2,400 feet long, and consists of a row of vaulted arcades: where the valley is deepest, the arcades rise in two stories up to a height of 100 Castilian feet, combining grace with firmness of structure. Owing to its excellent construction the aqueduct is still in good preservation.* The aqueduct of Tarragona is 876 feet long by 83 high.

So much about the aqueducts themselves. Many other contrivances were, however, required to make and keep the water fit for human use, as also to distribute it regularly. For the

* See Andres Gomez de Sommorostro, "El Acueducto y otras Antiguedades de Segovia." Madrid, 1820.

former purpose we mention, besides the shafts described above, the so-called *castella*, or reservoirs for collecting and purifying the water. At the beginning of the Anio Nova, for instance, lay a large mud-reservoir (*piscina limaria*), destined for filtering the water from the river. At the Aqua Virgo the waters of several springs had to be collected in separate reservoirs before being led into the common aqueduct.

The above-mentioned castella also served different purposes (see Fig. 379, representing a castellum of the Aqua Claudia).

Fig. 379.

According to Vitruvius, they had to be repeated at intervals of 24,000 feet, particularly in high aqueducts, their purpose being chiefly to give opportunities for distributing the water amongst the inhabitants of the surrounding countries; in case of stoppages, they also considerably facilitated the finding of the damaged places. Particular care was required for the castella at the ends of the aqueducts, from which the distribution of the water for the different purposes of the town took place. According to Vitruvius, the water seems to have been divided into three portions—one for the public fountains, the other for the thermæ, and the third for private use. For these three purposes three reservoirs served, each fed by a separate pipe; by means of other pipes the water was further distributed from these reservoirs. As, moreover, the water had to be divided over several quarters of the town, a number of smaller castella, and indeed a whole system of canals and reservoirs (247 of such are counted), became necessary, the excellent management of which, by a numerous staff, is a brilliant proof of the practical capacities of the Romans. Besides the usefulness of this quantity of water, it also served to embellish Rome. Numerous fountains adorned the city; M. Agrippa alone is said to have placed 105 jets. Rome still has the reputation of possessing a greater number of fountains than any other city in the world.

The above-mentioned *piscinæ* could also be constructed on a larger scale, in which case they became real reservoirs. In order to keep the water pure and cool a vault was constructed over the basin. As an example of these magnificent structures, we quote the piscina at Fermo (see section, Fig. 380), which contains in two stories six wide oblong compartments covered with so called barrel - vaults, and connected with each other by means of smaller openings. Fig. 381 shows the large reservoir still preserved near Baiæ, which is known as *Piscina Mirabile.* It is 270 palms long by 108 wide, and is covered with a vault broken by ventilation holes, and carried by forty-eight detached slender pillars. Two stairs of

Fig. 380.

forty steps each lead to the bottom of the reservoir, in the centre of which is a considerable cavity for the reception of the settling mud. Walls and pillars are coated with a peculiar kind of very hard stucco, impenetrable, it is said, even to iron.

Fig. 381.

75. In the private buildings of the Romans we discover the same mixture of old Italian and Greek elements as in their temples.

In order to understand the peculiarities of the Roman dwelling-house as distinguished from the Greek (see § 22) we have to consider the three most important parts of the former, as they can be plainly recognised from existing specimens. As is generally known, the three towns of Pompeii, Stabiæ, and Herculaneum were buried by an eruption of Vesuvius in 79 A.D. While the two latter towns were more or less destroyed by streams of lava, Pompeii was only covered with ashes; after, therefore, the ashes and the arable land on the top of them have been removed the buried buildings reappear in their original condition, unless they have been damaged by fire. In this way we gain a perfect idea of a provincial town, which, although Oscio-Samnitic by origin and Greek by development,* still, by its long connection with the Roman empire, may, in its present condition, be considered as essentially Roman.

---

* Some of the oldest buildings, as, for instance, the so-called temple of Hercules, show the old Doric style.

The dwelling-houses there preserved may therefore be fairly quoted as proofs, and indeed the only remaining proofs, of the Greek influence on private architecture.

The historic Roman house must be divided into a front space partly covered (*atrium*), a centre space wholly covered (*tablinum*), and adjoining it an open court surrounded by columns (*peristylium*). These three parts are found in the same order in almost every house, other smaller rooms being grouped round them in various ways. The atrium seems to be of exclusively Italian origin, as is proved by its mode of design entirely differing from Greek architecture, as also by its name. It consists of a square space covered by a roof which projects from the four walls, only a square opening being left in the centre. In this simplest form, of which several examples are known to us, the atrium is called *Tuscanicum*, for, like most other old Italian institutions, it was believed to owe its origin to the Etruscans (compare § 61 *et seq.*). Varro and other Roman antiquarians adhering to this notion have derived the name from the Etruscan town of Hatria; others derive the word from the Greek αἴθριον, or from the Latin *ater* (black). According to the former etymology, atrium would mean a room open to the sky (ὑπ' αἰθρίῳ); according to the latter, which is now generally accepted, a room blackened by the smoke of the hearth placed here. The latter explanation implies that the atrium was the chief room of the Italian house, owing to its containing the hearth, or, which is the same in other words, that, with the rooms immediately adjoining, it originally was the Italian house itself.

In sacred parlance, which retains the oldest ideas and expressions longer than any other, the house of King Numa is called *atrium regium*, which perhaps is identical with the *atrium Vestæ*, for this house lay close to the temple of Vesta, *i.e.* the common hearth of the Roman State. An old legal custom also proves the high age of the atrium. The opening in the centre of the roof was, as we said before, an essential feature of the atrium. Through it the smoke ascended, but also the rain entered, for which latter reason it was called, in conjunction with the slight excavation of the floor just underneath it, the *impluvium* and *compluvium*. The old law alluded to prescribed that if a man in fetters entered the house of the

Flamen dialis, these fetters were to be taken from him and thrown through the impluvium into the street, which proves sufficiently that at the time the law was made the atrium was an essential part of the house.

The simplicity of early times easily leads to the conclusion of the atrium having been the old Italian house itself; it was, like the court surrounded by columns in the Greek house, at once the starting-point and the remaining essential feature of later developments. Marini (see his "Vitruvius," c. III., Fig. 2) has attempted to reconstruct the old Italian house on this basis. As an important, though indirect, proof of our opinion we also mention an old Etruscan box of ashes discovered

Fig. 382.

at Poggio Gajello (see Fig. 382). It is evidently intended for the imitation of a house, as is not unfrequently the case with similar boxes. We can distinguish the protruding roof (mentioned by Vitruvius as a feature of the old Etruscan temple), the doors, and the impluvium, which is indicated by a cavity in the raised centre portion of the house, which accordingly consisted only of the atrium, surrounded perhaps by some smaller rooms.

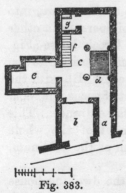

Fig. 384.

Fig. 383.

Amongst the numerous houses of Pompeii are moreover several which show this simple structure, and are evidently reminiscences of the original form. Fig. 383 shows the design, Fig. 384 (scale, 18 feet) the section, of one of these; besides a shop (*b*) lying towards the street, and a small passage (*a*), it consists exclusively of the atrium. The roof, protruding on three sides (on the fourth there is a simple wall), is supported

by two columns (*c*), to which correspond two semi-columns in
the wall; *d* indicates the impluvium. Within the atrium, and
under the same roof with it, we see a small separate compartment
(*g*), to the upper story of which (most likely the bedroom of the
slaves) leads a staircase (*f*); a larger room (*e*) adjoining the
atrium is evidently the sitting and bed room of the owner
(*cubiculum*), the small compartment observable in it being most
likely a sort of alcove for his bed.

Another house, the design of which is shown, Fig. 385
(scale, 18 feet), is of no less importance. Here again we see
nothing but an atrium (*c*), enclosed on two sides by the

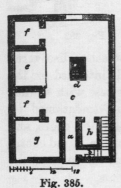

Fig. 385.

walls of the house, while the two other sides
open into various rooms. We first observe
the entrance-hall (*a*) and a small chamber (*h*),
to the upper story of which leads a staircase
(*b*); the other rooms (*f, f, g*) communicate
with the atrium by means of narrow doors.
The atrium itself, like the above-mentioned
Tuscan one, is without columns; the roof
protrudes equally from the four walls without
further props; the impluvium (*d*) is comparatively small. A particularly important
feature of this house is another room (*e*) not
hitherto met with, which adjoins one long side of the atrium, into
which it opens completely, and not by means of doors, as in other
cases. On comparing the design of the older Greek house (Fig.
92) we shall find that this room (*e*) lies in a similar position to the
atrium as the prostas (Fig. 92, C) does to the court (B), with the
only difference that in our present case, for want of space, the room
could not, like the prostas, be placed opposite the entrance. This
room (*e*) therefore becomes the chief apartment of the whole
house, and we recognise in it the simplest form of the tablinum,
to which we shall return presently.

The modifications of this original type of the dwelling-house
were, as in the temple, caused by the intrusion of Greek
elements. Here also they consist, first of all, of an enlargement
of the house. As we remarked before, the greater number of
existing Roman dwelling-houses contain, besides the atrium, a
second important part, viz. the court surrounded by a colonnade.

The mode of extending the house for natural reasons resembled
that explained by us with regard to the Greek dwelling (compare
Fig. 93 *et seq.*).   We there recognised the court and the prostas
as the oldest parts, to which afterwards a second back court was
added.   This court we also observe in most Roman houses.
Between it and the atrium lies an open hall, called *tablinum*,
which thus forms the centre of the house.   It lies in the same
place and served the same purpose as the prostas in the Greek
dwelling.   It was reserved to the master of the house, who from
it could overlook the two other divisions; here he kept his money
and documents, here he transacted his business.   Zumpt calls it
the office, or writing-room, of the owner, and derives its name
from *tabellæ* (writing-tablets); another derivation is that from
tabulæ, tabellæ, i.e. family-pictures, which are said to have hung
in the tablinum.*   Notwithstanding its being open and lying
between the atrium and peristylium, the tablinum was not used
as a passage between the two; slaves and other domestics rarely
entered it; some remaining traces seem to indicate that it could
be closed by means of sliding doors or curtains.   The communication between the atrium and peristylium was effected by means
of narrow corridors (*fauces*) running mostly alongside the tablinum.

The peristylium † is the court added to the Roman house at
a later period, after Greek architecture had become prevalent.
According to Greek patterns, it was surrounded by columns; its
name also is Greek; while tablinum and atrium are derived from
Latin roots.   It is natural, and moreover confirmed by Vitruvius's
statement and the remaining specimens, that in the houses of
the less wealthy classes the peristylium, if found at all, was
of secondary importance compared with the atrium; in many
cases it certainly was very unlike the regular court surrounded
by colonnades on its four sides prescribed by Vitruvius.   Some
houses in Pompeii have a court without any columns, instead
of the peristylium.   The Casa della Toeletta del Ermafrodito, or
di Adone ferito (called so from the pictures found in it), at

---

* According to other accounts, these family pictures were kept in separate rooms,
called *alæ,* the position of which seems uncertain but for the undisputed fact of
their being part of the atrium.

† The expression, *cavum ædium,* which occurs frequently, and has been explained
in various ways, seems to be applicable to the peristylium.

Pompeii shows a regular and spacious atrium; while the peristylium (the open part of which is not longer than the atrium) shows columns only on two sides, the two others being occupied by the walls, which enclose the house towards two streets crossing each other. A similar design we find in the peristylium of the Casa della Caccia, or di Dedalo e Pasifae, but for its being still more irregular, owing to the want of a rectangular termination; the atrium of this house also is spacious, and perfectly regular. The latter is the case also in the house of Sallustius, the peristylium of which is surrounded by columns on three sides.

We must omit other more or less irregular designs, and turn to a house at Pompeii which is remarkable both for the regularity of the *corps de logis* of the owner, and also for the manner in which other parts of the premises have been made useful for mercantile purposes, or let out to other persons. We are speaking of the house of Pansa, so called after the inscription on the façade, which, however, does not indicate the owner. The house, including the

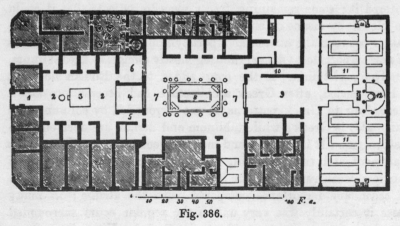

Fig. 386.

above-mentioned smaller habitations, is a complete oblong, surrounded by streets on all four sides (in front by that of Delle Terme), and therefore forming a so-called insula. The dwelling of the owner is surrounded on three sides by smaller houses (see Fig. 386), which appear hatched in our Plan. Part of the façade and the right side of the premises are occupied by various buildings, used partly as shops, partly let to so-called minor lodgers. The chief part of the opposite side is taken

up by a bakery, with the mill (12) belonging to it, and by
three shops (*tabernæ*) with small apartments attached to them. The
entrance to the dwelling-house lies between two shops, let separately. A narrow hall (*vestibulum*, 1),* the inner threshold of
which shows a "Salve" in mosaic, leads to the spacious atrium
(2 2), the impluvium of which is marked 3 in our plan. Six side-
chambers (*cubicula*) communicate with the atrium by means of
doors; two other rooms being entirely open towards it may
be considered as the side-wings of the atrium, whence their
name *alæ* (compare the Greek house, Fig. 92, 4, 5, and Fig. 93).
Opposite the entrance lies the tablinum (4), which, both by
its position and the beautiful mosaic on its floor, is marked as
the chief room of the house. Although open towards both sides
of the house, it did not serve as a passage, the communication
being effected by narrow corridors (*fauces*, 5) to the right of the
tablinum. On its left, towards the atrium, lies a good-sized room
(6), which shows a mosaic floor similar to that of the tablinum.
Remains of written documents have been found in it, whence
it is believed to have been the archive or library of the owner.
On the opposite side, separated from the tablinum by the fauces,
lies a smaller apartment, the entrance of which lies towards the
peristylium. Overbeck believes this to be a winter *triclinium*,
frequently met with in a similar situation. We now come to the
beautiful symmetrical peristylium (7) (20·15 × 13·10 metres),
the open centre space (8) of which is surrounded by sixteen
graceful columns of the Ionic-Korinthian order; its floor is
occupied by a fountain (*piscina*), the sides of which, two metres in
height, are painted with fish and water-plants. A narrow passage
between two of the out-houses led from the peristylium into
the side street. Several rooms open into the colonnade of the
peristylium, those to the left of the entrance being bedrooms
(*cubicula*); while a larger room on the right was the triclinium,†
or dining-room, the adjoining room serving as pantry, or as assem-

---

* Some authors (in accordance with Vitruvius, vi. 8) call vestibulum an open space
in front of the house. In Pompeii there is no example of such, unless we call the
small space immediately before the door (*ostium, janua*) by that name, in which case
the word *iter* (used by Vitruvius) would apply to the entrance-hall. Vestibulum
seems to have been used by the ancients in different senses.

† About the arrangement of the triclinium we shall speak at greater length (§ 88),
but we omit the description of the banqueting-halls (*œci*).

bling-room for the jugglers and dancers appearing towards the close of the meal. Behind the peristylium lies a garden, the connection between which and the peristylium is formed by a second kind of tablinum, the *œcus* (9) or state-room of the house. A corridor (10) by the side of the œcus, and communicating with it by means of a door, proves that the œcus itself was not used as a passage. To the left of the last-mentioned corridor lay the kitchen, and another room in which the dishes were dressed. The back façade, adorned with a portico, is joined by a garden (11), the regularly shaped beds (where most likely vegetables were grown), as also the lead pipes for watering the garden, are still visible; in the background, opposite the entrance to the œcus, seems to have been a sort of open hall (12).

One of the shops adjoining the dwelling-house was connected with the atrium by means of a back room (the blank compartment of our plan, the second to the left of the entrance). Perhaps the owner here sold the produce of his garden or estate. The largest and best preserved of the offices is the bakery (*pistrinum*), lying in the left division of the façade, next to the last-mentioned shop. Here we see the well-preserved oven, the mills, baking-table, water-reservoir, &c. Other shops were used for the sale of different goods, as, for instance, the colours used for wall-paintings. The owners lived in the dark rooms behind their shops, or in the rooms on the upper flats, to which led stairs from the shops. There are indisputable indications of the existence of a second story in this house, even parts of the floors of the upper rooms have been preserved. Mazois, to whom we owe a masterly publication of Pompeian buildings, remarks that here objects of female toilette have been discovered, which makes it appear probable that the sitting and bed rooms of the women lay on the second floor. According to Mazois's trustworthy design the rooms of this upper story were lower than those of the ground-floor; they were grouped round the two large open rooms of the house, so however that their walls did not take away air and light from the atrium and peristylium. Their windows, as far, at least, as the chief dwelling-house is concerned, looked towards the interior. The staircases in the outhouses here also prove the existence of a second floor, the windows of which, of course, lay towards the street (see Fig. 388).

Rome, of course, differed in many respects from provincial towns. Originally built without a plan and on uneven ground, its narrow angular streets were inhabited, about the time of the Antonines, by nearly a million and a half of people. Only the wealthy could have houses of their own, the middle and poorer classes living in hired lodgings. Speculators erected houses of many stories, of light woodwork or bad material, repairs were neglected, and enormous rents had to make up for the losses of the owners caused by their houses breaking down or being consumed by fire—daily occurrences in Rome. As early as the Republic houses of three or four flats were common in Rome. By a law of Augustus the street-frontage of no private house was allowed to exceed 70 feet (Roman measure), which limit was, after the fire of Nero, further reduced to 60 feet.

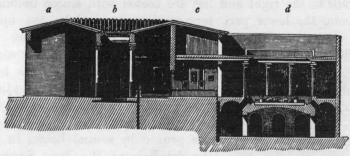

Fig. 387.

To conclude we add (Fig. 387) the section of a regular and tasteful middle-class house, the so-called Casa di Championnet, at Pompeii: *a* indicates the passage leading from the street to the atrium; *b* the atrium, the ceiling of which is carried by four slender columns: here lies the altar-like mouth (*puteal*) of a cistern, also met with in the peristylium of the house of Pansa; *c* is the tablinum, the walls of which are still adorned with paintings; *d* the peristylium, the open space of which is occupied by a cavity used as a conservatory; underneath this is a vaulted cellar (*hypogæum*) for the keeping of stores.

76. We add a few further remarks about the outward appearance of the houses, as also about certain modifications of their ordinary design. About the façades we know but little, seeing that in Pompeii all the upper stories of houses have

been destroyed. Most likely they were generally in very simple taste; for antique private architecture was chiefly intent upon the decoration of the inner apartments. The frontages of houses may, however, have been adorned in a simple way. We must distinguish between houses with or without shops in front. Of such shops we have already seen some examples (Figs. 385 and 386). They seem to have been open towards the street in their full width. The want of architectural beauty was supplied by a tasteful arrangement of the goods, in which the Italians of the present day, particularly with regard to fruit and other eatables, are still unsurpassed.

Of a house without a shop, opening towards the street only by a door, Mazois has attempted the reconstruction (Fig. 388), The façade shows a door in the centre between two Korinthian pilasters; the walls to the right and left are coated with stucco imitating freestone, the lower part representing large slabs, the upper

Fig. 388.

regular layers of small stones. A simple ledge finishes the lower story, over which a second story has been erected, with three small windows in it. The second story protruded from the surface in the manner of a bow-window, as is proved by several houses in the lane del Balcone Pensile at Pompeii. As to the manner of closing the window-holes we are uncertain in most cases. Sometimes movable wooden shutters have been used, as is proved

by the wooden frames found beside the windows of the house of the "tragic poet" at Pompeii; in other cases thin broken tablets of clay served the purpose, of which also several specimens have been preserved at Pompeii; we further hear of a transparent stone (*lapis specularis*) being used for the same purpose; window-panes of artificial glass have also been found at Pompeii.

Several specimens of doors (see Fig. 389) have been preserved to us: about the construction of their leaves and the manner of closing them we shall speak hereafter (§ 93). Fig. 389 shows a very simple door found at Pompeii. We there see the small window-like opening in the pilasters, through which the porter (*ostiarius*) could look at the callers after they had knocked with the knocker, also visible in our illustration. The most striking point on entering the house is the painting of the walls.

The thorough artistic taste of all classes is proved by the fact of the walls of even poorer houses being always either decorated pictorially or at least painted. The careful plastering of the walls, much superior to our present method, is equalled by the execution of the paintings themselves, which, although sometimes technically imperfect and mechanical in design, still give us some notion of the proportionately higher finish of real antique art. The large mythological figure-pictures painted on, or let into, the centre-pieces of walls at Pompeii and Herculaneum show the prevailing in-

Fig. 389.

Fig. 390.

fluence of Greek art, while the landscapes, still lives, and architectural decorations are more specifically Roman in taste.

To these wall-paintings also we shall have to return (see § 93). We add a few illustrations of single parts of houses, designed

in accordance with the remaining specimens. Fig. 390 shows
the open court of the house of Sallustius (also called the house of
Actæon) turned into a garden. One side of it is occupied by the
wall of the house, while the other shows a colonnade with a low
wall (*pluteus*) in the columnar interstices; on the third side, near
a fountain, the remains of which still exist, stands a sort of
verandah or bower, decorated by Mazois in the well-known
manner of a triclinium.

Fig. 391 shows the interior of the house of Pansa, from the
reconstructive design of Gell. We first see the atrium, containing statues and other objects; several alæ and cubicula open

Fig. 391.

into it (compare Fig. 386); we further see the triclinium, to the
left of which lies a cabinet; while to the right we discover the
corridors or fauces leading to the large peristylium, which itself
is visible in the distance with its lofty colonnades. Everything
gives the idea of a secluded comfortable home.

Where the wealth of the owner or the situation of the house
in the country gave additional space to the architect, he was
naturally tempted to develop new and enlarged modes of design.
This led, in the former case, to the palace; in the latter, to the
villa. This distinction, however, cannot always be preserved;
for, on the one hand, the town-palaces of later times sometimes
comprised pleasure-grounds, &c., belonging properly to a country

residence; while, on the other hand, the villa of a rich, luxurious Roman took the form of a monumental palace.

During the last century of the Republic the splendid mansions of private persons begin to be mentioned more and more frequently. We only remind the reader of the house built on the Palatine by M. Æmilius Scaurus, the stepson of the dictator, L. Cornelius Sulla, a man celebrated for his wealth. He first bought one of the most celebrated houses of the time, that of Cn. Octavius, with adjacent pieces of ground, to erect his own mansion on the site. As a specimen of great luxury Pliny mentions the marble columns, thirty-eight feet in height, which adorned the fore-court. They most likely had formerly belonged to the theatre built by Scaurus (see § 84), and their size certainly implies a locality of more than ordinary dimensions, even if compared with the larger dwelling-houses at Pompeii. Mazois has attempted a conjectural design of the palace of Scaurus, which gives an idea of the splendour and variety of its single parts. But all this was far surpassed by the buildings of imperial times, of which we will only mention the "golden house" of Nero, the product of an exaggerated love of splendid architecture which did not shrink from incendiarism to satisfy its craving on the ruins of Rome. The palace was built on the Palatine, and extended from there, by means of intermediate structures (*domus transitoria*), to the Esquiline, containing all the luxuries and conveniences imaginable. A fore-court surrounded by a triple colonnade (a Roman mile, or 1,478·50 metres, long) contained the statue of the emperor, 37 metres in height; ponds of the size of lakes, with rows of houses on their banks, gardens, vineyards, meadows, and woods inhabited by tame and ferocious animals, occupied the various courts; the walls of the rooms were covered with gold, jewels, and pearls; the ivory with which the ceiling of the dining-halls was inlaid was made to slide back, so as to admit a rain of roses or fragrant waters on the heads of the carousers. Under Otho this gigantic building was continued at an expense of about £525,000, but only to be pulled down for the greater part by Vespasian. On the site of the above-mentioned ponds stood the large amphitheatre finished by Titus (see § 85), and on the foundations of Nero's buildings on the Esquiline the thermæ of the same emperor were erected. The Palatine proper remained the

chief residence of the later emperors, who greatly altered the
original arrangements.   The excavations ordered by Napoleon III.
and Pius IX., and conducted by the architect Rosa, have yielded
the most important contributions to the history of the Palatine
edifices, from the oldest times of the Roma Quadrata down to
the Flavii.

A work of later date must serve to give us a more distinct
idea of Roman palatial architecture.   We are speaking of the
palace erected by the Emperor Diocletian on the coast of
Dalmatia, near his birthplace, Salona, where he spent the last
years of his life after his abdication.   On the few occasions when
this large and splendid building is mentioned by ancient authors
it is simply called a villa.   It might more properly be described
as a castle fortified in the manner of a camp (see § 70), for the
whole area occupied by the palace and other houses adjoining it
is enclosed on three sides by a solid wall, protected by square
or octagonal towers.   The whole space thus enclosed is about
500 feet wide by 600 long.   Amongst the ruins of the house
now lies a great part of the town of Spalatro.   Between the

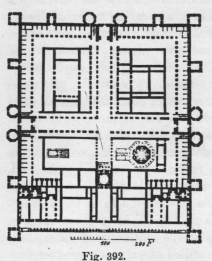

centre pair of the above-mentioned towers on each of the
three sides lies a gate (compare
Fig. 356), those on the two long
sides being connected by means
of a street, just as we found it
in the Saalburg, near Homburg
(compare Fig. 354).   Another
street, crossing the first in the
centre, starts from the gate
on the third, narrower side,
without, however, being continued to the opposite side.
This street, after passing between two temples, ends in
what may be considered as the
vestibule or entrance-hall of the

Fig. 392.

imperial palace proper. This palace occupied the fourth side towards
the sea.   Instead of the solid walls we here see an open passage
with arcades, into which open the numerous different apartments

of the imperial dwelling. The view of the sea and surrounding country is beautiful. The space of the whole area not occupied by the palace itself (see plan, Fig. 392) is divided into four quarters by means of the above-mentioned streets, the two outer ones being taken up by the houses for the body-guard and other attendants of the emperor, while the two remaining quarters form open spaces, with a temple standing in the centre of each. One of these temples, to the left of the palace-entrance is a simple prostylos of moderate dimensions; the other is a fine specimen of the vaulted round temple, for, although octagonal in its outer shape, it is circular in the interior. The wall is adorned with two rows of columns, one above the other, and by an elegant cupola.

There is no room within the enclosing wall for gardens and fields, and it is moreover mentioned expressly that these lay outside. The character of the architecture is rich and splendid, but shows a decline if compared with the purity of the end of the Republic and the beginning of the Empire.

Villas proper, *i.e.* country residences, were greatly in favour with wealthy Romans, and we in consequence possess numerous descriptions of them of various dates, on the authority of which architects and scholars since Pirro Ligorio have attempted various reconstructive designs. The old *villa rustica,* of which Cato and after him Varro speak, comprises a combination of the dwelling-houses and of the various buildings required for farming purposes. Varro already complains of the latter consideration being thrown into the background by the desire of transforming large agricultural districts into beautiful landscapes, the villas themselves being at the same time reconstructed on the luxurious system of town architecture (*villa urbana*). Vitruvius, whose statements about the villa rustica tally with those of Varro, says that the villa urbana was constructed like a town house, with the distinction of its being more regular in design, and that of its site being chosen better than the narrow space between the adjoining houses of a street would permit. The increasing scale of luxury and comfort may be marked by comparing the simplicity of the older Scipio's Linternum in Campania, or the family-seat of Cicero at Arpinum, with the more comfortable villa of the latter at Tusculum or his Formianum, and finally with the splendid

country residences of Metellus and Lucullus. We possess the
description and partly the remains of some of the villas of
imperial times, which give us a high idea of the variety and
splendour of their architectural arrangements. The younger
Pliny has described in two letters his Tuscum (Ep. V., 6; compare
§ 94) and his villa at Laurentum (II., 17). He there mentions
a great number of apartments, halls, courts, baths, and other
conveniences for the enjoyment of life in different weathers and
seasons; he at the same time notices the absence of fish-ponds,
museums, libraries, &c., such as were considered indispensable
at other villas. These statements refer to the time of Trajan.
Of the time of Hadrian we know the villa constructed for himself
by that art-loving emperor at Tibur, the former splendour of
which is still visible in the numerous remains of it found near
the modern Tivoli; a short description of the same villa by
Spartianus (v. Hadriani, 26) assists us further in realising its
grand design. The ground belonging to it had a circumference
of seven Roman miglie. We are still able to distinguish two
larger theatres, and an odeum, smaller in size, and destined, most
likely, for musical performances; a great number of chambers, still
recognisable, seem to have been destined for the pilgrims visiting
a temple and oracle here situated; other rooms in a still better state
of preservation ("le Cento Camarelle") may have belonged
to the emperor's body-guard. Near them lie the ruins of what
is supposed to have been the emperor's dwelling. Other structures
were called by the names of celebrated buildings in different
provinces of the empire. The Canopus (an imitation of the
temple of Serapis at Canopus) mentioned by Spartianus has been
recognised in the ruin of a round temple lying in a valley,
enclosed architecturally. It was adorned with numerous statues
in the Egyptian style, the remains of which are in the Capitoline
Museum. Other ruins containing the remains of baths are said
to have been the Lyceum and Academy; a large square surrounded
by columns was the Poikile, adjoining which lie a basilica and a
round building, most likely the Prytaneum mentioned by Spartianus. Even the valley of Tempe had been imitated, while
Hades is recognised by some in a still-preserved labyrinth of
subterraneous chambers. The architecture was technically perfect, as is shown by the remaining brick walls and vaults: some

of the ruins seem to prove that the walls were adorned with slabs of marble, and that the vaulted ceilings were coated with stucco. Numerous fragments of columns, beams, valuable pavements, and sculptures have been (during the last three centuries) and are still being recovered from the ruins.

To illustrate the simpler villas of the higher middle class we have inserted the plan of the so-called *villa suburbana* of M. Arrius Diomedes at Pompeii (Fig. 393; scale, 100 feet). It lies near the city in the street of graves, which passes the building in an oblique direction. The ground in this place slopes downwards

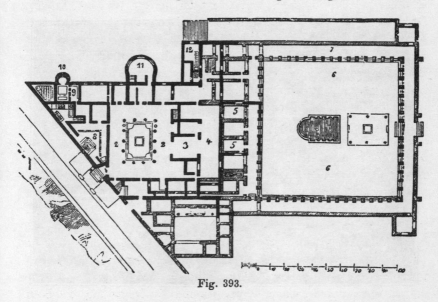

Fig. 393.

from the street; and as the house has to follow this declivity, the front parts (marked in our plan by black lines) lie higher than the back ones (marked by hatched lines), rising above them in the form of terraces. Near the entrance the pavement of the street is raised, and from it seven further steps ascend to the door (1) through which one enters the peristylium (2), quite in accordance with Vitruvius's (VI., 8) rules for such villas, called by him *pseudourbanæ;* in the position of the peristylium they therefore differ essentially from town-houses. Fourteen Doric columns (the lower third of which is not fluted, but painted red, while the two upper thirds are white and fluted) form the peristylium, and surround a compluvium, the water of which communicated with two fountains (*puteal*) between the columns. On the side opposite the door of the peristylium lies the tablinum (3), the other sides being adjoined by smaller chambers, some of which were bed-rooms, as appears from the beds worked into the walls. The tablinum opens into a sort of gallery (4), connected on one side with the peristylium by means of fauces, and opening on the other into a large hall (5), the œcus. This again opens into a second large court with colonnades by means of a window reaching almost to the ground. The enclosing walls of the space hitherto

Fig. 394.

described are marked black in our plan, the hatched lines between them being meant for the walls of smaller chambers on the ground floor underneath it. The just-mentioned court (6), mea-suring 33 square metres, was surrounded by a vaulted passage (7), supported by pillars (*cryptoporticus*), two sides of which are in perfect preservation; to judge by some of the remains it must have had a second story. In the centre of the court lies a large piscina adorned with a jet, and behind it an open structure resembling a temple, which most likely served as triclinium in the summer. The six columns formerly supporting it are partly

preserved. To the left of the street-door we notice a triangular
court (8) enclosed on two sides by a covered passage, the third
longer side being occupied by a cold plunging-bath. We also
find a tepidarium (9) and calidarium (10) for tepid and hot baths,
in the latter of which the tub for the hot water, the niche for the
labrum, and the heating apparatus are preserved (compare § 80).
Remarkable is also a beautiful bedroom (11), the semicircular
projection of which contains three large windows, to let in the
sun in the morning, afternoon, and evening ; the view from these
windows is beautiful. The back wall of this room contains the
alcove for the bed, that could be closed by means of a curtain,
as is proved by the rings still in existence ; 12 marks a small
chamber, through which, by means of a staircase, one passed
into the lower story and the rooms lying near the large court.
To conclude we add (Fig. 394) the view of a villa by the sea,
from a Pompeian wall-painting.

77. From the houses of the living we pass to graves and
grave-monuments. Amongst the numerous and variegated
Roman graves we must limit our remarks to a few specimens.
Almost all the different kinds of Roman tombs have their ana-
logies in Greek architecture. We cannot discuss the question
whether, as seems likely, the old Latin or Italian custom consisted
in simply covering the corpse with earth; neither will we try
to determine when this custom was superseded by the construction of grave-chambers or detached monuments for the reception
of the ashes of burnt bodies. Certain it is that at the time when
this was done models for all the varieties of tombs as developed
by the Greeks (see §§ 23 and 24) were to be found amongst
the neighbouring Etruscans. Amongst the Etruscan tombs we
distinguish the subterraneous grave-chamber, the tomb cut into
the rock with a more or less elaborate façade, and finally the
detached grave-mounds. Of the first kind the old graves of
Cære and the burial-places of Vulci and Corneto offer numerous
examples.

Amongst the former we have chosen the grave known as
Tomba delle Sedie (see plan, Fig. 395, and section, Fig. 396).
The plan shows an inclined passage leading (partly by means
of steps) down to a vestibule, into which open three doors ; the
two at the sides lead each into a chamber all but square in shape

(d); the third between these two is the entrance to the chief burial-chamber (a). It is an oblong, and shows on the wall opposite the entrance two stone chairs (see Fig. 396), whence the name

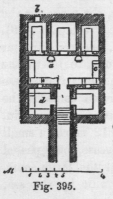

Fig. 395.

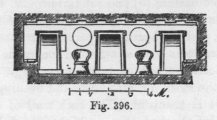

Fig. 396.

of the grave is derived; along the other three walls run benches (c). After this chief apartment follow three smaller chambers, of which that on the right contains a niche in the wall (b).

Of graves cut into the rock we find several examples in the narrow valleys of Norchia and Castell d'Asso, the steep slopes of which contain the entrances to the graves; steps lead up to them. Some of the façades are adorned with columns (compare Lenoir, "Tombeaux de Norchia." Ann. dell' Instit., IV. 289; "Mon. Ined.," I., tav. XLVIII. 4), while others (see Fig. 397)

Fig. 397.

show no artificial work beyond the doors and the steps leading up to them.

Of the third or detached grave we find numerous specimens in the burial-places of Vulci and other towns. Most of these resemble the above-mentioned grave-mound in the isle of Syme (see Fig. 98); our illustration (Fig. 398), the so-called Cucumella, differs from it only by its larger diameter (200 feet) and by the careful stone-border surrounding its whole circumference. On the slope of the mound we also discover ruins of old Etruscan structures which indicate a more elaborate architectural decoration of this grave.

Fig. 398.

We now come to the subterraneous Roman graves built after the Etruscan pattern. Like the Greek tombs they varied in design according to the conditions of the soil, being either cut into the hard rock, or dug into the earth and enclosed with walls where the softness of the soil required it; in the construction of the ceiling the vault became an important element. Of graves in rocks we possess a very primitive example in the tombs of the Scipiones—a kind of labyrinth of irregular subterraneous passages, previously used as a quarry. Originally

Fig. 399.

they lay outside the city in the Via Appia, but on the enlargement of Rome they came within the circle enclosed by the Aurelian wall. Of the monuments found there we quote (Fig. 399) the sarcophagus containing the remains of L. Cornelius Scipio Barbatus (Consul, 298 B.C.). It is made of common stone, and may be considered as one of the most important proofs of the early influence of Greek on Roman art, showing an ornamental border resembling the frieze of Doric art, and a cornice of dentils, which, like the volutes of the top decoration, remind one of Ionic patterns.

More regular is the tomb of the Nasones, in the Via Flaminia. It consists of a subterraneous chamber, with semi-circular niches for the coffins. The grave of the Gens Furia, near Frascati, consists of a semicircular chamber surrounded by a narrow passage, the entrance to which, on the slope of the mountain, is adorned with a façade.

We finally mention the subterraneous grave-chambers common to a tribe or to the slaves and freedmen of the imperial or other noble families. The urns (*olla*), with simple covers to them, stand in niches somewhat resembling pigeon-holes, whence the name of *columbarium* (dovecot) applied to these graves; a small marble tablet

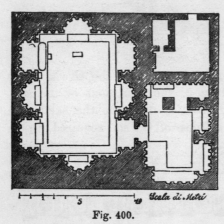

Fig. 400.

above each niche records the name of the deceased. Several of these columbaria have been found in and near Rome. Figs. 400 and 401 give the plan and view of the columbarium in which the freedmen of Livia, the wife of Augustus, were buried. It lies in the Via Appia, and consists of several apartments, of which the one nearest the entrance is very simple, while the larger ones, reached by descending a staircase, are decorated more richly. Large niches,

Fig. 401.

square or circular in shape, were destined for the reception of sarcophagi; while seven ascending rows of smaller openings in the walls contained the cinerary urns. Another columbarium in the Vigna Codini contains 425 niches in nine rows.

The interior arrangements of detached graves are of a similar kind (compare § 78). Fig. 402 illustrates the interior of a detached tomb, the exterior of which we shall consider hereafter (see Fig. 412). The simple room covered with a barrel-vault receives its light from a single window in the ceiling. Niches in the walls

Fig. 402.

and in the benches contain the urns, others of which are standing on these benches.

78. The simplest forms of detached graves aboveground are nearly related to Etruscan structures of the same kind. We pass from the simple earth-mounds (*tumuli*) to those tombs which show a distinct architectural design. Fig. 403 shows Hirt's reconstructive design of a partly destroyed, but still recognisable, grave

Fig. 403.

Fig. 404.

near Naples, generally called the tomb of Virgil. It consists of a square base made of bricks, the frontage of which contains a round-arched door leading into the grave. On this base stands a flattened cone, also made of bricks, except the bottom layers, which consist of hewn stones.

A similar, though more artistic, design appears in the so-called tomb of the Horatii and Curiatii, standing on the road from Rome to Albano, near the last-mentioned place (see view and design, Figs. 404 and 405). It seemingly belongs to the time of the Republic. Its material is a stone found in the quarries of Albano, generally called "Peperin." The substructure is nineteen metres in circumference, and shows a base and a cornice

carefully worked out. On it stands a conical structure, similar to that of the grave of Virgil. Here, however, several smaller cones are grouped round the centre one, the former occupying the four corners of the substructure. The centre cone is

Fig. 405.   both thicker and higher than the others. Perhaps an individual Etruscan model has here been imitated; the descriptions, at least, of the tomb of the Etruscan King Porsenna indicates a similar arrangement of four conical turrets.

Akin to these conical erections is the round tower on a square base, such as found in the grave in the Via Appia belonging, according to its inscription, to Cæcilia Metella, daughter of Q. Creticus, and wife of the triumvir C. Crassus, celebrated for

Fig. 406.

his riches (Fig. 406). The base is made of quarry-stone, the round tower being carefully faced with freestone, and adorned with frieze and cornice. The decoration of the frieze is composed of alternating flowers and skulls of animals, whence the popular name of the monument "Capo di Bove." A small door leads into the circular grave-chamber. What the original roof of the building has been can no more be ascertained; the battlement seen in our illustration dates from the Middle Ages, when the Cætani turned the tomb into a tower of defence, connecting it with other fortifications still preserved.

Another monument built in imitation of the Egyptian pyramids belongs to the age of Augustus (Fig. 407). The pyramid is of rather steep ascent, its base being 30 metres in circumference, its height 37 metres. It is built of a very firm composition of mortar and small stones faced with tablets of white marble. The grave-chamber is comparatively small, and still

Fig. 407.

shows traces of beautiful wall-paintings. The original entrance was effected by means of an inclined shaft about half-way up the northern side of the pyramid. This shaft, covered outside with a stone, led straight to the centre of the vault, covering the grave-chamber. Columns and statues adorned the exterior. Several inscriptions record the dignities of the deceased inmate, amongst which we count those of prætor and tribune of the people. His name was C. Cestius. The monument was erected to him by his heirs, one of whom was M. Agrippa. In accordance with the last will of the deceased it had been completed in 330 days.

Other forms of the grave resemble the design of a temple, as does, for instance, a monument discovered near the northern

Fig. 408.

corner of the Capitol (Fig. 408). It is built of freestone, and shows on its base an inscription, according to which it was dedicated by the people and senate to the memory of the ædile Caius Poblicius Bibulus. The upper part contains on the side shown in our illustration a door between two Doric or Tuscan pilasters, which at the same time carry the beams, with a sort of balustrade on the top of them. The frieze shows a decoration of flowers and skulls of bulls, similar to that of the tomb of Cæcilia Metella. Another tomb at Palmyra shows a still closer resemblance to the temple;

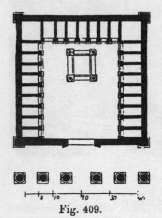

Fig. 409.

it may, indeed, be described as a prostylos hexastylos (see Fig. 409; scale, 40 feet). It forms an all but perfect square, with a portico of six detached columns added to it. The arrangement of the interior proves its destination as a family-grave: on three sides we see rows of narrow cellæ or grave-chambers, while almost in the centre of the building stands a structure of four columns (*tetrastylos*), most likely destined for the reception of the chief sarcophagus. Another grave in the form of a tower is also found at Palmyra (Fig. 410 ; scale, 24 feet), the front side of which shows the statue of the deceased in a lying position ; while the interior contains, in different stories, a number of niches for the reception of cinerary urns.

All the monuments hitherto mentioned are, if not small, at least of moderate dimensions; the increasing luxury of later times, however, also extended to grave monuments. This was particularly the case where the dignity of the State itself was

represented by the deceased person. The monument erected by
Augustus to himself and his descendants shows colossal dimensions.
On a square base rose an enormous round building (similar to
that of the tomb of Cæcilia Metella), on which
was heaped an additional tumulus, while underneath it lay the imperial grave-chambers. The
enclosing walls are preserved sufficiently to give
an idea of the original grandeur of the structure.

When, in the course of a century, it had been
filled with the remains of emperors, Hadrian
determined upon erecting a similar structure for
himself and his successors.

The site chosen lay on the other side of the
Tiber, opposite the tomb of Augustus, connected
with the city by means of the above-mentioned
Pons Ælius (Figs. 369 and 370), at present
called Ponte S. Angelo. This tomb also con-
sists of a square basis (90 metres), and, standing on it, a colossal
round tower (67 metres in diameter by 22 high), originally faced

Fig. 410.

Fig. 411.

with Parian marble, and decorated more richly than the mausoleum
of Augustus. According to a tradition, the twenty-four Korinthian

columns in the centre nave of St. Paul's Basilica originally belonged to this Moles Hadriani, which indicates its having been surrounded by colonnades in the manner of a round peripteros. This conjecture becomes still more probable from the fact of plastic works of art being mentioned in connection with the mausoleum, which statues most likely stood in these colonnades: excellent works of art have indeed been found in the neighbourhood. The chief part of the edifice has been preserved in the round tower of the Castello S. Angelo, which makes a careful investigation of the interior a matter of some difficulty. Several

Fig. 412.

designs of the original form of the building have been attempted. Fig. 411 shows that of Canina, who, in opposition to Hirt, assumes the existence of two external colonnades. Canina crowns the building with a pyramidal roof, the top ornament being a large pineapple of bronze, found in the neighbourhood, and at present in the garden of the Vatican.

Of other smaller grave-monuments, partly containing the grave-chambers, partly built above them, we possess a variety of forms. They either resembled small round or square altars (*cippi*), or they consisted of simple pillars (*hermæ*), the tops of which were rounded on one side, so as to almost resemble a human head cut in half. Of all these forms we see specimens in the street of graves at Pompeii (Fig. 412). On both sides of the street (our view is taken from a point near the villa of Diomedes, Fig. 393) we see numerous graves, generally with the names of individuals or families inscribed on them. Where space permitted the monument was, like the temple, surrounded by a small court, separated from the street and other graves by a wall. These enclosures, besides indicating the hallowed character of the place, were, in some cases, used for the solemn burning of the body and the collecting of the remains according to prescribed rites (*ossilegium*). In case the enclosure served this purpose it was denominated *ustrina* (from *urere*, to burn). In some places, however, the burning of the body near the grave was forbidden, besides which the poorer classes could not afford separate enclosures; for these reasons public ustrina had to be provided, one of which, in the form of a square space enclosed by a wall, has been discovered at Pompeii. Another large public ustrinum, in the Via Appia, about five miglie from the Porta S. Sebastiano, has been discovered by Piranesi, and described by him in his "Antichità di Roma" (III., 4). It is a vast square, surrounded on all sides by walls of large blocks of Peperin stone. On the wall is a path with a low parapet, evidently intended to enable the mourners to witness the burning of the body in the square, after which the collecting of the ashes took place.

Amongst the tombs of the Pompeian street of graves (Fig. 412) we discover on the left, first a small monument like a temple, with two columns; it lies just opposite the villa of Diomedes, and was, according to its inscription, the common grave of the family of M. Arrius Diomedes; to it belong the two cippi which lie on a common base with the chief monument, and are inscribed to two members of the same family. The second larger monument on the same side is devoted to the memory of L. Ceius Labeo; his and his wife's busts, which formerly stood on the grave, are now in the Museo Borbonico. On the right side of our illustration we see a wall covered by a gable; a low door in this wall leads into an uncovered square court adjoining one corner of the villa of Diomedes, in which court the arrangements for the funereal repast, the last ceremony of the burial, have been found. In this court we recognise a *triclinium funebre* resembling the dining-rooms of private houses, with their gently inclining couches; its walls were covered with paintings, now in an all but destroyed condition. Next to this triclinium stands, on a rich base, an altar-like monument, which is amongst the finest and best pre-served tombs of Pompeii. It lies in a court, the wall of which is adorned with small turrets; a door in this wall opens into the street. The grave-chamber lies inside the base (see the view of the interior, Fig. 402); the cippus, resembling an altar, which rises above the base on several steps to a height exceeding

Fig. 413.

that of the enclosing wall, is richly adorned with bas-reliefs. The inscription on its front side says that Nævoleia Tyche, the freedwoman of Luccius Nævoleius, has erected the monument during her lifetime to herself, to L. Munatius Faustus, and to their liberated slaves of both sexes. Amongst the monuments following on the same side, and still visible in our illustration, we mention the cenotaphium of C. Calventius Quietus, in the form of an altar. After it follows a family-grave without inscription, consisting of a round flat tower surrounded by a wall, crowned by turrets, with decorations in relief. We further mention the tomb of

Scaurus, interesting by its bas-reliefs representing gladiators
(compare Figs. 505, 507, 508).

To conclude we add an
illustration of a portion
of the Via Appia, near
Rome. This important
highway was peculiarly
adapted to be adorned
with tombs and other
monuments, the traces of
which have been disco-
vered for a distance of
several miles from Rome.
After carefully examin-
ing the remains and com-
paring them with other
monuments, the architect
Canina has tried to illustrate parts of the Via in
their original appear-
ance. Fig. 413 is a re-
production of one of these
attempts.

79. We now come to
those monuments which,
instead of being the re-
ceptacles of dead persons,
served to prolong the
memory of their deeds
and merits. Some monu-
ments served both as
tombs and memorial
structures (compare our
remarks about the keno-
taphion of the Greeks,
§ 24, c). The most
striking illustration of

Fig. 414.

the combination of these two different purposes is the column
of the Emperor Trajan, to which we shall have to return. Fig.

414 shows a monument, which in a manner forms the connecting link between the two species of edifices alluded to. It
lies near the village of Igel, in the vicinity of Treves ; our
illustration shows the north side. It is built of freestone, and
rises in several divisions to a height of 64 feet, according to the
lowest of the different measurements. The sides towards north
and south are 15, those towards east and west 12 feet wide. The
steep roof, resembling a pyramid with curved outlines, is adorned
with decorations not unlike scales. It is crowned by a sort of
capital, adorned with human figures in the four corners, on which
rests a globe supported by four small sphinxes. Some fragments
on the top of this globe seem to indicate that here was placed
originally an eagle carrying a human figure to heaven—an
apotheosis of the persons to whom the monument was dedicated.
Besides these greatly injured sculptures we observe a profusion of
figures in relief on all sides and in all divisions of the structure.
Like the chief representation on the south side they refer partly to
the individuals to be honoured by the monument, partly to mythological objects (the centre bas-relief visible in our illustration, for
instance, shows the god of the sun in his chariot), partly also they
illustrate scenes of actual life in reference to the persons alluded to.
Of this more anon. The style of the sculptures and architecture
belongs to late imperial times. An inscription, although partly
destroyed, and explained in many different ways, seems to prove
beyond doubt that the monument was erected by L. Secundinius
Aventinus and Secundinius Securus in honour of their parents
and their other blood-relations. It was the common monument
of the Secundinii, several members of which family are mentioned in inscriptions found near Treves as holding offices of
various kinds. Similar monuments of Roman origin have been
found by Barth in the south of the Tripolitan country (the
Syrtica Tripolitana of the Romans), in the Wadi Tagidje, and
near the fountain of Taborieh (see H. Barth, " Reisen und
Entdeckungen in Nord- und Central-Afrika," I., pp. 125
and 132).

In turning to the monuments of honour proper we must
premise that amongst such may be counted all structures, be they
temples, halls, theatres, columns, pillars, or gates, erected in
honour of a person or in celebration of an event. To Cæsar and

several emperors temples have been erected; small buildings resembling chapels, built in honour of individuals, occur at Palmyra; halls and colonnades in Rome served, as they did amongst the Greeks, to perpetuate the memory of great men; even a theatre in Rome was built in honour of a favourite of the Emperor Augustus. We must refrain from describing these and similar structures. We mention only two forms of the monument of honour, one of which has been invented, the other applied in preference, by the Romans. To the latter class belong the columns; to the former the triumphal arches. Columns were frequently erected by the Greeks for the same purpose, and in that case bore the statue of the person to be honoured (as, for instance, that of the orator Isokrates), or some object referring to the deeds or merits of this person. A second column erected to the same Isokrates showed the image of a syren as a symbol of eloquence; other columns, partly still preserved, carried tripods, such as were awarded to the victors of the agones.* Sometimes the columns showed only inscriptions without sculptural decorations. Columns of all three kinds may have occurred amongst the Romans, who at an early date adopted this mode of honouring meritorious citizens from the Greeks. Originally they were awarded only by the senate, afterwards also by the people, the expenses being either raised by private collections or paid by the State. Having frequently described the architectural characteristics of the column, we shall here refer to such columnar monuments only as greatly deviate from the common type. We first mention the oldest of all such columns, viz. the Columna Rostrata, built in the Forum, and adorned with the prows of ships, to celebrate the naval victory of C. Duilius over the Carthaginians (B.C. 261). A modern imitation of it with the antique inscription is preserved in the Capitoline museum. This venerable monument became the model of other *columnæ rostratæ* found on various coins of imperial origin, struck in celebration of naval victories. Whether these columns (as, for instance, those on silver coins of Augustus and Titus, with the statues of these emperors on the top of the columns) were actually erected remains uncertain. Other columns

---

* On the south side of the Akropolis, near the castle-wall, above the theatre of Dionysos, are still standing several columns of this kind, the Korinthian capitals of which have been made triangular, so as to fit the tripods to be placed on them.

show the deeds of their heroes in relief representations, winding generally in a spiral line round the shaft of the column from base to capital. A column of this kind was the chief ornament of the Forum built by Trajan, to which we shall later have to return (see § 82). The column stands on a square base covered with the inscription and with numerous warlike trophies of various kinds. The pedestal is 17 feet high; the column itself, including base and capital, 92 feet. Above the capital rises a pedestal, on which the bronze statue of the emperor stood: it has been lost and replaced by that of St. Peter. The column itself, consisting of twenty-three drums of marble, is in surprisingly good preservation. The bas-reliefs surrounding it, in twenty-two spiral curves, form a consecutive number of scenes from Trajan's wars with the Dacians. The inscription on the base gives the date and purpose of its erection.* According to a doubtful tradition the ashes of the emperor were enclosed in a globe held by the statue; while, according to another more trustworthy account, Hadrian deposited the remains of his predecessor in a golden urn underneath the column. A winding staircase of 185 steps inside the column (the entrance to which lies in the pedestal) leads to the top of the capital.

Resembling the column of Trajan, although not equal to it in workmanship and beauty, is the column erected by senate and people to the memory of the noble Marcus Aurelius Antoninus. It seems to have been connected with a temple devoted to the same emperor. Like the column of Trajan, it is well preserved, and, like it, it has lost the original statue of the emperor, the present one of St. Paul having been placed on it by the same pope, Sixtus V., who put the statue of St. Peter on the column of Trajan, on the occasion of both these monuments being cleaned and restored. Fig. 415 shows a design of Canina of the column with its original surroundings. Like the first-mentioned column, it consists of large cylindrical blocks of marble worked, on the inside, into a winding staircase of at present 190 steps. According to an inscription found near it, its height is 100 old Roman feet.

---

* SENATUS POPULUSQUE ROMANUS IMP CAESARI DIVI NERVAE F NERVAE TRAIANO AUG GERM DACICO PONTIF MAXIMO TRIB POT XVII IMP VI COS VI P P AD DECLARANDUM QUANTAE ALTITUDINIS MONS ET LOCUS TANTIS OPERIBUS SIT EGESTUS.

The shaft is like that of the column of Trajan, but the pedestal is considerably higher in this case; part of it is now hidden by the earth. The bas-reliefs winding round the column in twenty spiral curves refer to the wars of the emperor with the Marcomans and other tribes to the north of the Lower Danube (compare § 107).

Triumphal arches were frequently erected by the Romans, in

Fig. 415.

this case without the aid of numerous models in Greek architecture. Both by their character and destination these structures are essentially Roman. The custom of arranging festive pageants in celebration of happy events soon led to the erection of triumphal gates for the procession to pass through. Besides decorating the gates of the city for the occasion, the Romans used to erect detached gates of a monumental character. Such triumphal arches might be the reward of all kinds of civic merit. An arch erected to Augustus at Araminium (Rimini) celebrated his construction of the Flaminian road from that town to Rome ; an arch, still standing, on the jetty of Ancona records Trajan's restoration of that harbour ; another arch at Beneventum was dedicated to the same emperor for his restoration of the Via Appia ; an arch still preserved, near the Olympicum, commemorates the building of a new splendid quarter of Athens by Hadrian. The so-called arch of the Sergii at Pola records the merits of a family ; a small but richly decorated triumphal gate in the Forum Boarium in Rome was erected to Septimius Severus by the goldsmiths and cattle-dealers.

In most cases, however, these arches were designed for the triumphal entrance of a commander at the head of his army after a victorious war. These triumphal entrances (compare § 109) are essentially representative of the national spirit of the Romans, quite as much as the public games were of that of the Greeks. The sculptural decorations of the arches generally represent the processions that were to pass through them : on the arch of Titus we even see a sculptural reproduction of this monument itself. As the arch itself is a product of Roman national spirit, so its design is pre-eminently representative of that specifically Roman element in architecture — the vaulting or arching principle. Nowhere is this principle displayed more simply and more effectively, nowhere does the mixture of Greek columnar architecture with Roman elements appear in a more striking manner, than in these detached triumphal gates, the arcades of which are in a manner framed with columns or semi-columns appearing to support the flat coverings of the arches and the second lower stories on the top of them. Into the architectural varieties of the triumphal arch we cannot enter here ; we only shall quote two examples, representative of the two principal divisions of these monuments. Like the city gate, the triumphal arch can have either one (compare Fig. 356) or three openings (358—360), the possibility of two openings occurring in some Roman gates (Fig. 357) being naturally excluded.

A beautiful example of the first species is the arch of Titus

in Rome, built of Pentelic marble (see design, with the statue
of the emperor in a quadriga added to it, Fig. 416). Its height
is 15·40 metres, its width 13·50, its depth 4·75 metres. The
arched opening is 5·36 metres wide by 8·30 high. In the
Middle Ages a tower of fortification had been built on it; but it
was restored to its present form in 1822. Its construction is very
simple: two strong piers have been connected by means of an arch
for the triumphal procession to pass through. To right and left of

Fig. 416.

the arch the piers show two fluted semicolumns of the "composite"
order, being the earliest specimens of that order (the two outside
ones in travertine and without flutes are a modern addition); they
stand on a common base, and enclose on each side of the arch a
so-called false window. The beams, which are supported by the
columns, and which at the same time cover the arch, are richly
decorated; the frieze shows a small bas-relief representation of
a sacrificial pageant. Above the beams rises the attic, divided,
like the lower story, into three parts, the centre one of which

shows the inscription. The sculptural decorations of the arch itself are beautiful; the triangular surfaces between the arch and the columns are occupied by winged Victories with warlike attributes. Inside the opening the walls to right and left are adorned with bas-reliefs, one of which represents the emperor in his triumphal chariot, the other groups of soldiers with the booty of the Jewish war, amongst which we discover the seven-branched candlestick of the temple of Jerusalem (compare § 109). The barrel-vault of the archway is adorned with laquearia, a bas-relief in the centre showing the apotheosis of the emperor, who is carried to heaven by an eagle. According to the inscription, the monument has been erected to the memory of Titus by senate and people in the reign of his successor Domitian. It lies in a beautiful position, between the temple of Venus and Roma and the Coliseum above the Via Sacra, and is one of the most remarkable architectural monuments of Rome.

Still more important for the history of art, although of later date, is the triumphal arch of the Emperor Constantine. In it the traces of two very different periods are distinguishable. For it marks the closing period of the old empire and the rise of Christianity, being erected in celebration of the victory of Constantine over his rival Maxentius, by means of which Christianity was established as the official religion of the Roman State. On the other hand, it takes us back to one of the most glorious epochs of Roman history, viz. the time of Trajan's victories over

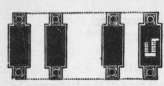

Fig. 417.

the Dacians. For when, after the victory at the Pons Milvius (A.D. 312), people and senate decided upon erecting an arch for the victor, the shortness of time or the want of artistic means at their disposal compelled them to make use of the plastic and architectural decorations of an older monument for their new structure.* This latter (see plan, Fig. 417) has three openings, the centre one of which is both higher and wider than the two others, being destined for the triumphal chariot of the emperor. The three entrances were enclosed by detached columns, instead of

* Height, 21 metres; width, 25·70; depth, 7·40. Height of centre arch, 11·50, of side arches 7·40.

the usual semi-columns (see Fig. 418), four of which, made of yellow Numidian marble (*giallo antico*), stood on each side of the structure. According to Hirt, their workmanship denotes the purer style of the reign of Hadrian. The greater part of the sculptures, on both sides of the structure and inside the centre arch, are taken from the triumphal gate (according to Hirt, two different gates) erected to Trajan for his victories over the Dacians and Parthians. The arrangement of these sculptures is very tasteful. They begin at the bases of the columns, which are adorned with

Fig. 418.

large relief-figures in standing postures; on each side of the richly decorated arch-enclosures we see two seated Victories. After them follows, in the manner of a frieze, over the smaller entrances, a series of smaller bas-reliefs; above each of these lower bas-reliefs are two circular bas-reliefs ("medallions," eight in all), representing scenes from the private life of Trajan, to which correspond eight square bas-reliefs with larger figures in the so-called Attic. The scenes represented by the last-mentioned sculptures begin, according to Braun's description, on the side turned towards the Aventine. "They commence," he says,* "with an illustration of the triumphal entrance of Trajan after

* In his work on the Ruins and Museums of Rome, p. 8.

the first Dacian war, and then turn to his merits in conducting the Via Appia through the Pontine marshes, and in founding an orphanage. They also refer to his relations to Parthamasires, King of Armenia, and to Parthamaspates, to whom he gives the Parthian crown ; also, finally, to Decebalus, king of the Dacians, whose hired assassins are brought before the emperor. The remaining groups show the emperor addressing the soldiers, also the usual sacrifices of pigs, sheep, and oxen." About the "medallions" representing the private life of the emperor, " in simple and graceful compositions," Braun makes the following remarks:—"They begin with the setting out for the chase. The second group represents a sacrifice to Sylvanus, the protecting god of the forest. The third shows the emperor on horseback hunting a boar ; the fourth, the thank-offering to the goddess of the chase. The groups on the side of the Coliseum show a boar-hunt, a sacrifice to Apollo, the inspection of a killed lion, and, lastly, an unexplained oracular scene, most likely referring to the miraculous escape of Trajan from an earthquake at Antiochia."

The above-mentioned frieze continued over the central opening represents consecutively the battle, the flight, and chase of the enemy, and the crowning of the emperor by the Goddess of Victory. It is dedicated to Constantine as the "founder of peace," and the "liberator of the city ; " which inscriptions refer to Constantine's victory over Maxentius, and his occupation of Rome. Only the latter sculptures—the seated Victories, and the standing figures on the pedestals of the columns—date from Constantine's time. By their bad execution and clumsy compositior they denote the decline of Roman art ; while the bas-reliefs from the time of Trajan, together with the figures of captive barbarians over the columns, are perfect in both these respects (compare §§ 107 to 109).

80. We have described (§ 25) the development of the Greek gymnasia from private institutions for the requirements of individuals to centres of public intercourse and recreation. A similar position in Roman life was held by the public baths. They also grew from private into public institutions of great magnificence indispensable to the Romans, and, therefore, found in all important towns.

These baths, from the greater importance of the warm baths

contained in them, generally called *thermæ,* are, in many respects, comparable to the Greek gymnasia, which name was, indeed, occasionally applied to them in later times; in other points, however, the two differ entirely. Although the gymnastic exercises, together with their Greek names, were adopted by the Romans, they never gained national importance amongst them : war, and warlike evolutions in the field, remained the chief means of their corporeal education. In their bathing-establishments the thermæ or baths had, therefore, the largest space assigned to them, smaller localities being reserved for agonistic games; the Greek notions about the relative importance of these two purposes were thus exactly reversed. Common to both Greek and Roman institutions were the localities serving as walks and places of meeting and conversation to all visitors. The luxury of imperial times added to the thermæ means of intellectual enjoyment, such as libraries and museums.

In older times, before bathing had become a necessity of daily existence, the *lavatrina,* or washhouse, lying next to the kitchen, and connected with it by a heating-apparatus, served also as bath-room. But this simple arrangement soon became insufficient. Hot, sudatory, tepid, and cold baths, shower-baths, rubbing and oiling of the body—all these required separate apartments, to which, at the thermæ, were added dressing and undressing rooms and other apartments for conversation and various kinds of amusement. From numerous remains of baths discovered in various points of the Roman empire we have a distinct idea of their original arrangements; these remains, moreover, tally in a remarkable degree with Vitruvius's rules. We ought to add, that the picture of the interior of a bath supposed to have been found in the thermæ of Titus, and reproduced in most compendiums of Roman antiquities for a century and a half, has been proved by Marquardt* to be an invention of the architect Giov. Ant. Rusconi (1553).

All the bath-rooms lay over a substructure (*suspensuræ*) about two feet high, the ceiling of which rested on rows of pillars standing at distances of one and a half foot. The furnace (*hypocausis*), with the firing-room (*propnigeum, præfurnium*) lying

* In "Handbuch der römischen Alterthümer, etc., begonnen von W. A. Becker, fortgesetzt von J. Marquardt," Part v. Division i., p. 283 *et seq.* Leipsic, 1864.

in front of it, occupied the centre of the establishment. From
here the heat was diffused through the basement, and ascended in
earthen or leaden pipes (*tubi*) in the walls to the bath-rooms.
The cold, tepid, or hot water required for the baths came from
three tanks lying above the furnace, and connected with each
other by means of pipes. The bath-rooms, over the basement,
grouped round the furnace at greater or less distances, were
divided, by the different degrees of heat attained in them, into
tepidaria (sudatory air-baths), *caldaria* (hot baths), and *frigidaria*
(cold baths). Tanks (*piscina*), or tubs (*solium, alveus*), occupied the
centre of the caldaria and frigidaria; benches and chairs were
ranged along the walls, or stood in niches; a flat tub (*labrum*, see
Fig. 202), placed in a niche on the narrow side of the oblong
calidarium, was filled with cold water for a plunge after the hot
bath. In larger, particularly public, baths separate rooms served
for dressing and undressing (*apodyterium*), rubbing (*destrictarium*)
and oiling the body (*unctorium*). In smaller baths, the latter
process was occasionally gone through in the tepidarium. After
the end of the Republic, larger establishments used to have a
separate steam-bath (*laconicum*) in imitation of the Greek
πυριατήριον. Next to the tepidarium, but separated from it by
a wall, lay, according to Vitruvius, a small circular building
covered by a cupola, which received its light through an aperture
in the centre of the dome. By means of a separate heating
apparatus its temperature could be increased to an enormous
degree. A brass plate (*clypeus*) was suspended on chains from
the dome; by lowering it, or pulling it up, the hot air in the
apartment became more or less condensed.

So much about the general arrangements of the bath. We
now must turn our attention to some of the remains of baths
preserved to us. A house at Pompeii shows very simple arrangements. A small dressing-room (*apodyterium*), with a chamber
for a tepid air-bath (*tepidarium*) and a hot bath (*caldarium*), may
still be recognised. A similar arrangement we see in the above-
mentioned *villa suburbana*, where to the tepid and hot baths (Fig.
393, 9 and 10) is added a court for a cold bath (8). The reservoir
of the latter, as well as the apparatus for heating the water of the
hot bath, is still recognisable.

The same arrangements, although increased in number and

varied in form, we meet with in the thermæ proper, or public
baths; as the simplest specimen of such we quote the thermæ
of Veleia. Veleia, or Velleia, was built in the first century of
the Christian era by the Veleiates, a Ligurian tribe dwelling
previously in villages in the country traversed by the Via Æmilia,
not far from the modern Piacenza. Under one of the successors of
Constantine the town was buried by the fall of a mountain, and
all knowledge of it was lost till 1747, when the discovery of the
largest existing bronze inscription, the so-called *tabula alimentaria*
of Trajan, near the village of Macinisso, indicated the existence
of a Roman settlement. In 1760, by command of Don Philip
of Parma, systematic excavations were begun, which, after five
years, resulted in the discovery of a moderate provincial town of
the first centuries of the Empire. Fig. 419 shows the plan of the

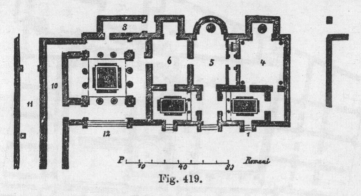

Fig. 419.

partly destroyed thermæ of Veleia according to the design of the
architect Antolini. The façade (1 to 12) contains several
entrances. That lying on the extreme right (1) leads into the baths
for women, consisting of a sort of entrance-hall (2) and of a larger
apartment for hot baths (4). The smaller room lying between the
two may have contained the heating apparatus (*hypocaustum*).
On the other side of the vestibule common to both divisions lies
the entrance-hall of the men's baths (3). After it follows the
bath-room for men (5), separated from that for women by a space
containing a staircase. The room adjoining it (6) was intended
for social intercourse, after it follows the swimming-bath (*natatio*)
of the men (7), surrounded by a colonnade. Into this peristylium
open a narrow apartment (8), in which a mosaic floor has been

discovered, and a covered passage (*crypta*, 10). The street (11)
runs parallel with the latter : on the opposite side of the building
was also a street, while in front of it seems to have been an open
square.

More complicated in design and larger in size are the thermæ
excavated at Pompeii in 1824 (see plan, Fig. 420). Like the
house of Pansa (Fig. 386), they are surrounded by a number of
shops and lodging-houses, which, however, are unconnected with
the bathing-establishment. The whole block of houses (*insula*)
forms an irregular square bordered on all sides by streets. Here,

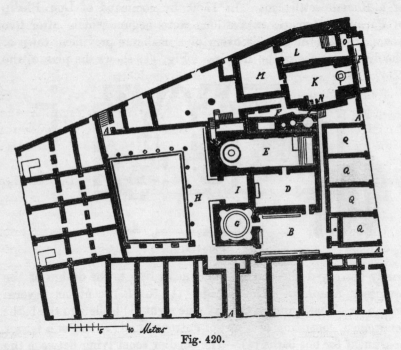

Fig. 420.

also, the baths of women and men are separate, and have different
entrances. The former comprise the rooms *K L M N O P*, the
entrance being near *O* ; the latter, the rooms *B D E G H I*.
Four entrances lead into them from the street on three different
sides (*A A A*). The heating-apparatus (*F*) is common to both
divisions, and lies between them. The remainder of the area
(marked in our plan *Q*, or left blank) is occupied by shops and
private lodgings belonging to them. *O*, as we mentioned before,

marks the entrance to the women's bath in a projection of the wall. To the left of it lies a small apartment furnished with benches, undoubtedly a sort of waiting-room. The larger room *L* is generally believed to be an apodyterium; it also is fitted up with stone benches. In the small alcove-like part of it nearest the entrance we recognise the frigidarium, with the piscina belonging to it, to which latter descend steps (see Plan). From the apodyterium one enters the tepidarium (*M*), under the floor of which, as well as under that of the caldarium (*K*) adjoining it, the suspensuræ for the diffusion of the hot air are still recognisable. In a sort of niche in the latter room we discover the labrum, intended for cold ablutions. Near *N* is the opening of the canal through which the hot air and hot water were conducted from the firing-room (*F*) to the caldarium. Here we see the heating-apparatus enclosed in thick walls : it consists of a circular furnace, about 8 to 9 feet in diameter, from which the hot air was conveyed to the two caldaria for women (*K*) and men (*E*) by means of canals of brickwork which pass underneath the raised floors. We also mention two cauldrons in which the bathing-water was heated ; they were filled with cold water from a quadrangular reservoir lying behind them. The fuel was kept in a court, perhaps covered, and connected with *F* by means of narrow passages.

The rooms for the baths of the men were also grouped round this central heating-apparatus, those requiring the greatest heat lying nearest to it. The caldarium of the men (*E*), lying close to the furnace, consists of an oblong apartment, covered with a barrel-vault, containing openings to admit the light and let out the steam. The slightly raised floor of the centre part lies above the suspensuræ. On the sides narrow openings were left between the stones of the wall and its outer surface to let the hot air pass through. On the narrow eastern side of the room lies a large tub for hot baths (*lavatio calda*) ; several steps led up to this tub or tank, which is connected with the wall itself. The opposite western side, ending in a semicircular niche, contains a detached round labrum, for cold ablutions, about eight inches deep and raised above the ground by one metre; a bronze pipe at the bottom of it admitted the water. An inscription in bronze letters on the border of the tub says, that it had been purchased by decree of the *decuriones* for the sum of 5,250 *sestertii* (about £38).

A door connects the caldarium with the tepidarium (*D*), smaller in size, but more richly decorated with sculptures and paintings: a bronze hearth and three benches of the same material have been discovered in this elegant and comfortable apartment (Fig. 421). Inscriptions on the seats of the benches name M. Nigidius Vaccula as the donor. Parallel with the tepidarium, and connected with it by means of a door, we see another slightly larger room (*B*). It also has a barrel-vault, but

Fig. 421.

is decorated less richly than the tepidarium. It served as apodyterium, and was surrounded by stone benches with a low step in front of them. On one of the narrow sides of this room lies a small chamber (*A*) belonging to the keeper of the bathers' clothes (*capsarius*, from *capsa*, *i.e.* cupboard where valuables are kept). On the opposite side the apodyterium is adjoined by a round room (*rotatio*, *G*), covered with a cupola, in which room a round marble basin served for cold baths, and which may therefore be described as frigidarium. A small aperture in the conical ceiling admitted the light, while the tepidarium was lighted by means of a window closed with *one* pane of ground glass. In accordance with its destination, the tepidarium was connected with the street (*A*) by means of a narrow corridor. In the wall opposite the opening of this corridor, by the side of the entrance to the frigidarium, lies the door of another narrow corridor leading to an open court (*H*). This court, accessible from the street by two other entrances (*A A*), resembles a peristylium, two of its sides being occupied by covered Doric colonnades, while on a third lies a vaulted hall, *crypto-porticus*, receiving its light from several large windows. One of the colonnades is adjoined by a hall (*I, exedra*), serving for purposes of conversation and amusement. The court itself was used for gymnastic exercise and walks, whence its name *ambulatio*. It was particularly adapted to advertising purposes, whence the numerous inscriptions on the walls, most of which, however, are no longer legible. Here has been found a box, in which, most likely, the entrance fees were collected by the janitor.

Much larger than those just described are the so-called "new thermæ" at Pompeii, the excavation of which was finished in 1860. Here all the walls are covered with rich paintings; the upper rooms, moreover, are larger in size, and several new accommodations have been added. Amongst these, we principally count an uncovered marble swimming-bath (*natatio* ; compare Fig. 419, 7), 16·5 by 8 metres in size, opening with its full width towards the palæstra.

The thermæ of Pompeii were naturally surpassed by those of Rome ; nevertheless, they are to us of almost greater importance than the latter, owing to their better state of preservation. The dimensions and splendour of the Roman thermæ may, for instance, be seen from the fact that the Pantheon itself, one of the grandest monuments of Roman architecture, formed only a small portion of the thermæ built by M. Agrippa. In later imperial times, even this splendour was surpassed : Seneca already mentions the coating of the walls with the most valuable kinds of marble, the introduction of silver mouthpieces for the water-pipes, and the placing of numbers of columns and statues in the public baths— a statement which is confirmed by the fragments of beautiful statues found amongst the ruins of thermæ ; an ancient author justly compares their extensive grounds to whole provinces.

Fig. 422 shows the plan of the thermæ of Caracalla, designed

by Cameron. His design, however, only represents the chief
building: an enormous court with which the emperor Decius
afterwards surrounded it has been omitted; but, even without
this addition, the thermæ finished by Caracalla in the fourth year
of his reign (A.D. 217) must be considered as the most magnificent Roman structure of the kind. The walls and part of the
vaults are well preserved; the latter are made of porous tufa,
lighter than the common one, which adds to the boldness of
their design. This applies particularly to the magnificent
entrance-hall, a rotunda (A) with eight niches, similar in design
to the Pantheon, which it almost equals in size, its diameter being

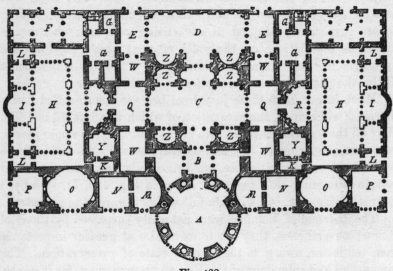

Fig. 422.

111 feet. The vault is not, as in the Pantheon, spherical,
but surprisingly flat in design, and has, for that reason, been
compared by the ancients with a sole, whence the name of the
structure *cella solearis*. The architects of the time of Constantine
explained the possibility of this kind of vaulting by presuming
that metal sticks were placed in the interior to support the
ceiling; Hirt, however, thinks that the lightness of the material
is sufficient to account for the difficulty. After having passed
through the cella solearis one entered the apodyterium (B), behind
which lay the chief hall—the ephebeum (C) (compare the

gymnasium of Ephesos, Fig. 154, *C*), by Roman authors also called
xystus. Eight colossal granite columns, one of which now stands
in the square S. Trinità in Florence, carried the intersecting
vaults of the ceiling (see view of the interior, Fig. 423) : the
length of the whole room was 179 feet. Adjoining the two
narrow sides of the ephebeum, and separated from it by columns
only, lay smaller rooms (*Q Q*) destined for spectators or wrestlers ;
exedræ resembling niches (*Z Z Z Z*) lay on the longer sides of
the hall. We next come to another hall (*D*) of equal length, in
which lay the swimming-bath (*piscina*) ; this room also was

Fig. 423.

adjoined by niches (*Z Z*) and other apartments for the spectators
(*E E*). The rooms hitherto mentioned formed the chief part of
the building, distinguished from the other divisions by its greater
height. The destination of these latter lying to both sides of the
centre structure cannot always be determined with certainty.
According to Cameron, *F* marks vestibules or libraries; *G*, the
dressing-rooms for the wrestlers, near which the remains of staircases to the upper stories have been found. He further mentions
peristylia with swimming-baths (*H*), rooms for practising (*I*),
elæothesia (*K*), with konisteria (*Y*) adjoining them ; also vestibules (*L*), above which rooms with mosaic pavements have been

discovered. *M, N, O, P,* respectively mark the laconicum, caldarium, tepidarium, and frigidarium; *R* indicates larger rooms (*exedræ*) for conversation. Fig. 423 shows the interior of the chief hall (*C*) in its original condition, for the reconstructive design of which the analogous hall of the thermæ of Diocletian, preserved in the church S. Maria degli Angeli, has been of considerable assistance. Other reconstructive designs of the whole building may be found in the comprehensive work, " Les Thermes de Caracalla," by the French architect, Abel Blouet.

81. The enormous development of their political power naturally reacted on the architecture of the Romans; its tasks were greater and more varied than those of Greek architecture. With the extension of the empire, the number of officials in the central seat of government increased proportionately, for whose accommodation large public buildings were required. Other buildings served to supply the demands of the more extensive and varied judicial and commercial developments of the people, while further structures were required to satisfy the craving of the populace for pageantry and theatrical splendour. Hence the number of basilicas (both for judicial and commercial purposes), of colonnades (for social intercourse), of forums and theatres; hence, also, the enormous extension of the circus to accommodate the cruel populace of the metropolis : the amphitheatre of Vespasian may, in a manner, be considered as the embodiment of the power and splendour of the empire. The same phenomena, though on a smaller scale, we see repeated in the provincial towns in proportion to their growing wealth and independence.

The remains of political buildings of the time of the republic are scarce; republican Rome soon became transformed into imperial Rome, the different phases of which latter are illustrated by numerous monuments. Our knowledge of the official buildings of republican magistrates is, to a great extent, conjectural; sometimes their meetings may have taken place in certain parts of the Forum or in temples. About the meeting-place of the senate, generically called *curia,* we know little,— neither as regards the *curia Hostilia* belonging to the times of the kings, nor the *curia Julia* instituted by Cæsar, nor, indeed, those other curiæ called by the names of Marcellus, Pompey, &c. Most likely they were roomy oblong halls of some kind, which view is supported by the fact that the cellæ of the temples, where the sittings of the senate frequently took place, show the same form. Of particular importance, in this respect, are the remains of the temple of Concordia in the Forum Romanum, already described by us (see Fig. 334) : it was here that Cicero delivered his fourth oration against Catilina and several of his Philippics ; here also the condemnation to death of Ælius Seianus, the notorious favourite of Tiberius, was pronounced by the senate.

The meeting-place of the quæstors also was a temple, viz. that of Saturn, of which eight columns on a high base are still preserved in the Forum. Here the treasure of the State (*ærarium*), with the documents belonging to it, as also the standards of the army, were kept. The tablets of the law and other political documents (*tabulæ*) were kept in the so-called Tabularium or archive. This building, lately investigated, rests on a large sub-structure, seventy-one metres in length, which seemingly adds to the firmness of the Capitoline Hill on the side of the Forum. It lies immediately above the just-mentioned temple of Concordia (compare Fig. 428, *E F G H*). One wall of the Tabularium, and a row of arcades erected on it, are still in existence (see Fig. 334, *a*). The arcades rest on strong separate pillars of freestone, adorned, towards the Forum, with Doric semi-columns. Above them rises the "Palazzo del Senatore," built in the sixteenth century, and supposed to occupy the site of the Tabularium, which, therefore, must have been of considerable dimensions. According to an inscription, both the substructure and the Tabularium itself were built by Q. Lutatius Catulus (B.C. 78). Under Nero the Capitol and the archives were destroyed by fire. Vespasian undertook the new building. According to Suetonius (Vespas. 8), "the emperor restored 3,000 bronze tablets melted by the fire after having searched for copies of their contents, the finest and oldest collection of documents (*instrumentum*) of the empire, in which, since the foundation of the city, all the decrees of the senate, and the plebiscites with regard to the right of confede-ration, and the privileges granted to each community, were kept."

The censors had their office in the so-called *atrium libertatis*—to judge by its name, a building of some religious character (com-pare what has been said about the atrium in § 74). The prætors performed their judicial function at first in "tribunals" (*i.e.*

square raised substructures standing in the Forum), afterwards in basilicas. Before describing the latter most developed form of Roman architecture we must mention a few smaller buildings as examples of simple meeting-places of municipal officials and boards.

We are alluding to three buildings in the immediate vicinity of the forum of Pompeii (see their plans, Fig. 424). They consist of three halls (9 to 10 metres broad by 16 to 18 long) of simplest design. The entrances lie on the narrow side towards the forum, separated from the latter by a double colonnade. On the side opposite the entrances there are niches, destined evidently to receive the seats of the functionaries. In *a* this niche (*tribunal*) is semicircular in form; in *b* it is smaller,

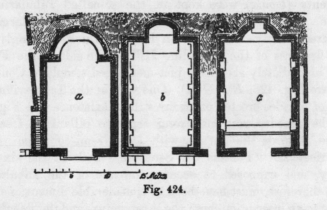

Fig. 424.

and appears terminated by two parallel walls to which a flattened segment has been affixed; in *c* we see a further square indenture in the centre of the wall of the otherwise semicircular niche. Everything indicates that these buildings were used for the meetings of some board, and not as temples or treasure-houses as has been conjectured.

The destination of another building in the forum of Pompeii as the meeting-house or *senaculum* of the decurions can be determined with more certainty. It consists of a large square hall (20 by 18 metres), to the back of which is added a semicircular apse 11 metres wide (at the opening) by 6·50 deep. In the background of this apse is situated a broad daïs for the seats of the presiding magistrates. These and similar buildings may be safely classed as *curiæ*, a name which was generically applied to council-houses of magistrates: a building, for instance, devoted to Mars, where the priestly college of the Salii held their meetings, was called a curia.

Still more often occurs the name of *basilica*, a kind of structure frequently described by antique authors, and, moreover, sufficiently illustrated by the remaining specimens. The name was derived from the kingly hall (στοὰ βασίλειος) at Athens where the archon basileus sat in judgment. This derivation is confirmed by the fact that the first basilica was erected at a period when the influence of Greek on Roman architecture had already become powerful. When, during the consulate of Q. Fabius Maximus and M. Marcellus (B.C. 214), a fire destroyed part of the Forum, no basilica was in existence: a fact which Livy (XXVI.— 27) thinks it necessary to tell his contemporaries, to whom the ideas of forum and basilica had become inseparable. About thirty years after this event, M. Porcius Cato, while censor (B.C. 184), erected the first basilica at public expense, after having purchased two plots of ground in the Latomia, besides four shops, for the site of the building. The latter lay beside the curia in the Forum, of which it was in a manner a continuation, being destined for commercial and judicial purposes. For which of these two purposes Cato intended the building, called by himself Basilica Porcia, is difficult to decide, seeing that written testimony is wanting, and that the building itself has been totally destroyed during the riots of Clodius. Vitruvius (Arch., V. 1) seems to think only of commercial convenience. "Basilicas," he says, "ought to be built in the warmest quarters of the market-places, in order that, in winter, the merchants assembling there may not be inconvenienced by bad weather." In his description, on the other hand, of the basilica built by himself at Fanestrum (the modern Fano), he mentions the "tribunal," which he calls "hemicyclium;" but says that the curve was not a complete semicircle, its depth being 15 feet by 46 wide, "in order," he adds, "that those who stand near the magistrates may not be disturbed by those doing business in the basilica."* The twofold use of the basilica appears suffi-

---

* The first passage (edition of Rose and Müller-Strübing) reads, *Ut per hiemem sine molestia tempestatium se conferre in eas negotiatores possint;* the second, *Uti qui apud magistratus starent negotiantes in basilica ne impedirent:* according to this version, here also the commercial interest is put in the foreground.

ciently from these two passages. With regard to the construction
of such buildings Vitruvius adds the following rules. "Their
width must not be less than one-third, and not more than one-
half, of their length, providing the nature of the locality does not
necessitate different proportions. If the site is of considerable
length, *chalcidica* ought to be added at both ends of the building."
The latter seem to have been halls added to the narrow sides of the
basilica, in order to make use of the whole space at disposal. The
basilica is divided lengthwise into three parts, the two at the sides
being called *porticus;* their width is to be equal to one-third of
that of the centre space ; the height of the columns is to be equal
to this width ; above the first porticus lies a second, with columns
lower by one-quarter than the bottom ones; between these lies a
high parapet. From the further description of the basilica of
Fanestrum, it appears that all the rooms were covered. All these
rules, however, must be taken in a general sense only ; individual

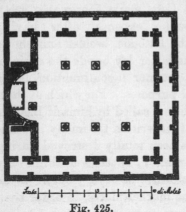

Fig. 425.

buildings frequently deviate from
them. One class of exceptions
are, for instance, the basilicas with
one instead of three naves; other
basilicas occurring at an early
period had as many as five
naves. Of such with one nave, and
therefore without porticus, we
mention the remains of a basilica at
Aquino (the old Aquinum in
Latium), where the walls of the
tribunal built of freestone are
still recognisable ; also that at
Palestrina (the old Præneste), where the "hemicyclical"
tribunal, with a "chalcidicum," has been preserved. The design
of the three tribunals in the forum of Pompeii is, in a more
or less modified way, repeated in most of these buildings ; this
is, for instance, the case in a basilica at Palmyra, consisting of
an oblong hall, to one of the narrow sides of which a perfectly
semicircular niche has been added, while the opposite side shows
an entrance-portico of four columns. To the other sides of the
building wings have been added, which, however, are enclosed
by detached columns instead of walls. Each of these wings

contains twenty columns arranged in five rows of four columns
each; they were covered with roofs, and thus formed convenient
places of meeting for the merchants whose disputes were decided
in the interior of the building.

We also possess several specimens of basilicas with three
naves; one of them has been discovered near the modern Otricoli,
in 1775. It has been recognised as the basilica of the old Roman
municipium of Ocriculum, one of the larger towns of Umbria,
situated on the Via Flaminia (Fig. 425). The shape of the
basilica considerably differs from Vitruvius's rule, forming an all
but perfect square. It is divided by two rows of columns (three
in number) into three naves, the centre one of which is the widest.
To this has been added a semicircular tribunal, up to which lead

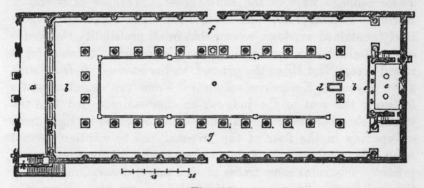

Fig. 426.

steps. On the floor of the first a second daïs seems to have been
raised. On both sides of the hemicyclium lie two small quadrangular chambers, accessible also from the two side naves, besides
being connected with the niche of the tribunal. A narrow
passage (*cryptoporticus*) surrounds the space on three sides. Of
other basilicas with three naves, we mention the church of Alba
on the Fucine Lake, and a basilica at Treves (233 by 88 feet); as
also the so-called " Temple of Peace " in Rome, lying between the
Coliseum and the temple of Venus and Roma. It was begun by
Maxentius, and finished by Constantine; its ruins are amongst the
most splendid of Rome. Four enormous piers divided the inner
space into a wide centre and two narrower side naves, the former
being covered with an intersected vault, the two latter with barrel-

vaults. Two apses were reserved for the seats of the judges. The form of the principal hall in the thermæ of Caracalla (Fig. 423) is exactly like that of the present building, but for the absence of a tribunal in the former.

Fig. 426 (scale 36 feet) illustrates the basilica with three naves at Pompeii, from which we are able to derive a distinct idea of the arrangement of such buildings. With its narrow side it touched the forum, the colonnade of which hid the front of the basilica. *a* in our plan marks a small fore-hall, most likely a chalcidicum. On four steps of the same width as the building we ascend the basilica proper—an oblong edifice with five doors, surrounded on all four sides by a colonnade (*porticus*, *b b*, *f g*), by means of which the whole is divided lengthwise into three naves. These columns were of the Ionic order. Thinner pilasters, of Korintho-Roman order, were let into the walls, which latter most likely contained windows, seeing that in all probability the centre space (*c*) also had a roof to it. The quadrangular tribunal (*e*) is raised several feet above the ground, and is adorned in front with a row of smaller Korinthian columns. From two chambers stairs led up to this seat of the judges; another staircase led into the vaulted chamber under the tribunal, which received its light from an opening in the floor of the tribunal, not to mention several small side openings. This chamber was most likely a temporary prison. The ruins show traces of rich mural decorations all over the building; the pavement consisted of marble. Near *d* a pedestal has been discovered, which, to judge by some sculptural fragments, carried an equestrian statue. According to Mazois, the three naves were of nearly equal height, the centre one only being raised a little. The entire length of the basilica was 67 metres, by a width of 27·35 metres. The staircase (*h*) in our plan is not connected with the basilica; it leads up to the roof of the colonnade surrounding the forum.

Of basilicas with five naves we mention the Basilica Julia, built by Cæsar for the centumviral courts of justice in the Forum, between the temple of the Dioscuri and that of Saturn. According to the latest excavations, it was a large building surrounded by a double porticus, and divided by four rows of strong travertine stone pillars into five naves. The pavement consists of grey, reddish, and yellow slabs of marble, which are in an excellent state of preservation. The building (some arches of which were still in existence in 1849) was so large that four judges could sit in its different parts simultaneously. Fig. 427 shows the plan of the Basilica Ulpia, built by Trajan as part of the splendid decoration of his forum. A fragment of the antique plan of Rome,* frequently mentioned by us, distinctly shows the five naves, and even the large niche of the tribunal. The covering of the building with beams of bronze is mentioned with admiration by ancient writers.

82. About the places where public meetings were held in republican times we know but little. In most cases open spaces

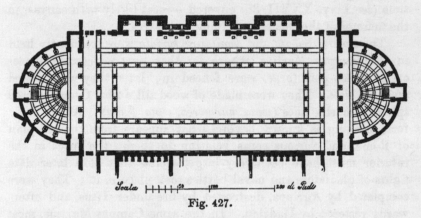

Scala ⊢⊢⊢⊢⊢50   100   200 di Piedi

Fig. 427.

without much monumental decoration served the purpose. Only the *curiæ, i.e.* the divisions of the people according to old tribal traditions, form an exception to this rule. The buildings where they met, originally situated in the old parts of the town, were for the greater part afterwards transferred to the more modern quarters, whence the distinction between *curiæ veteres* and *curiæ novæ.* The importance of the curia as a tribal community, although to a great extent divested of its political character, remained unaltered. Their original places of meeting were undoubtedly of the simplest construction, the curiæ of later date, mentioned in § 81, being most likely fashioned after their model.

* This plan engraved on slabs of marble, represents Rome under Septimius Severus and Caracalla. Fragments of it were found, under Pope Pius IV., behind the church of SS. Cosmo e Damiano, and deposited by Benedict XIV. in the Capitoline Museum founded by him. According to Canina, the scale of the plan barring some inaccuracies, was 1 : 250.

They were connected with sanctuaries (*sacella*) of Juno Quiritis, the protecting goddess of the old tribal unions. They were destined for deliberations and sacrificial acts under the presidency of the *curio*, as also for common meals of the members (*curiales*). The *comitia*, on the other hand, were the places of meeting of the whole sovereign people : the name was applied both to the assemblies themselves and to the place in the upper part of the Forum Romanum where they were held (see Fig. 428, R). The meetings were held in the open air till 208 B.C. (546 of the city), in which year, on the occasion of a census (which fixed the number of citizens at 137,108), the comitium was for the first time (see Livy, XXVII. 36) covered,—most likely with canvas, in the manner of the theatres and amphitheatres.

The *comitia tributa* and *comitia centuriata* were frequently held in the Campus Martius, where for that purpose certain places called sheep-pens (*ovile*) were fenced in ; later they were called *septa*, or lists. They were made of wood till Julius Cæsar erected splendid marble ones (*septa marmorea, septa Julia*). About their form nothing is known, beyond what appears from the old plan of Rome, and various coins relating to them : the space in the interior must have been very large, seeing that at a later date fights of gladiators and naval battles took place in it. They were completed by Agrippa, destroyed by fire under Titus, and afterwards restored by Hadrian. In the same Campus Martius, most likely connected with the septa, lay the *diribitorium*, a splendid building, used for counting, perhaps also for giving, votes ; of its original roof, a beam 100 feet long used to be shown in the septa as a curiosity.

We have to add a few remarks about the market-places (*fora*), in which many of the public buildings mentioned by us were situated. Their importance for political life was still greater amongst the Romans than amongst the Greeks (compare § 26). Particularly the Forum Romanum appears like the heart of the body politic. In the course of centuries it was adorned with numerous structures of both historic and artistic importance. Fig. 428 shows the plan of the Forum Romanum in accordance with the latest investigations by Reber and Detlefsen : we shall, in the following remarks, attempt to convey to the reader an idea of what the Forum was during the first centuries of the empire. Upon a discussion of controverted minor points we cannot enter.

The Forum (A) occupies the valley to the north-west of the ridge of mountains connecting the two Capitoline hills (S S) ; to the south-east it extends as far as the Velia, a part of the Palatine (T). Its shape is an irregular oblong, the south-western long side of which is determined by the recently discovered antique pavement of the Via Sacra and several buildings touching it. The north-eastern side is still covered by a mass of rubbish (30 feet deep), on which later structures have been erected. The antique buildings formerly situated there are for that reason indicated in our plan by dotted lines, with the exception only of the Mamertine prison and the temple of Faustina. Of the two narrow sides, that lying towards the slope of the Capitoline hills has been determined by the discovery of the substructures of several temples, identifiable both by their inscriptions and by the testimony of ancient authors ; the opposite side (at a distance of 570 feet) can be distinguished from the vicinity of the Rostra Julia (W) ; the arch of the Fabii, formerly standing there, has, on the other hand, entirely disappeared. We first enumerate the buildings bounding the south-western side of the Forum, also called *sub veteribus sc. tabernis.* According to antique authors, the Atrium of Vesta (Q) lay at the foot of the Palatine (T); its exact situation can no more be determined. By the side of it rose the temple of Castor and Pollux, of which three Korinthian columns, connected by a richly ornamented architrave, are still standing erect. It was devoted to the memory of the victory near the Regillus Lake (B.C. 485), but was most likely burnt down together with the Basilica Julia in its vicinity. Tiberius rebuilt it A.D. 6. The excavations, begun in October, 1871, have already laid open three sides of the building, the pavement of which lies 10 metres below the surface of the modern street. The above-mentioned Basilica Julia (C) was separated from this building only by a street ; its substructure has been laid open in its full length. After it follows the temple of Saturn, the *ærarium* or public treasury (D), eight granite columns of which (six belonging to the frontage, the two others to the two long sides), with the architrave resting on them, are still in existence. The first erection of this temple dates back to early republican times ; it

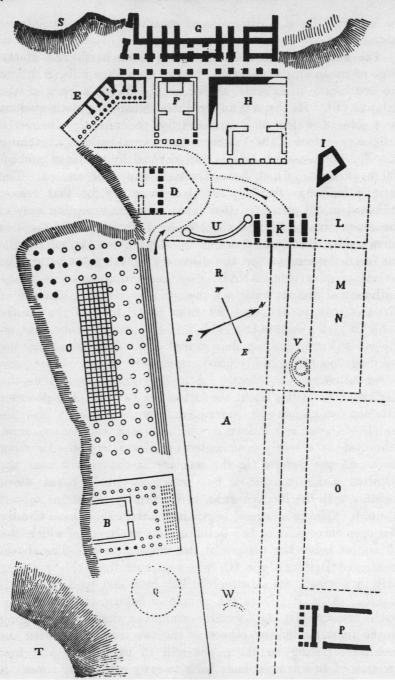

Fig. 428.

was, however, restored repeatedly, for the last time in bad style, under one of the later emperors.

The north-western side of the Forum was bounded by four buildings, viz. the porticus of the Dii Consentes (E), the temple of Vespasian (F, formerly called temple of Jupiter Tonans), the temple of Concordia (H, see also Fig. 334), and, towering above them all, the Tabularium (G) already mentioned. The porticus of the advice-giving gods (Dii Consentes), or twelve chief Roman deities, has been partly restored in modern times with the aid of excavated fragments of antique columns and architraves. The statues of the gods stood, most likely, in front of, or between, the columns. Of the temple built by Vespasian in honour of Domitian (a prostylos hexastylos), three Korinthian columns with their beams are still standing.

Our knowledge of the buildings on the north-east side of the Forum is to a great extent conjectural. Only the two corners are distinctly marked by the ruins of the Mamertine prison (I) and those of the temple of Antoninus and Faustina (P). The foundations of the intervening buildings, viz. the Curia Hostilia (M; the senate-house till B.C. 55, when it was destroyed by fire), the Curia Julia built by Augustus (N), and the Basilica Æmilia et Paulli (O), have been built over at a later date. The Mamertine prison lies underneath the church S. Guiseppe de' Falegnami and the chapel S. Pietro in Carcere, from which a modern staircase leads down to the uppermost of the two subterraneous chambers (according to tradition the prison of the Apostles Peter and Paul). From here another staircase descends to the lower chamber, under which lies the so-called Tullianum (from the old Latin word *tullii*, which, according to Festus, means "fountain-vault"), in which Jugurtha, Sejanus, and others found their death. No trace remains of the notorious staircase leading from the prison to the Forum, on which the corpses of the executed were exhibited, and on which the Emperor Vitellius was killed. In comparatively the best state of preservation is the temple of Antoninus and Faustina (P), a prostylos hexastylos, inside of which the church S. Lorenzo in Miranda has been erected.

The upper part of the space surrounded by these buildings was, in republican times, occupied by the comitium (R); the lower part formed the Forum proper. The two divisions were of about equal size : on the north-east side stood the old tribune for the orators, the *rostra vetera* (V), protected from the populace thronging the Forum by a semicircular balustrade ; behind it lay the above-mentioned Curia Hostilia and the older Græcostasis, an uncovered terrace (*locus substructus*) surrounded by a balustrade, where foreign ambassadors waited for the decision of the curia. After Cæsar's time the rostra was transferred to the lower Forum, where it existed during the two first centuries of the empire under the name of Rostra Julia (W). After the downfall of the Republic, the comitium and the whole republican arrangements of the Forum lost their political significance ; new buildings were erected, the old ones remodelled. Septimius Severus at last (203 A.D.) built a triumphal arch (K), of Pentelic marble, on the north-west side of the Forum, and at the same time transferred the Via Sacra (which previously ran along the older booths—*sub veteribus*—on the south-west side of the Forum) to the opposite side, directing it straight towards the triumphal arch ; behind the latter the road most likely turned westward in a curve (marked by a bent arrow), joining the old Via Sacra at the foot of the Clivus Capitolinus. Near the arch of Severus lies, at present, a terrace (U), slightly curved towards the Forum, and showing the remains of a marble balustrade ; a brick base in the corner nearest the arch of Severus is believed to be a remnant of the milliarium aureum, built by Augustus, *i.e.* the central milestone, and at once the centre (*umbilicus*) of the Roman empire. The terrace itself is, by some modern archæologists, believed to be the Rostra Capitolina of imperial times ; others call it Græcostasis.

Vitruvius (V. 1), in his rules for the building of regularly planned fora, says that their shape ought to be oblong, instead of showing the square form of the older Greek agora ; the reason for this modification being the public games (combats of gladiators) which, according to old Italian custom, were held in them. For this purpose the oblong form seems to have been the more convenient one. In order not to obstruct the view of the spectators the columns of the surrounding colonnades ought to stand at considerable distances from each other. Inside these colonnades shops (*tabernæ argentariæ, i.e.* money-changers' offices) ought to be built, with a second story above them. The width of the

forum ought to be equal to two-thirds of its length. The latter
rule is strictly followed in the forum of the Ligurian town of
Veleia, formerly mentioned by us (see Fig. 429, from Antolini's
design). The open space (1) is 150 Roman palms long by 100
wide; it is surrounded on three sides by colonnades (14), the
single Doric columns of which are ranged at considerable distances
from each other. In the open space several pieces of solid
masonry (2), most likely the remains of decorative monuments,
have been discovered. A still-existing canal surrounded the
whole area, in order to drain off the water; a stripe of marble
(marked in our Plan by thinner lines), with a bronze inscription

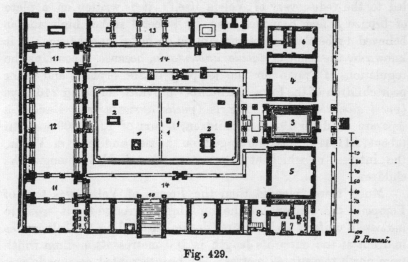

Fig. 429.

on it, lay right across the Forum: according to the inscription,
L. Lucilius Priscus had the Forum paved with stone slabs (*laminis
stravit*) at his expense. A temple (3) occupies the centre of the side
on which one enters the square, the entrance being through small
passages leading past the temple, not unlike the fauces of private
houses.* To right and left of the temple lie two good-sized
rooms, one of them (4, 6) believed to be the dwelling of the priest,
the other (5) a meeting-hall (*comitium*) reserved for the deliberations of religious communities. On entering the forum through
the temple or the fauces, one sees to the left a row of shops (9),

* The temple itself has been mentioned by us (§ 63) as one of the rare examples
of an amphiprostylos.

opening into the surrounding colonnades; 10, on the same side, marks another entrance, through which one ascends the forum by means of steps; 7 and 8 have been explained as prisons. Opposite the temple lies a large building, generally called a basilica (12), with chalcidica (11) on both sides; it bounds the area in its full width. 13 is supposed to be another larger and detached chalcidicum: an inscription found there says that Bæbia Basilla presented a chalcidicum to her fellow-citizens. The space between this chalcidicum and the supposed dwelling of the priest is generally considered as the site of the ærarium. In this Forum was undoubtedly kept the large inscription, the finding of which led to the rediscovery of Veleia itself: it is written on a plate of bronze 8 feet 8 inches long by 4 feet 4 inches high, and is believed to be the largest inscription on metal in existence; it is known by the name of *tabula alimentaria*, because it contains the regulations of Trajan for the keeping of the orphans and other poor children of the town, the number provided for being 246 boys (*pueri alimentarii*) and 35 girls (*puellæ alimentariæ*). Besides a separate fund for 19 other children, a sum of 1,044,000 sestertii (about £11,344) was mortgaged on houses and land in Veleia, the interest of which at 5 per cent. was divided amongst the children.

Much more splendid than the Forum of Veleia was that of Pompeii: the remains of the buildings surrounding it seem to indicate a uniform architectural design. Including the colonnades in front of the curiæ its length is 160 metres, its medium width from north to south 42 metres. An uninterrupted colonnade surrounds the forum on the western long side, the southern narrow side, and part of the eastern long side. On the remaining sides the colonnade is interrupted in several points. The continued colonnades carried (in accordance with Vitruvius's precept) a second story, the former existence of which is proved by the preserved staircase leading up to it. On the north side stands the temple of Jupiter, already described (see Figs. 332 and 338); to both sides of it lie two gates, that on the right being, to judge by its remnants, a triumphal gate. It was, at the same time, the chief entrance to the Forum. On the eastern long side, to the left of the triumphal arch, lie the so-called Pantheon, with the money-changers' shops (*tabernæ argentariæ*) in front of it, the curia of the decuriones, the small so-called temple of Mercury or Quirinus, the chalcidicum of Eumachia, and, separated from these by a street, another edifice, perhaps a public school. On the south side (adorned with a double colonnade), opposite the temple of Jupiter, lie the council-houses (shown in Fig. 424) ; on the west side the basilica (see Fig. 426) and the so-called temple of Venus, the long side of which latter, with its splendid colonnade, is turned towards the Forum, but is accessible from it only by a gate, the chief entrance to the temple lying in a street leading to the Forum. By the side of the last-mentioned gate, in a niche, stands an interesting monument, viz. the gauging-stone, consisting of two tables, one on the top of the other, into the slabs of which the normal measures have been inserted. The original is at present in the museum of Naples, being supplied at Pompeii by a rough imitation. On the same side of the forum and opening on to it lies also a large hall (10 metres deep by 34 wide), considered by some as a picture-gallery (*stoa pœkile*); by Overbeck, with better reason, as a public room for conversation.

Hitherto we have considered only the fora reserved for civic intercourse (*fora civilia*), from which mercantile pursuits (barring the shops of the money-changers) were excluded. Market-places for the latter purposes (*fora venalia*) also occur in Rome and other towns, as, for instance, markets for vegetables (*forum olitorium*), oxen (*f. boarium*), pigs (*f. suarium*), fish (*f. piscarium*), meat and vegetables conjointly (*f. macellum*), &c. In Rome itself there were, besides the Forum Romanum, several other fora civilia, originated by the increasing number of citizens and by the desire on the part of the emperors to gain popularity by the erection of splendid structures for common use. Whole blocks of houses had frequently to be bought and levelled for the purpose. The Forum of Julius Cæsar, surrounded by double colonnades and adorned with the splendid temple of Venus Genitrix, has almost entirely disappeared. We mention besides the fora of Augustus, Vespasian, Nerva (also called *Forum Transitorium* or *Palladium*), and of Trajan, the last of which surpassed all the others in size and splendour. All these fora lay grouped together on the north side of the Forum Romanum, of which they were in a manner a splendid continuation.

83. Our remarks about the buildings for public games and

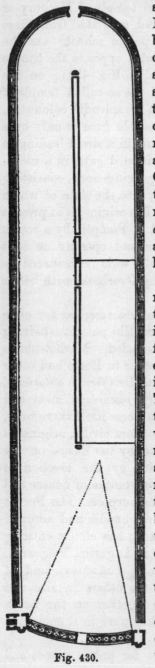

Fig. 430.

similar enjoyments, so important for Roman life, and so fully illustrated by the remaining specimens, can be couched in few words. What we have said about the Greek hippodrome (§ 28), stadion (§ 29), and theatre (§ 30) applies to a prevailing extent also to the Roman circus and theatre. Peculiar to the latter nation is only the amphitheatre ; but here also the architectural principles of the Greek theatre in conjunction with those of the stadion and hippodrome may be recognised. About the games of the circus (*ludi circenses*), the theatrical representations, and the fights of the gladiators, we shall have to speak at greater length hereafter.

Fig. 430 shows the plan of a *circus* or racecourse discovered, in 1823, amongst the ruins of the old Bovillæ, a small town in Latium lying on the Via Appia, at the foot of the Albanian mountains. It is comparatively small, much smaller, for instance, than the racecourses in Rome. The foundations are of simple construction, and show a very moderate use of the vault, generally one of the grandest and most characteristic features of similar structures. On the other hand, it is more than usually well preserved, particularly that part of it where the race began ; it resembles the hippaphesis of the hippodrome of Olympia, and is one of the most essential features of the whole arrangement. We are speaking of the compartments for the single chariots (*carceres*), being placed in a line at once curved and oblique, in order to produce equal distance from the point where the real race began (see Plan, Fig.

430). The number of these carceres, in the middle of which lay the entrance-portal, was twelve: on the two sides are tower-like buildings (*oppida*), occurring also in other racecourses. In one of these towers we discover steps leading to the seats on the roofs of the carceres. In the middle of the course lies the *spina* (a raised line), with the *metæ* (goals) at both ends; round these the chariots had to race a certain number of times. In the centre of the semicircular curve of the course, opposite the carceres, lies the triumphal gate (*porta triumphalis*) through which the victor left the circus.

Fig. 431.

The same arrangements, on a large scale, we find repeated in the numerous racecourses of Rome itself. We mention only the Circus Maximus, lying in the broad valley between the Palatine and Aventine hills. This circus (afterwards, in comparison to other smaller ones, called "the largest") is said to have been built by King Tarquinius Priscus, who also arranged the seats of the people, according to their division, into thirty curiæ. In Tarquinius Superbus's time already the circus was enlarged and the seats re-arranged, which process of enlargement and embellishment was, in the course of a thousand years, repeated frequently, the last restorer being Constantine or his son Constantius. The additions consisted of massive buildings in several stories, by means of which the number of seats was gradually increased from 150,000 to 260,000, according to a later account even to 383,000.* The circus has entirely disappeared, the regulated formation of the sides of the valley being the only trace of its existence. Fig. 431 shows its original aspect ; we there see the raised substructure (*podium*) and the different stories of the spectators' seats (*mæniana*), overlooked on the left by the imperial palaces, also the spina with its manifold decorations (the goals, several sanctuaries, an obelisk, &c.) and the porta triumphalis.

The stadia, of which there was a considerable number in Rome, exactly resemble those of the Greeks.

84. " After the market-place has been designed," Vitruvius continues (V., 3 *et seq.*), " a very healthy spot must be chosen for the theatre, where the people can witness the dramas on the feast-days of the immortal gods." Unless a natural rising of the ground had been made use of, as was mostly the case in Greece, foundations and substructures had to be built. " On this basement marble or stone steps (*gradationes*) must be raised." The latter remark refers to the place for the spectators, which, in analogy to the κοῖλον (see § 30), was called *cavea* (hollow). Part of it was the orchestra, which was not, as in Greek theatres, used for the performance, but contained seats for the spectators. The seats were, as in the Greek theatre, interrupted by parallel passages (*præcinctiones*—διαζώματα), the name of the several divisions being *mæniana*.

" The number of the præcinctiones," Vitruvius continues, "must be in proportion to the height of the theatre. They ought not to be higher than they are broad ; for if they were higher they would throw the voices back towards the top, and thus prevent those occupying the uppermost seats above the præcinctiones from hearing the words distinctly. A line drawn from the highest sitting-step (*gradus*) ought to touch all the corners or edges of the steps, so as nowhere to impede the voice." After having treated in the following chapters (IV. and V.) of several acoustic calculations and contrivances, Vitruvius (chapters V. and VII.) adds some prescriptions as to the size and proportions

---

* According to the latest calculations, the circus, in late imperial times, must have had contained 480,000 seats. It is about 21,000 feet long by 400 wide.

of the stage and of the place for the spectators. The orchestra, like the sitting-steps rising round it, ought to be semicircular in shape. Between the orchestra, where the arm-chairs of the senators are placed, and the back wall (*frons scenæ*) lies the stage (*pulpitum*), which ought to be twice as long as the diameter of the orchestra, and wider than the Greek stage, because in the Roman theatre "all the actors act on the stage." "The height of the pulpitum must be above five feet, so as to enable those sitting in the orchestra to see the gestures of the actors."

The sitting-steps of the spectators are to be divided not only horizontally by the præcinctiones, but also into wedge-like parts (*cunei*) by means of stairs. In the same manner, radiating from the centre of the orchestra, are to be designed the entrances, lying between the walls of the substructure (also designed as radii).

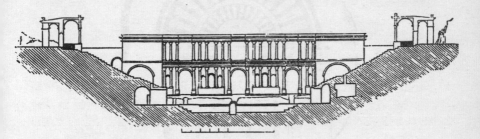

Fig. 432.

Care must be taken not to let the entrance-passages to the upper seats cross those to the lower, so that on leaving their seats the people may not press on each other (chap. III.).

Having considered Vitruvius's precepts, we now must turn to some of the remaining specimens of theatres. Fig. 432 (scale, 100 Sicilian palms) shows the cross-section of the theatre of Syracuse, being, as we mentioned before (§ 30), a Greek structure with Roman additions. The cavea lying on the slope is of Greek origin. The seats are made of the rock itself. The remaining parts of the stage-wall indicate Roman origin : with the aid of these remnants a reconstructive design of the two stories of the skene has been attempted. The colonnade of the spectators' place also is a Roman addition.

Of Roman theatres we mention that built by Pompeius, B.C. 55.

All previous theatres, although splendidly decorated,* had been
built of wood, to be pulled down after the festive performances
were over.   Of the theatre of Pompeius little remains; but a
fragment of. the old plan of Rome enables us to distinguish its
general design, and even the arrangement of the single parts
(see Fig. 433).   The cavea (*a*) contained, it is said, 40,000 seats;
it shows the above-mentioned radiating direction of the walls,
between which the entrance-passages of the spectators lay, and

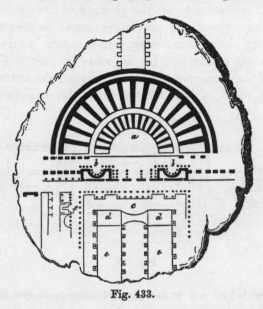

Fig. 433.

on which the sitting-steps rested.   The stage (*b b*) shows a skene-
wall richly decorated with columns and semicircular niches.
"Behind the stage lies a portico (*c*), in order," as Vitruvius adds
(chapter IX.), "that, in case the play is interrupted by a shower of
rain, the people may find refuge there; also in order to give the
choragi room for arranging the chorus."   The design of this
portico indicates various embellishments : the ancients indeed boast

* The theatre of Scaurus already mentioned, built 52 B.C., had 80,000 seats. The
stage-wall was three stories high and adorned with 360 marble columns partly of
colossal size. The wall of the first story was coated with marble, that of the
second with glass (most likely coloured glass mosaic), that of the third with plates
of gilt metal. Between the columns bronze statues, to the almost incredible number
of 3,000, were placed, not to mention various other decorations.

of its statues and valuable tapestry, also of the groves, fountains, wild animals, &c., found in it.

Another theatre, in a better state of preservation, is that built by Augustus (after a plan of Cæsar), and called by him after the name of his nephew Marcellus. It was opened B.C. 13, the same year in which the theatre of Cornelius Balbus was completed. These three were the only theatres in Rome. The theatre of Marcellus stood near the hall called after his mother Octavia : during the Middle Ages the Savelli family used the remains of the theatre for the erection of their palace, at present owned by the Orsinis. The passages between the foundation-walls of the theatre are at present used as offices, and part of the old wall of the cavea may still be recognised in the enclosing wall of the palace. The cavea was semicircular in shape, and rose in three stories, the two lower of which were adorned with arcades and Doric and Ionic semi-columns, while the upper one consisted of a massive wall adorned with

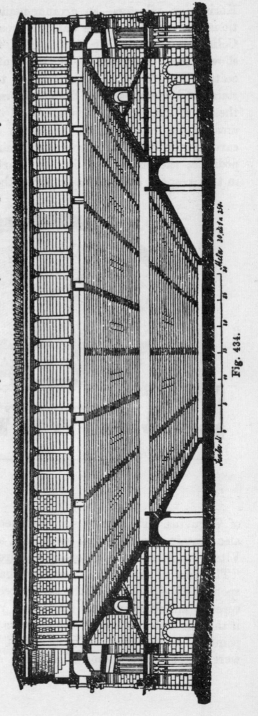

Fig. 434.

Korinthian pilasters—an arrangement which (but for the additional fourth story, here wanting) resembled that found in the Coliseum (compare Fig. 439). Fig. 434, after Canina's design, shows the cross-section of the interior, containing 30,000 seats. We there see the form of the substructure with the stairs and passages, also the corridors, already described in the theatre of Pompeius, which surround the cavea and open into the arcades, also mentioned in the above. The rows of seats of the cavea rise in beautiful proportions from the orchestra and the low podium; they are divided into two parts by a præcinctio, tallying in this respect, and also as regards the cunei, with the precepts

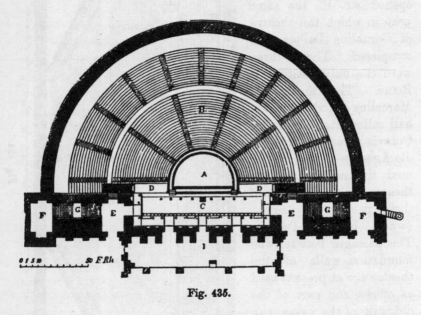

Fig. 435.

of Vitruvius. The upper end is finished off by a colonnade, which also contains places for the spectators, and which is mentioned by Vitruvius amongst the necessary requirements of a Roman theatre. "The roof of the arcade," he says (chap. VII.), "ought to correspond with the height of the skene, because in that case the voice spreads simultaneously to the upper ranks and the roof; while if the two differ in height the voice is broken by the first lower point it encounters." On the roof of the arcade the ropes were fastened, by means of which a canvas could be stretched

over the cavea, so as to protect the spectators from the sun
(see § 85).

About the stage itself little was known till the discovery of
the theatre of Aspendos in Pamphylia; the closer investigation of
the Roman theatre at Orange, in the south of France, has also
yielded interesting results as to this important portion of the
antique theatre (see Lohde's work, "Die Skene der Alten").
Besides these two buildings we mention the theatre of Herod at
Athens, the stage of which seems to show a similar arrangement.
The latter theatre, counting amongst the best-preserved antique
buildings of Athens, lies on the western side of the southern slope
of the Akropolis, the seats being worked into the rock. Skene
and paraskenia have been well preserved, rising partly up to
three stories, interrupted by arcades. The end wall of the
hyposkenion, which carried the logeion, and the stairs leading up
to the stage have been partly recovered by recent excavations.
These arrangements have been imitated from Greek architecture,
while the magnificent stage-building itself shows the Roman
method. The cavea (Fig. 435, B) lying towards the rock of the
Akropolis is divided into two ranks of sitting-steps by means of a
præcinctio 4 feet wide: the lower division contained twenty, the
upper most likely thirteen steps; the latter are completely destroyed.
The height of each step is $1\frac{1}{4}$ foot: the lower section of steps is again
divided by six, the upper one by twelve, staircases. The orchestra
(A) is semi-elliptical in shape, its diameter being 60 feet long; it
is paved with square slabs of white Pentelic marble and of
Cipollino from Karystos, the latter with green, yellow, or grey
veins. As in Greek theatres, the lowest row of steps does not
immediately touch the stage, but is divided from it by the
parodoi (D D). The stage, 24 feet deep, lies $4\frac{1}{2}$ feet above the
floor of the orchestra. The skene-wall contains three doors,
through one of which one enters a room (I), the remains of which,
like those of the rooms marked E E and F F, show the traces of
a vaulted ceiling. The theatre was built between 160 and 170 A.D.
by Herodes Atticus of Marathon, celebrated for his wealth and
his oratorical talents: to him Athens also owes the Panathenaïc
stadion on the Ilissos. When Pausanias visited Athens this
theatre had not yet been erected; in another passage he speaks of
it as an odeum, and counts it amongst the most splendid buildings

in Greece. Philostrates calls it the theatre of Annia Regilla, the deceased wife of Herod, in whose honour her husband erected it. According to the same author its roof consisted of cedar-wood, a remarkable feature in a building of such dimensions.

Fig. 436 gives a perspective view of the repeatedly mentioned theatre of Orange, the stage of which is in perfect preservation. The cavea lies on the slope of a hill. Behind the richly decorated skene-wall lies a narrow building of three stories, the façade of which, adorned with arcades, is seen in our illustration. Between the wall of the skene and the outer wall are several staircases. The stage-building is 103·15 metres long by 36·821 high; the length of the proskenion, from paraskenion to paraskenion, is

Fig. 436.

61·20 metres; the distance between its facing wall and the centre door of the skene-wall is 13·20, that from the two side doors 18 metres: an oblique roof of timber covered this whole space (see Lohde, " Die Skene der Alten," p. 5 *et seq.*).

Of a similar kind was the arrangement of the theatre of Aspendos (see Fig. 437, where the position of the oblique roof of the stage may be distinguished). The spectators' seats lie on the slope of the hill on which the town of Aspendos is situated. The rows of seats rise from the semicircular orchestra, which first is surrounded by a podium of considerable height. A diazoma divides the rows of seats into two stories, the upper one of which

is surrounded by arcades, with a barrel-vaulted niche attached
to each of them. The cavea is more than usually well preserved. The top of the arcades is on a level with that of the skene-
wall, in accordance with Vitruvius's precept. The wall of the
skene rises in three stories, richly adorned with columns, which
have disappeared; the projecting beams carried by them are,
however, still visible, as are also the gables. All these projecting
parts, and the window-sills of the first stories, are made of marble;
the wall itself consists of large blocks of a kind of *breccia*, joined
together without mortar; the whole back wall of the skene
was once adorned in an encaustic manner. Above the third series

Fig. 437.

of columns lay the oblique roof covering the whole stage: traces
of its insertion into the wall of the proskenion may be discovered
in our illustration. Besides the usual three doors, two apertures
in the wall of the paraskenion opened on to the stage, similar
to those in the theatres of Herod and at Orange. Above each
of these two doors the walls of the proskenion contain two other
openings, leading, most likely, to small balconies or boxes for
distinguished spectators. The building behind the wall of the
skene is narrow, as at Orange. It had three stories, the middle
one of which communicated by a door with the space which lay

between the wall of the skene and the back scene, put in front of it during the performance.

85. We now have to mention a building unique as regards mechanical appliances, and important for us in so far as it undoubtedly was the intermediate step to another class of edifices for public amusement. We are speaking of the building erected by C. Curio during his tribunate (B.C. 50) for an enormous sum of money, given to him by Cæsar for the furthering of party-

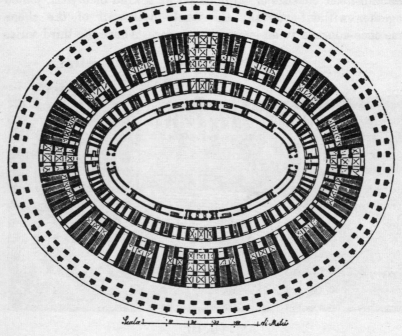

Fig. 438.

purposes. Both the stone theatre of Pompey (55 B.C.) and the wooden one of Scaurus were already in existence. A new contrivance of astonishing boldness had to be invented, so as to excite the admiration of the multitude. Pliny (Hist. Nat., XXXVI., 24, 8) gives the following description of the astonishing structure. " He (Curio) built two wooden theatres by the side of each other, each of them kept its balance by means of movable pegs. In the forenoon comedies were performed on them, and the two theatres were turned away from each other, so that the noises on the two stages should not interfere with each other. All of a sudden they were whirled round, so as to stand opposite each other; in the evening the wooden partitions of the stages were removed, the ends of the sitting-steps (*cornua*) touched each other, and an amphitheatre was thus created, in which Curio, after having endangered the lives of the people themselves, arranged battles of gladiators." Pliny strongly reproves both tribune and people for trusting their lives to a fragile wooden machinery.

Whether this was the first attempt at constructing an amphitheatre we cannot tell; certain it is that four years later Cæsar built an edifice for the battles of gladiators and the fights of animals, which resembled the bold attempt of Curio, and to which the name of *amphitheatrum* was technically applied.* It was built of wood, but richly decorated. The first stone amphitheatre in Rome was built during the reign of Augustus by Statilius Taurus, the friend of that emperor; it was destroyed by fire under Nero. The amphitheatres, to which the gladiatorial battles formerly fought in the forum or circus were transferred, became so popular in consequence, that even provincial towns went to enormous expenses in erecting them. Fig. 438 shows the plan of the amphitheatre of Capua, consisting of an oval arena surrounded by rows of seats. It was built at the expense of the town, after the model of the Flavian amphitheatre in Rome, from which the substructure, and the arrangement of the sitting-steps and of the stairs leading up to them, are imitated almost exactly. It nearly equalled the size of its model, being the second largest of all the amphitheatres known to us. An inscription says that the Emperor Hadrian added the columns and their roof, meaning the colonnade surrounding the highest row of steps, as in a theatre (compare Fig. 434). Underneath the arena were vaulted chambers (also found in the Flavian amphitheatre), destined

---

* Amphitheatrum means literally a building with a θεάτρον, spectators' place or cavea, on two sides. The buildings for the so-called naumachia (naval battles) also had the form of amphitheatres. Hirt (*loc. cit.*, III., 159) points out that the elliptical shape was chosen in preference to the circular as it held more spectators on an equal space; the greater length of the arena, moreover, left more freedom to the movements of men and animals than a circle would have done. Acoustic considerations were out of the question, as there was nothing to be heard, but only something to be seen.

for the keeping of the wild animals, also for making the necessary preparations for the performances.

The Flavian amphitheatre, better known as the Coliseum, was begun by Vespasian, and completed by his successor Titus, on the site of a large pond (*stagna Neronis*) in the "Golden House" of Nero. Augustus is said to have planned an amphitheatre to be erected on the same spot. It is said to have contained 87,000 seats (*loca*), and was, owing to its central situation, one of the most favourite places of amusement of the Roman people. Its plan is shown in Fig. 438. The arena, underneath which vaulted

Fig. 439.

chambers have been discovered, has the form of an ellipse, the larger diameter measuring 264, the smaller 156 feet. The surrounding edifice has a uniform depth of 155 feet, which gives a total diameter of 574 feet, or of 466 feet for the enclosing outer wall. The latter was interrupted by eighty arcades, forming the openings of the numerous systematically arranged corridors and staircases of the interior. The lowest row of these arcades (*vomitoria*) is adorned with Doric, the second story with Ionic, and the third with Korinthian semi-columns. The fourth story consists of a wall adorned with Korinthian pilasters, and inter-

rupted by windows. The total height is 156 feet. Figs. 439 and
441 show views of the exterior and interior of the Coliseum in
its present state. In the upper story 240 small projections are
conspicuous, to which answer as many openings in the chief
cornice. These were destined to carry masts, to which ropes were
fastened, to support an awning (*velarium*) stretched across the
enormous space. The section (Fig. 440, from a design by Fontana,
modified by Hirt) serves to illustrate the interior arrangements
(compare also Fig. 434). The Coliseum consists almost entirely of
travertine freestone, carefully hewn ; the interior, partly built of

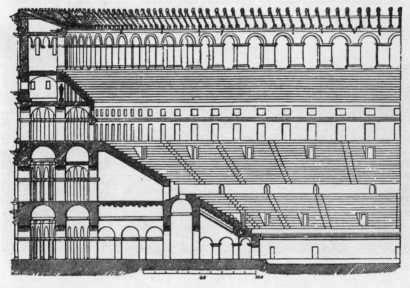

Fig. 440.

bricks, has considerably suffered during the Middle Ages. At
one time it served as the castle of the Frangipani family ; at
another it was systematically ransacked for building materials
(the Palazzo della Cancelleria, Palazzo Farnese, and Palazzo di
S. Marco have been built of such) ; but its grand forms have
withstood all these attempts at destruction. In the substructure
of the rows of seats, the corridors (*itinera*), passages, and stairs
leading up to them are still recognisable. The lowest part of the
spectators' place, viz. the *podium*, has been built higher than was the
custom in theatres : as a further means of protection against the

wild animals in the arena other contrivances were added. Near the podium were the seats of the imperial family, of the highest magistrates, and of the Vestals; at the back of them followed the ordinary rows of seats in three stories (*mœniana*, corresponding to those of the exterior arcades), the lower of which, containing about twenty steps (*gradus*, no more in existence), was reserved for magistrates and knights, the next following one (of about sixteen steps) for Roman citizens. The præcinction-wall, between the second and third stories, is higher than usual, and the upper rows themselves show a steeper ascent than the lower ones, in order to enable the spectators seated there to overlook the arena. This high præcinc-

Fig. 441.

tion-wall, called *balteus*, was richly decorated (according to Hirt, with glass mosaic) in the same manner as that of the theatre of Scaurus. The fourth story, the steps of which were considerably higher than those of the lower rows, was surrounded with an open portico, also richly decorated. Here were the seats for the women, and, perhaps at both ends of the longer diameter, those for the common people. The differences of rank and station co-existing with the legal equality of the Roman people appear thus distinctly marked in the Coliseo, which, in a manner, becomes the symbol of the grandeur and variegated development of the nation itself.

86. We now turn to the consideration of the implements of domestic use; our knowledge of these is much more accurate than of those of Greek origin, owing, to a great extent, to the preservation of the dwelling-house itself, to which these utensils belong. We have mentioned before how, during the eruption of Vesuvius (79 A.D.), Herculaneum and Stabiæ were more or less destroyed by a stream of lava, while Pompeii was first covered with a shower of glowing *rapilli*, on which lava afterwards collected. Only in 1748 Pompeii was rediscovered by an accident. At Herculaneum the hardened lava could only partially be removed; at Pompeii, on the other hand, the layers of loose ashes, to a depth of seven to eight metres, offered comparatively little difficulty to attempts at excavation. At first these excavations were made without plan or system; the recovered objects were left for a long time at the mercy of the weather, not to speak of the spoliation of uncultivated or unprincipled persons. Arditi, in 1812, was the first to bring system into the work; and, after the expulsion of the Bourbons, Fiorelli has continued his predecessor's efforts, introducing at the same time a new method, viz. that of horizontal instead of vertical digging; in this manner the former danger of the houses breaking down as soon as their props were taken away, has been removed. A little less than one-half of Pompeii has thus been discovered. The wall, about 10,000 feet long, surrounding the whole town in the shape of an irregular oval, shows Pompeii to have been of moderate dimensions; but the numerous public buildings and the comfort of many of the private houses proves the wealth of the citizens. Pompeii, and (in a lesser degree) many other seats of Roman culture, have yielded from amongst their ruins a rich harvest of utensils and implements of daily life and

intercourse, such as vessels (of metal, glass, and earthenware), lamps, armour, jewellery, coins, &c.   Most of these have passed into private and public collections ; numerous valuable objects have been purloined and destroyed by the finders.

In looking at these utensils, and comparing them with similar objects of Greek origin, we have to consider the question whether they were really of Roman make,—that is, worked by Roman artificers.   In trying to answer this question we must briefly touch upon the political history of Rome.   To south and north of the Roman territory, the country was inhabited by nations superior to the Romans in both material and intellectual respects.   We are speaking of the Greek colonies in the southern, and of the Etrus-can cities in the more northern, parts of Italy.   The splendour of both nations, however, was waning when they came into contact with their less-civilised neighbours : first the Etruscans, and after them the Greeks, had to submit to the superior military tactics of the Romans.   The military spirit of the conquerors prevented them at first from adopting the higher culture of the vanquished. At the same time it must be remembered that at an early period Etruscan artists adorned the public edifices of Rome with the works of their handicraft ; moreover, the statues of gods and other works of art, brought to Rome as booty from the conquered and devastated Etruscan cities, formed an intellectual and religious link between conquerors and conquered.   Political motives thus co-operated with growing artistic culture.   The statue of the Juno Regina was brought from Veii by Camillus, that of Jupiter Imperator from Præneste by Cincinnatus, with a view to amalga-mating the nations.

Of still greater importance was the treasure of masterworks of art and culture found by the Romans in the cities of Magna Græcia and Sicily, such as Capua, Tarentum, and Syracuse, further augmented by the spoils of the Greek peninsula, Macedon, and the Asiatic empires.   The art-treasures paraded in the three days' triumph by Quinctius Flaminius and Paullus Æmilius, the conquerors of Philip and Perseus of Macedon, were of enormous value.   Roman prætors used to ransack their Greek provinces for valuable objects of art : Scaurus, for instance, adorned his theatre with Greek statues and pictures acquired in this manner ; and when his villa at Tusculum was burnt by his enraged slaves, Greek works of art to the value of about £600,000 are said to have perished in the flames. Omitting many other instances of spoliation, we remind the reader only of that of Nero, by which Delphi and Olympia were deprived of the statues still remaining there. Thus Italy was flooded with the creations of Greek genius, and the craving for foreign art diffused amongst all classes of the Romans could not but throw into the background the productions of native artists. Many Greek artificers, moreover, came to Rome as the best market for their wares: even amongst the Greek slaves artistic talent was of no rare occurrence. In this way Greek patterns became prevalent, not only in high art but also in mechanical handicrafts. Even at a later period, when Greek art itself had declined, and Roman customs and ideas had, to a great extent, absorbed the national peculiarities of the conquered races, the artistic creations of what is generally called the national Roman style are, for the greater part, only reminiscences of originally Greek ideas. At Pompeii also, much of what we now call Roman is undoubtedly of Greek origin; the compositions of the best wall-paintings and mosaics breathe Greek spirit, as might be expected in a town which, although Romanised to a great extent, still retained traces of its Greek origin. Nevertheless, most of these wall-paintings, mosaics, and other objects of art and industry, although perhaps composed by Greek artists, or after Greek patterns, are justly denominated Roman, as they undoubtedly belong to the period of municipal power and independence, which fostered the growth of the Roman national element.

87. Seats and couches are sufficiently illustrated by wall-paintings at Pompeii and Herculaneum, and by the remaining specimens. The simple folding-stool with crossed legs, the backless chair with four perpendicular legs, the chair with a low or high back, and the state-throne (see § 31),—all these were made after Greek patterns. The word *sella* is the generic term for the different classes of chairs comprised in the Greek diphroi and klismoi; only the chair with a back to it is distinguished as *cathedra*. The form of the cathedra resembles that of our ordinary drawing-room chairs but for the wider, frequently semicircular, curve of the

back, which greatly adds to the comfort of the seated person.
Soft cushions, placed both against the back and on the seat, mark
the cathedra as a piece of furniture belonging essentially to the
women's apartments; the more effeminate men of a later period,
however, used these *fauteuils* in preference.   The marble statues

of the younger Faustina (Fig. 469)
and of Agrippina the wife of Germanicus, both in the gallery of Florence (Clarac, "Musée," Pls. 955, 930),
are seated on cathedræ.   The legs of
the chairs were frequently shaped in
some graceful fashion, and adorned
with valuable ornaments of metal and
ivory; tasteful turnery was also often
applied to them: all this is sufficiently proved by the wall-paintings
(compare Fig. 471).   Different from
these chairs is the *solium*, the dignified
form of which designates it as the seat
of honour for the master of the house,
or as the throne of rulers of the State and gods; it answers,
therefore, to the *thronos* of the Greeks.   The richly decorated
back rises perpendicularly sometimes up to the height of
the shoulders, at others, above the head, of the seated person;
two elbows, mostly of massive workmanship, are attached to
the back.   The throne stands on a strong base or on high legs;
it was generally made of solid, heavy materials.   Of the wooden
solium, seated on which the patron gave advice to his clients,
naturally no specimen remains; but we possess several marble
thrones, most likely the seats of emperors, and others placed,
according to Greek custom, near the divine images in the temples.
A marble throne of the first-mentioned class, richly decorated with
sculptures, is in the Royal Collection of Antiques at Berlin.   Fig.
442 shows a throne from a temple—one of the two of the kind
preserved in the Louvre.   The symbolical sculptures on the inner
surface of the back, both above and below the seat, consisting of a
pair of winged snakes, the mystical basket, and the sickle, also
the two torches serving in a manner as props of the back, seem

Fig. 442.

to indicate its connection with the worship of Ceres. The seat is supported by two sphinxes, the wings of which form the elbows of the chair. The companion chair in the Louvre shows the Bacchic attributes arranged in a similar manner. Similar thrones of gods occur frequently in Pompeian wall-paintings and on Roman coins; we also mention in connection with the subject a wall-painting at Herculaneum ("Pitture antiche d'Ercolano," vol. i. p. 155). These thrones generally show light, graceful forms of legs, and broad seats covered with soft cushions; the back and elbows are frequently enveloped in rich folds of drapery. Of the two thrones in the Herculaneum wall-painting referred to, one has a helmet, the other a dove, on its seat—the respective emblems of Mars and Venus. The solium used by the magistrates of the republic was without back or elbows.

Peculiar to the Romans was the *sella curulis*, a folding-stool with curved legs placed crosswise; at first it was made of ivory, afterwards of metal: it most likely dates from the times of the kings. At that period it was in reality a seat on wheels, from which the kings exercised their legal functions: afterwards the sella curulis, although deprived of its wheels, remained the attribute of certain magistrates; it was placed on the tribunal, from the height of which the judge pronounced his sentence. The use of the sella curulis was permitted to the consuls, prætors, proprætors, and the curulian ædiles; also to the dictator, the magister equitum, the decemviri, and, at a later period, the quæstor. Amongst priests, only the Flamen Dialis enjoyed the same privilege, together with a seat in the senate. On some of the *denarii* of Roman families, such as the Gens Cæcilia, Cestia, Cornelia, Furia, Julia, Livineia, Plætoria, Pompeia, Valeria, we frequently see the sella curulis connected with the names of those members of the gens who held one of the curulian offices. Fasces, lituus, crowns, and branches frequently are arranged round the chair to indicate the particular function of the magis-

Fig. 443.

trate. Fig. 443 shows the reverse of a coin of the Gens Furia, with a sella curulis depicted on it. On the chair are inscribed the words P. FOVRIVS; underneath it we read, CRASSIPES: the other side of the coin shows the crowned head of Cybele

with the inscription, AED. CVR.   The emperors also claimed
the privilege of the sella curulis.   The marble statue of the
Emperor Claudius in the Villa Albani (Clarac, "Musée," Pl.
936, *B*) is, for instance, seated on a sella curulis, or rather *sella
imperatoria.* Several bronze legs of chairs, in the Museo Borbonico,
worked like necks of animals and placed crosswise, most likely belonged to chairs of this kind.   The *subsellium*, a low bench with

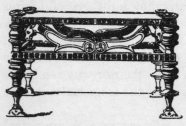

room for several persons, was
destined for the magistrates of the
people, *i.e.* for the tribuni and ædiles
plebis.   Silver coins of the Gens
Calpurnia, Critonia, Fannia, and
Statilia show this bench always
occupied by two ædiles (see
Riccio, "Le Monete delle antiche
Famiglie di Roma," Tavs. X.,

Fig. 444.

XVII., XX., XLV.). Another seat of honour was the *bisellium*,
a very broad chair, or rather double chair, without a back,
destined for the decuriones and augustales.   Two bronze bisellia
have been found at Pompeii, one of which is shown, Fig. 444.

88. The couches and beds show the same elegance and comfort
as the chairs.   We need only add a few remarks to what we
have already said about Greek couches (§ 32).   The body of
the bed, made either of wood inlaid with ivory and tortoiseshell,
or of valuable metal (*lecti eborati, testudinei, inargentati, inaurati*),
rested on gracefully formed legs.   Sometimes the whole bed-
frame was made of bronze, and in a few cases (*e.g.* the bed of
Elagabalus) of solid silver.   A bronze bed-frame somewhat
resembling our iron truckle-beds may be seen on an Etruscan
tomb (see "Museum Gregorianum," vol. i., Tav. 16).   A bronze
trellis-work here carries the mattrass, instead of the more usual
webbing (*fasciæ, institæ, tenta cubilia*).   The mattrass (*torus*), originally filled with straw, was afterwards stuffed with sheep's wool
(*tomentum*) or the down of (particularly German) geese and swans;
Elagabalus chose the soft plumage under the wings of the partridge
for his mattrasses.   Bolsters and cushions (*culcita*) were stuffed
with the same material (see, for instance, Zahn's "Schönste
Ornamente," Series III., Taf. 41).   Blankets and sheets (*vestes*

stragulæ), according to the owner's wealth, made either of simple material or dyed and adorned with embroidered or woven patterns and borders, were spread over the cushions and bolsters. One or several pillows (*pulvinus*) served to prop the head (whence their name *cervicalia*) or the left elbow of the sleeping or reclining persons (compare the couches in Fig. 232 and those in Figs. 187—190, the latter of which, although taken from Greek vase-paintings, are equally illustrative of Roman forms). Footstools (*subsellia, scabella, scamna*), used for mounting high thrones and beds, or with cathedræ for resting the feet, were as general amongst the Romans as amongst the Greeks. Wooden bed-frames, like all other wooden utensils, have been destroyed at Pompeii; but we see many couches (on the average 2·50 metres long by 1 wide) let into the walls of the niches of bedrooms; these niches, as, for instance, that in the villa of Diomedes, could be closed by means of curtains or pasteboard partitions ("Spanish walls").* As we said before, the couch was used, not only for sleeping, but also for meditating, reading, and writing in a reclining position, the left arm leaning on the cushions. This custom was undoubtedly adopted from the Greek. The two names, derived from the different purposes, *lectus cubicularius* and *lectus lucubratorius*, most likely apply to one and the same kind of couch; perhaps in the latter there was attached to the back of the couch (*pluteus*) nearest the head a contrivance like our reading-desks, to put books and writing materials on; a similar contrivance is mentioned in connection with the cathedra.

In later times, when the simpler custom of sitting at their meals was abandoned by the Romans, men used to lie down to their meals on couches. The wife sat on the foot end of the lectus, the children on separate chairs, and the servants on benches (*subsellium*). This custom, as illustrated by numerous bas-reliefs, was limited to the family circle. In the dining-rooms (*triclinium*), where guests were received, a particular arrangement of the couches became necessary. A square table stood in the centre of the triclinium (several of which are perfectly preserved at Pompeii) surrounded on three sides by so many low couches

* See a picture of the remains of such a partition found at Pompeii in Overbeck's "Pompeji," 2nd ed., ii. p. 48.

(*lectus triclinaris*), while the fourth side remained open to the access of the attending slaves. Fig. 445 shows the arrangement of a triclinium. M indicates the table surrounded by the three couches. The latter, as is proved by several couches made of masonry

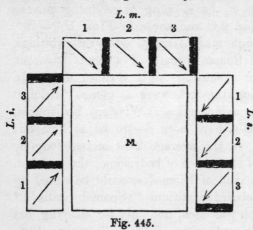

Fig. 445.

at Pompeii (Mazois, "Ruines de Pompei," t. i., Pl. 20), had the edge nearest the table slightly raised (compare the summer triclinium in the background of Fig. 390). The couch was ascended by the guests (*accubare*) on the lower side, the space between the edge of the table and the couch being too narrow for a person to pass.

Each couch had room for three persons reclining in the direction of the arrow in our plan; the left arm rested on the cushions, while the disengaged right hand was used for eating. *L. i.* mark the lowest (*lectus imus*), *L. m.* the middle (*lectus medius*), and *L. s.* the highest (*lectus summus*) couch. In the same manner the single seats on each couch were distinguished as *locus imus, medius*, and *summus*. On the lectus imus 1 marks the lowest, 3 the highest, and 2 the middle places. On the lectus medius 3 marks the highest, 1 the lowest, and 2 the middle. The last-mentioned place was the place of honour; 1 was called the *locus consularis*, because if a consul was present this place was occupied by him, in order that he might be able to receive important communications during dinner. The place on the lectus imus (3) touching his was occupied by the host. On the lectus summus the places followed in the reverse order of that on the lectus imus. The stronger lines on the edges of the loci summi mark the low backs against which the cushions belonging to these seats were placed; the cushions belonging to the other places lay in the middle of the couch, and, therefore, did not require a prop. In later times three or more triclinia were frequently placed in one dining-room, which must have been of considerable size, taking into account the additional space required for the servants, dancers, musicians, &c.

About the end of the Republic the use of round tables (*orbes*) instead of square ones became more frequent; the three couches standing at right angles were accordingly transformed into one, the shape of which, following the curve of the table, became semicircular, resembling the form of a Greek C, whence its name *sigma* or *stibadium*. The two corner seats (*cornua*) now became the places of honour, that on the right (*in dextro cornu*) being considered superior to that on the left (*in cornu sinistro*). On a sigma of this kind are reclining several Cupids, round a table covered with drinking-cups (see the graceful Pompeian wall-painting, "Museo Borbon.," vol. xv., Tav. 46). One large bolster on the edge of the couch nearest the table serves as prop for the left arms of the topers; a light awning protects them from the sun. A different arrangement we see in the wall-painting found near the tomb of the Scipiones in the Via Appia (Campana, "Di due Sepolcri Romani del Secolo di Augusto, &c." Roma, 1840. Tav. XIV.). Here the table has the form of a crescent (*mensa lunata*); along its outer edge is placed the sigma, on which eleven persons are reclining, partaking of the funereal repast (compare the description of a similar scene in "Bullettino arch. Napoletano," 1845, p. 82). We refrain from describing the rich ornamentation of these couches, with their bolsters and valuable carpets, harmonizing with the wall-decorations and the mosaic pavement of the dining-room itself.

To conclude, we mention the benches of bronze found in the tepidarium of the thermæ at Pompeii (Fig. 421), as also the *hemicyclia*, semicircular stone-benches, holding a greater number of persons, such as were placed in gardens and by the side of public roads. Two marble hemicyclia may be seen by the side of the street of graves, near the Herculanean gate at Pompeii; a third bench occupies the background of a small portico opening into the street (see "Mus. Borb.," vol. xv., Tav. 25, 26).

89. We have already made mention of square, round, and crescent-shaped tables. The brick leg of a table, the wooden slab of which has disappeared, may be seen in the *triclinium funebre* at

Pompeii; it is surrounded by three well-preserved couches. The above-mentioned mensa lunata in a wall-painting is, on the other hand, supported by three legs shaped like animals. Besides these larger tables, others of smaller size, and more easily movable, were in frequent use. They might be either round or square, and were placed by the side of the couches : like the dining-tables, they were not higher than the couches. For their various forms we refer the reader to the Greek tables shown in Fig. 191. The way of ornamenting the tables was far more splendid and expensive amongst the Romans than amongst the Greeks. Not only were the legs beautifully worked in wood, metal, or stone (the graceful forms of the numerous marble and bronze legs found at Pompeii have become the models of modern wood-carvers), but the slabs also consisted of metal and rare kinds of stone or wood wrought in elegant and graceful shapes. Particularly the slabs of one-legged tables (*monopodia, orbes*) used to be made of the rarest woods; the wood of the *Thyia cypressiodes*, a tree growing on the slopes of the Atlas, the stem of which, near the root, is frequently several feet thick, was chosen in preference ; the Roman name of this tree was *citrus*, not to be mistaken for the citron-tree. The value of large slabs of citrus-wood was enormous. According to Pliny, Cicero (by no means a wealthy man according to Roman notions) spent 500,000 H S. (about £5,400), Asinius Pollio £10,800, King Juba £13,050, and the family of the Cethegi

£15,150, for a single slab of this material. The value of this wood consisted chiefly in the beautiful lines of the veins and fibres (*maculæ*), shown to still greater advantage by the polish. The Romans classified the slabs by their designs into tiger, panther, wavy, and peacock feather, &c., patterns. The enormous price of the massive

Fig. 446.

slabs naturally led to the custom of veneering other wood with citrus. Valuable tables of this kind were taken out of their covers only on festive occasions. The plate and nicknacks, always found in elegant Roman houses, were displayed on small one or three legged tables (*trapezophoron*), the slabs of which (*abacus*, a word which, like trapezophoron, is sometimes used for the whole table) had raised edges round them : several richly ornamented specimens of such tables have been found at Pompeii. Fig. 446 shows a small abacus resting on three marble legs, which has been found in the house of the "Little Mosaic-Fountain" at Pompeii. Another table ("Museo Borb.," vol. xv., Tav. 6), with a slab of *rosso antico* resting on four graceful bronze legs, deserves attention on account of an ingenious contrivance between the legs, by means of which it could be lowered or heightened at will: a similar contrivance occurs in several tripods.

A table of a different kind was the tripod (*delphica sc. mensa*), imitated from the Greek τρίπους, and used chiefly at meals to put vessels and dishes on : several elegant specimens of the tripod have been discovered at Pompeii. The ends of the three legs were generally shaped like the paws of animals; the legs, connected by means of metal bars and generally ornamented with figures or foliage, carry a metal basin, either flat-bottomed or of semi-globular shape (Fig. 447). Whether the tripods found in the rooms of houses were used for sacred or profane purposes cannot always be decided with certainty. The skulls and garlands surrounding the top of our tripod (Fig. 447) seem to indicate

Fig. 447.

its sacred character: other tripods are without any decoration. The top of the sacred tripods generally consisted of deep caldron-like basins: specimens of them have been found in Etruscan graves ; they also occur in various forms on coins and vases.

90. The numerous vases found in the graves of Italy (see § 38 *et seq.*) are, as we have seen, of Greek origin, although frequently manufactured on Roman territory. The pictures

on them illustrate myths, or scenes from the daily life of Greeks
or Etruscans; we therefore have refrained from referring to
them in speaking of Roman customs and artistic achievements.
As to the degree of skill with which native Roman artificers
worked after Greek patterns we are unable to judge, seeing that
most of the specimens of Roman native pottery preserved to us
belong to a low class of art. Local potteries were found in almost
all places of any importance; and the former existence of manu-
factures is betrayed by the heaps of potsherds found in such
places,—as, for instance, in the valley of the Neckar. Whole
vessels are, however, found very rarely. More numerous are the
specimens of clay vessels found in Roman graves: their style and
material are far inferior to those of Greek make. About the forms
of the smaller drinking and drawing vessels and ointment-bottles
(to which classes they chiefly belong), we have spoken before
(compare Fig. 198): new to us only are the kitchen utensils of
clay, numerous interesting specimens of which have been dug
up. The destinations of most of these can be determined from
their similarity to vessels now in use. Besides these earthen-

a   b   c   d

Fig. 448.

ware vessels a great many others made of bronze have been found
at Pompeii and other Roman settlements; their elegant and, at
the same time, useful forms excite our highest admiration. In
most cases the names occurring in ancient authors cannot, unfortunately, be applied with certainty to the remaining specimens.
Figs. 448 and 449 show a variety of vessels, all found at Pompeii,
Fig. 448, c, shows a kettle, semi-oval in shape and with a comparatively narrow opening, to the rim of which the handle is
fastened; it rests on a tripod (tripes). Similar kettles, with covers
(testum, testu) fastened to their necks by means of little chains,

have been found in several places ("Mus. Borbon.," vol. v., Tav.
58). A pot (*olla, cacabus*), similar to those now in use, the handle
of which is made in the shape of a dolphin, is represented,
Fig. 448, *d*. Porridge, meat, and vegetables were cooked in it.

Of pails we possess a considerable number (Fig. 448, *a, b*).
Their rims are adorned with graceful patterns, and the rings to
which the handles are fastened often show palmet to ornaments.
The pail, Fig. 448, *b*, shows small pegs on both sides of the rings
to prevent the heavy handle from falling on the graceful rim of
the vessel; the double handle (Fig. 448, *a*) served to steady the
vessel while being carried; thus usefulness and elegance of
form were combined.

Fig. 449, *f*, resembles our saucepan. Two vessels of this kind,
the ends of whose horizontal handles are shaped like heads of

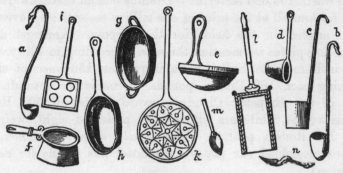

Fig. 449.

swans, have recently been found, the one at Teplitzin Bohemia,
the other at Hagenow in Mecklenburg; both show, on the upper
surface of the handle, the stamp of the same manufacturer—
TIBERIVS ROBILIVS SITALCES. The vessel found in
Bohemia shows underneath this inscription another name,
GAIVS ATILIVS HANNO, which Mommsen (*Archäologischer
Anzeiger*, 1858, Nos. 115—117) takes to be that of the modeller.
The flat pan (*sartago*, Fig. 449, *h*) was used to heat the oil—an
important ingredient of Southern cookery. Fig. 449, *i*, shows a
pan with four indentures, used most likely for poaching eggs;
Fig. 449, *l*, a sort of shovel with a handle and an elegant border-
pattern; and Fig. 449, *g*, a two-handled vessel, also for kitchen
use. In Fig. 449, *m* and *n*, we see two forms of the spoon

(*cochlear, ligula*) ; they were used not only for eating soup and porridge, but also for the opening of eggs, oysters, and snails, whence their pointed ends. Fig. 449, *e* and *d*, show ladles for drawing water ; Fig. 449, *a, b, c*, specimens of the long-handled *trua* or *trulla* (the Greek kyathos, compare Fig. 303), to draw the wine from deep butts, &c. Of sieves (*colum*, Fig. 449, *k*), funnels (*infundibulum*), and similar kitchen utensils, most of the larger museums contain specimens; we refer the reader to the numerous works illustrative of the kitchen utensils found at Pompeii.

Meat and fish were put on small or large flat dishes (*patina*) with raised edges, mostly made of clay. Those of rich people were made of precious metals beautifully chiselled (*argentum cælatum*). But even those made of clay frequently were bought at enormous prices. Pliny relates that the tragic actor, Clodius Æsopus, possessed a dish worth 100,000 sestertii. Vitellius had an earthenware dish made for himself at the price of one million sestertii; an oven had to be erected in the fields for the purpose. Amongst dishes resembling plates we mention the *lanx*. According to Pliny, there were in Rome, after Sulla's wars, more than 150 *lances* of silver, weighing each 100 Roman pounds. Drusilianus Rotundus, the slave of the Emperor Claudius, owned a dish of 500 Roman pounds weight, while his fellow-slaves possessed eight, weighing each 250 Roman pounds. The *patella, catinum, catillum*, and *paropsis* resembled our plates ; the latter was chiefly for dessert (*opsonium*).

91. The names of Roman drinking-vessels, *calix, patera, scyphus, cyathus*, sufficiently indicate their Greek origin; their shapes show the same variety as those of their Greek models (see § 38). Their names cannot always be identified, but the existence of a few measuring-vessels with the gauge marked on them enables us to speak with certainty about the cubic contents of some of their forms.* Here, however, we must limit ourselves to the outer appearance of the vessels, and the material of which they are made. All vessels made of precious metals were either *pura*, i.e. without any relief-work, and therefore of smooth surface, or they were *cælata*, that is, adorned with bas-reliefs, either wrought of the material itself or soldered to its surface. Many

* Compare Hultsch, "Griechische und römische Metrologie," p. 87 *et seq.*, and Becker's "Gallus," herausgegeben von Rein, Third Edition, Part III. p. 280 *et seq.*

Greek and Oriental vessels of great value were brought to
Rome, and kept in Roman families as precious heirlooms; others
made of precious metals were melted and recast according
to Roman taste. The custom of adorning drinking-vessels with
precious stones, known to the Greeks, was exaggerated by the
luxurious Romans of imperial times to an unprecedented degree
(Pliny, "Hist. Natur.," XXXIII. 2). Such vases (*gemmata potaria*)
were sent by foreign kings to the Roman people, and with them
the emperors rewarded the services of their generals or of the
chieftains of Germanic tribes (Tacitus, "Germania," V.). We
possess numerous vessels of earthenware, adorned with garlands of
leaves and flowers, and inscribed with gay devices; such as, COPO
IMPLE ; BIBE AMICE EX ME ; SITIO ; MISCE ; REPLETE,
&c. Vessels of precious metal are of rarer occurrence.

We have mentioned before the luxurious custom, common
amongst the Romans after the conquest of Greece and Asia, of
having their utensils of the table, and even of the kitchen, made
of solid silver. Valuable plate (*argentum escarium* and *potorium*)
was of common occurrence in the houses of the rich. According
to Pliny, common soldiers had the handles of their swords and
their belts studded with silver; the baths of women were covered
with the same valuable material, which was even used for the
common implements of kitchen and scullery. Large manufactories of silver utensils were started in which each part of the
work was assigned to a special artificer ; here the orders of the
silver-merchants (*negotiatores argentarii vascularii*) were executed.
Amongst the special workmen of these manufactories were the
figuratores (modellers), *flatuarii* or *fusores* (founders), *tritores*
(turners or polishers), *cælatores* (chisellers), *crustarii* (the workmen
who attached the bas-reliefs to the surface of the vessel), and the
inauratores or *deauratores* (gilders). Many valuable vessels have
been recovered in the present century; others (for instance, several
hundred silver vessels found near the old Falerii) have tracelessly
disappeared. Amongst the discoveries which happily have
escaped the hands of the melter we mention the treasure of more
than one hundred silver vessels, weighing together about 50 lbs.,
found by Bernay in Normandy (1830). According to their
inscriptions, these vessels belonged to the treasury of a temple
of Mercury; they are at present in the late imperial library at

Paris. In the south of Russia the excavations carried on in 1831, 1862, and 1863, amongst the graves of the kings of the Bosphoric empire, have yielded an astonishing number of gold and silver

Fig. 450.

vessels and ornaments belonging to the third century of our era. At Pompeii fourteen silver vases were discovered in 1835; at

Fig. 451.

Cære (1836) a number of silver vases (now in the Museo Gregoriano) were found in a grave. One of the most interesting discoveries was made near Hildesheim, 7th October, 1868, consisting of seventy-four eating and drinking vessels, mostly well preserved; not to speak of numerous fragments which seem to prove that only part of the original treasure has been recovered; the weight of all the vessels (now in the Antiquarium of the Royal Museum, Berlin) amounts to 107·144 lbs. of silver. The style and technical finish of the vases prove them to have been manufactured in Rome; the form of the letters of the inscriptions found on twenty-four vessels indicates the first half of the first century after Christ. The surfaces of many of them are covered with alto-relievos of beaten silver—a circumstance which traces back their origin to imperial times, distinguishing them, at the same time, from the bas-relief ornamentations of the acme of Greek art. The gilding of the draperies and weapons, and the silver colour of the naked parts, in imitation, as it were, of the gold-and-ivory statues of Greek art, also indicate Roman workmanship. Figs. 450 and 451 show some of the finest pieces of this treasure. The composition of the figures on the surface of the vase in Fig. 450 shows true artistic genius: naked children are balancing themselves on water-plants growing in winding curves from a pair of griffins; some of the children attack crabs and eels with harpoons, while others drag the killed animals from the water. The graceful groups on the drinking-vessels in Fig. 451 are mostly taken from the Bacchic cycle of myths.

Besides vessels of precious metals and stones, those of glass were in favourite use amongst the Romans. The manufactory of glass, originating in Sidon, had reached its climax of perfection, both with regard to colour and form, in Alexandria about the time of the Ptolemies. Many of these Alexandrine glasses have been preserved to us, and their beauty fully explains their superiority in the opinion of the ancients to those manufactured in Italy. Here also, after the discovery of excellent sand at Cumæ and Linternum, glass works had been established. Most of our museums possess some specimens of antique glass manufacture, in the shape of balsam or medicine bottles of white or coloured glass. We also possess goblets and drinking-bottles of various shapes and sizes, made of white or common green glass; they generally taper towards the bottom, and frequently show grooves or raised points on their outer surfaces, so as to prevent the glass from slipping from the hand; urns, oinochoai, and dishes of various sizes made of glass are of frequent occurrence (Fig. 452). Some of these are dark blue or green, others party-coloured with stripes winding round them in zigzag or in spiral lines, reminding one of mosaic patterns. Pieces of glittering glass, being most likely fragments of so-called *allassontes versicolores* (not to be mistaken for originally white glass which has been discoloured by exposure to the weather), are not unfrequently found. We propose to name in the following pages a few of the more important specimens of antique glass-fabrication. One of the finest amongst these is the vessel known as the Barberini or Portland Vase, which was found in the sixteenth century in the sarcophagus of the so-called tomb of Severus Alexander and of his mother Julia Mammæa. It was kept in the Barberini palace for several centuries, till it was purchased by the Duke of Portland, after whose death it was placed

Fig. 452.

in the British Museum. After having been broken by the hand of a barbarian it has fortunately been restored satisfactorily. Many reproductions of this vase in china and terra-cotta have made it known in wide circles. The mythological bas-reliefs have not as yet been sufficiently explained. Similar glass vases with bas-relief ornamentation occur occasionally either whole or in fragments. The present writer saw in the collection of the late Mr. Hertz in London a small tablet of transparent green emerald resembling a shield, in the centre of which appears an expressive head of a warrior in gilt opaque glass similar to the bas-reliefs of the Portland vase; this tablet is said to have been found at Pompeii. According to a story told by several writers in the time of Tiberius, a composition of glass had been invented which could be bent and worked with a hammer.

We further mention a small number of very interesting goblets, which, to judge by their style, evidently belong to the same
place of manufactory as the Portland vase. They perhaps belong
to the class of goblets known as *vasa diatreta*, some specimens of
which were sent by Hadrian from Egypt to his friends in Rome.
The goblet, Fig. 453, found near Novara may serve as specimen.
Winckelmann, in his "History of Art," gives a description of it.
He speaks of a reticulated outer shell at some distance from the
glass itself, and connected with it by means of thin threads of
glass. The inscription : BIBE VIVAS MVLTIS ANNIS, is in
projecting green letters, the colour of the net being sky-blue, and
the colour of the glass itself that of the opal, *i.e.* a mixture of red,
white, yellow, and sky-blue, such as appears in glasses that have
been covered with earth for a long time. Three vases of a similar
kind have been found at Strasburg and Cologne (see "Jahrbücher
des Vereins von Alterthumsfreunden im
Rheinlande," Year v., p. 337, Tafs. XI., XII.);
all these distinctly show that they have been
made of solid glass by means of a wheel,
together with the net and letters. The highest
prices were paid for the so-called Murrhine
vases (*vasa Murrhina*) brought to Rome from the
East. Pompey, after his victory over Mithridates, was the first to bring one of them to

Fig. 453.

Rome, which he placed in the temple of the Capitoline
Jupiter. Augustus, as is well known, kept a Murrhine goblet
from Cleopatra's treasure for himself, while all her gold plate
was melted. The Consularis T. Petronius, who owned one of
the largest collections of rare vases, bought a basin from Murrha
for 300,000 sestertii ; before his death he destroyed this match-
less piece of his collection, so as to prevent Nero from laying hold
of it. Nero himself paid for a handled drinking-goblet from
Murrha a million sestertii. Crystal vases also fetched enormous
prices. There is some doubt about the material of these Murrhine
vases, which is the more difficult to solve, as the only vase in
existence which perhaps may lay claim to that name is too thin
and fragile to allow of closer investigation. It was found in the
Tyrol in 1837 (see *Neue Zeitschrift des Ferdinandeums*, vol. v.,
1839). Pliny describes the colour of the Murrhine vases as

a mixture of white and purple ; according to some ancient writers, they even improved the taste of the wine drunk out of them.

Fig. 454 shows two bronze jugs, at present in the Museo Bor-

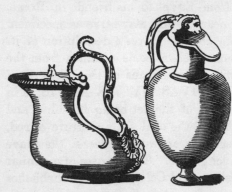

Fig. 454.

bonico, for the drawing or pouring out of liquor (compare the corresponding Greek forms, Fig. 198). The metal admitted of a more artistic treatment than the clay used by the Greeks. The more or less bent handles are adorned at their ends with figures, masks, or palmetto ornaments ; the gracefully curved mouths of the vessels frequently show borders of leaves and branches ; the body of the vessel is either smooth or decorated by toreutic art. These vessels served for domestic uses, such as pouring water over the hands of the guests after dinner, or keeping the wine in. One particular kind of them, similar in form to the wine-vessels found on Christian altars, was reserved for libations (compare § 103).

We finally mention two graceful vessels, one of which, made of

Fig. 455.

bronze (Fig. 455), represents a Roman fortified camp ; the walls, as well as the towers flanking them, are hollow ; into these boiling water was poured, in order to keep warm the dishes placed on the parapet of the walls, or fitted into the centre hollow, which was also filled with water. The tower in the right corner of our illustration shows a lid ; the water ran off through a tap on the left. The handles visible in Figs. 455 and 456 tend to show that both vessels were meant to be lifted on to the table. The construction of the latter heating apparatus is of a complicated kind. A square box on four graceful legs supports a high barrel-like vase with a lid to it; the mask just underneath serves as a safety-valve for the steam inside the vases; a similar contrivance appears on a semicircular water-box connected with the former. Three birds on the upper brim of the latter served as stands for a kettle. Whether the open box contained hot water or burning coals seems uncertain.

The Greek custom mentioned in § 39 of decorating buildings with ornamental vases was further developed by the Romans, who

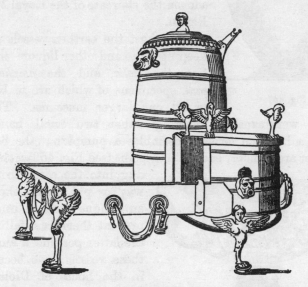

Fig. 456.

loved to place krateres, amphoræ, urns, and pateræ in their rooms or on the outsides of their houses; open halls and gardens were adorned in the same manner. Marble, porphyry, bronze, and precious metals were used for these ornamental vases, several specimens of which, in stone and bronze, have been preserved to us. The Museo Borbonico in Naples possesses a pitcher or kettle with a richly ornamented border, resting on three fabulous animals; also a bronze krater of great beauty. Fig. 457 shows a bronze mixing-vessel of Etruscan workmanship, of noble simplicity in form and decoration. Another vase of marble (Fig. 458) belongs both by its graceful shape and by the execution of its ornamental details to the finest specimens of antique art. It most likely came

from a Greek workshop (some say from that of Lysippus), and has been found amongst the ruins of Hadrian's villa at Tivoli; at present it is in Warwick Castle, whence the name of Warwick Vase by which it is generally known. It has been frequently reproduced on a smaller scale; a copy, in the original size, adorns the staircase of the Royal Museum, Berlin.

Amongst the earthen vessels used for keeping wine and other liquors we mention the *dolia,* and the *amphoræ* and *cadi,* specimens of which are to be found in all our larger museums. They are

Fig. 457.

of rude workmanship, showing either two small handles or none at all. The former resembles a pumpkin; the bodies of the latter are slender, ending in a point (see Fig. 459); they were

dug into the earth about half-way, or put against the wall in an oblique position in order to prevent them from falling. In the latter position a number of these vessels have been found in the house of Diomedes at Pompeii.

We subjoin a few remarks about the Roman way of making wine. After the grapes

Fig. 458.

for eating had been sepaated, the remainder was put into coops and stamped on with the feet. After this the grapes were once more operated upon with a wine-press. The juice thus produced was poured into *dolia* or large tubs, and taken to the wine-cellars (*cella vinaria*), which, in order to make them cool, were always built facing the north. In these open tubs the wine was left to ferment for a year: after that it was either drunk or (in case its quality was to be improved by longer keeping) poured from the dolia into the amphoræ and cadi (*diffundere*). The amphoræ, after having been pitched (hence *vinum picatum*) and cleaned with sea or salt water, were further rubbed with ashes of vines and smoked with burnt myrrh, after which they were closed with clay stoppers, and sealed up with pitch, chalk, or cement (*oblinere, gypsare*). A small tablet (*tesseræ, notæ, pittiacia*) attached to the body of the vessel indicated the size of the vessel and the name of the wine, also the consul under whom it had been stowed away. One amphora, for instance, bears the following inscription—RVBR. VET. V̄. P. CII. (*rubrum vetus vinum picatum CII.*), *i.e.* old pitched red wine, contents 102 lagenæ. The amphoræ were put in the upper story of the house, in order that the ascending smoke should give the wine a mild flavour (compare Horace, Od. III., 8, 9). Owing to the copious sediment produced by this method, the wine had to be strained each time before it was drunk. Several strainers (*colum*) made of metal have indeed been found at Pompeii. Sometimes a basin filled with snow (*colum nivarium*) was put on the top of a larger vessel. The wine was poured on the snow, through which it dripped into the amphora both cooled and filtered. Wooden barrels were not used in Rome in Pliny's time; they seem to have been introduced from the Alpine countries at a later period.

Innumerable different kinds of wine were grown in Italy, not to mention the Greek islands. The Romans became acquainted with the vine through the South Italian Greeks, who brought it from the mother-country. Italian soil and climate were favourable to its growth, and Italian growers were moreover encouraged by laws prohibiting the planting of new vineyards in the provinces. According to Pliny ("Nat. Hist.," XXXIII., 20), the Surrentum (*sc. vinum*) was the favourite wine of earlier times, afterwards supplanted by the Falernum or Albanum. These and other celebrated wines were frequently imitated. Of great celebrity were also the Cæcubum (afterwards supplanted by the Setinum), the Massicum, Albanum, Calenum, Capuanum, Mamertinum, Tarentinum, and others. Altogether eighty places are mentioned as famous for their wines, two-thirds of which were in Italy. Besides these we count about fifty kinds of liqueurs made of odoriferous herbs and flowers, such as roses, violets, aniseed, thyme, myrtle, &c., also several beverages extracted from various fruits.

We possess several representations of vintages and of the process of pressing the grapes. In the centre of a bas-relief in the Villa Albani (Panofka, "Bilder antiken Lebens," Taf. XIV., 9) we see a large tub, in which three boys are stamping with their feet on grapes brought to them in baskets. The must runs from the large tub into a smaller one, whence another boy pours it into a vessel made of osiers secured with pitch; to the right another boy pours the contents of a vessel of the same kind into a dolium. A wine-press is seen in the background. In another picture (Zahn, "Die schönsten Ornamente," &c., 3rd Series, Taf. 13) we see three Sileni occupied in the same manner as the three boys.

We mentioned before (§ 38) that the custom, still obtaining

Fig. 459.

in the South, of keeping the wine in hides of animals is of antique origin. The hairy part, rubbed with a resinous substance, was turned inside. Both Roman and Greek peasants brought their cheap wines to market in such skins (*uter*). In case larger quantities had to be transported, several skins were sewed together, and the whole put on a cart. Fig. 459 shows a wine-cart from a wall-painting, with which the interior of a tavern at Pompeii is appropriately decorated. The picture, which requires no further explanation, gives a vivid idea of a Roman market-scene.

92. Amongst all domestic utensils dug up, the lamps, par-

ticularly those made of bronze, claim our foremost attention,
both by their number and by the variety of their forms. Lamps,
like other earthenware utensils, were made in the most outlying
settlements, or were (in case their designs were of a more elaborate
kind) imported there from larger towns. The older Greek custom
of burning wax and tallow candles (*candelæ cereæ, sebaceæ*), or
pine-torches (see § 40) was soon superseded by the invention of
the oil-lamp (*lucerna*) ; these candles, moreover, were always of
a primitive kind, consisting of a wick of oakum (*stuppa*) or the
pith of a bulrush (*scirpus*) dipped into the liquid wax or tallow,
and dried afterwards. Even the lighting of the rooms by lamps

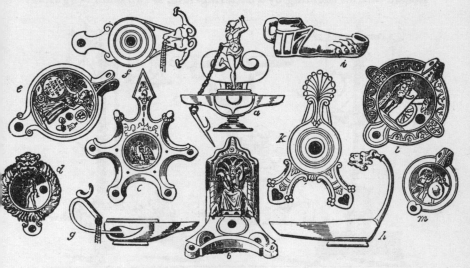

Fig. 460.

(notwithstanding the elegant forms of the latter) was not on a
par with other comforts and luxuries of Roman life. Glass
chimneys were unknown, and the soot of the oil-lamps settling on
furniture and wall-paintings had to be carefully sponged off by
the slaves every morning.

The lamp consisted of the oil-reservoir (*discus, infundibulum*),
either circular or elliptic in form, the nose (*nasus*), through which
the wick was pulled, and the handle (*ansa*). The material
commonly used was terra-cotta, yellow, brownish red, or scarlet
in colour, frequently glazed over with silicate. The simplest

forms of the lamp are specified in Fig. 460, *d, e, l, m.* All these
lamps have only *one* opening for the wick (*monomyxos, monolychnis*),
others (*b, c, k*) have two such openings (*dimyxi, trimyxi, polymyxi*).
Birch ("History of Ancient Pottery," vol. ii., pp. 274 and 275)
gives earthenware lamps with seven, and even twelve, *nasi* from
originals in the British Museum. The Royal Antiquarium in
Berlin also possesses two earthenware lamps with twelve nasi. The
disks and handles of many of these lamps are adorned with graceful bas-reliefs, representing mythological events, animals, domestic
life, or battles, fights of gladiators, flowers, garlands, &c., frequently original in composition. Fig. 460, *d,* shows Apollo, *l* a
Roman warrior standing by a battering-ram, *m* two soldiers fighting.

b   a   c

Fig. 461.

Of particular interest is Fig. 460, *e,* representing an earthenware
lamp, which, according to its inscription, was intended for a New
Year's present (*strenæ*).* The device on the shield of the Goddess
of Victory reads: ANNO NOVO FAVSTVM FELIX TIBI.

A number of lamps show on their bases inscriptions, either
incised or in relief, indicative of the name of the potter, the
owner, or the reigning emperor, &c.; sometimes we also meet with
trade marks affixed to the lamps.

* Several lamps, intended as new year's gifts, such as were habitually exchanged
by friends amongst the Romans, are in the R. Antiquarium of Berlin.

The forms of the lamps in Fig. 460, *b*, *i*, are of an unusual kind. The former shows a sacellum with the enthroned figure of Pluto; the latter has the semblance of a sandalled foot. Greater elegance and variety are displayed in the bronze lamps frequently found in our museums (Fig. 460, *a*, *f*, *g*, *h*, *k*). Herculaneum and Pompeii have yielded a number of beautiful specimens, counting amongst the most graceful utensils of antique times. To snuff the wick (*putres fungi*) and to pull it out small pincers were used, numbers of which have been found at Pompeii; another instrument serving the same purpose appears in Fig. 460, *a*, where the figure standing on the lamp holds it by a chain.

In order to light up larger rooms these lamps were either put on stands or they were suspended by chains from lamp-holders or from the ceiling. These stands or lamp-holders (*candelabrum*) were, amongst the poorer classes, made of wood or common metal; the rich, on the other hand, had them executed in the most graceful and elegant forms. The thin stem, sometimes fluted, sometimes formed like the stem of a tree, rises to a height of 3 to 5 feet, on a base generally formed by three paws of animals; on this stem rests either a diminutive capital or a human figure, destined to carry the plate (*discus*) on which the lamp stands. The shaft is frequently adorned with figures of all kinds of animals. Sometimes we see a marten or a cat crawling up the shaft of the candelabrum, intent upon catching the pigeons carelessly sitting on the disk— a favourite subject, which occurs, with many variations, in the candelabra found in Etruscan grave-chambers. Besides these massive candelabra, there were others with hollow

Fig. 462.

stems, into which a second stem was inserted, which could be
pulled out and fastened by means of bolts; in this manner
the candelabrum could be shortened or lengthened at will.
Fig. 461, *a*, shows a candelabrum in the shape of a tree, the
branches of which carry two disks for lamps. At the foot of the
tree a Silenus is seated on a rock—an appropriate ornament,
seeing that the lamp was destined to give light to merry
topers.

Different from the candelabrum is the *lampadarium*. Here

the stem resembles a column or pillar, and is
often architecturally developed; from the capital
at the top issue several thin branches gracefully
bent, from which the lamps are suspended by
chains. Fig. 461, *b* and *c*, represents two elegant
specimens of lampadaria; in the latter the base
takes the shape of a platform, on the front part
of which we see an altar with the fire burning on
it, and on the opposite side Bacchus riding on a
panther. Each of the four lamps is made after
a different pattern, which is also the case with
the lamps in Fig. 461, *b*.

All the candelabra and lampadaria hitherto
mentioned could be placed and replaced as convenience required; others were too heavy to be
moved. We are speaking of the long marble
candelabra, specimens of which are shown in
Figs. 462 and 463; they were placed as anathe-
mata in temples, or in the halls of the rich, and on
festive days blazing fires were lit on them.
The sacred character of the candelabrum (Fig.

Fig. 463.

462) is proved by the altar-like base resting
on three sphinxes, and by the rams' heads at the corners.
Cicero, in his impeachment of Verres, mentions a candelabrum
adorned with jewels destined by the sons of Antiochus for
the temple of the Capitoline Jupiter, but appropriated by
Verres before it had reached its place of destination. The
candelabrum (Fig. 463), the stem of which is supported by
kneeling Atlantes, most likely belonged to a private mansion.

Lanterns also (*laterna*) have been found at Pompeii; they

consist of cylindrical cases protected by a cover, and attached to a chain. Transparent materials, such as horn, oiled canvas, and bladder, were used instead of glass, which was introduced at a later period.

To conclude we mention some Greek lamps, mostly found in Roman catacombs, which, by the Christian subjects of their bas-reliefs and by the sign of the cross and the monogram of Christ frequently found on them, can be distinguished from other contemporary lamps, from which, however, they do not differ in form.

93. To complete our description of domestic utensils, we must once more pass through the different rooms of the Roman house with the assistance of our Plan (Fig. 386). Entering the ostium from the street we first observe the folding-doors (*fores, bifores*), made of wood, frequently inlaid with ivory or tortoiseshell; in public buildings, particularly in temples, these always open out-wards, in private houses inwards. They, however, did not, like the doors of our rooms, move on hinges, but on pivots (*cardines*) let into the lintel (*limen superum*) and the stone sill (*limen inferum*). Holes for this purpose have been found in the thresholds of houses at Pompeii. Like the threshold, the doorpost (*postes*) in good houses consisted of marble or of elegant woodwork. Knockers, fastened in the centre of the panel, may be seen in wall-paintings; a few specimens of these have been preserved. The janitor or porter (whose office was held in every good house by a particular slave, and whose box, *cella ostiarii*, was near the door) opened the door by pushing back the bolt (*pessuli*) or bar (*sera*, whence the expression *reserare*, to unbolt). Doors opening outward, particularly those of cupboards,
&c., were not bolted, but closed with lock and key. Most of our larger museums possess specimens of iron or bronze keys (Fig. 464). They are of all sizes, from the small ring-

a   *b*   *c*

Fig. 464.

key (Fig. 464, *a*) attached to the finger-ring, or the small skeleton-key (Fig. 464, *c*), to the large latch-key. Frequently they are of a peculiar shape (Fig. 464, *b*), and the locks to which they were fitted must have been contrived with great mechanical ingenuity. A few locks have been preserved; but most of them, like, for instance, those found at Neuwied, are in an almost decayed condition.

There were no separate doors to the single rooms, which were closed only by curtains (*vela*), so as not to shut out the fresh air from the generally small bedrooms and sitting-rooms. Poles and rings for these curtains have been found at Pompeii.

We now enter the interior of the house, undeterred by the rod (*rirga*) or threatening fist, which the porter (*ostiarius*) was wont to oppose to unwelcome visitors. A "SALVE" on the threshold bids us welcome. We first come to the atrium, the centre of house and family, where stood the hearth with its Lares and Penates and the venerable marital couch (*lectus genialis*). Here, in ancient times, the matron, surrounded by her children and hand-maidens, used to sit and weave. These old customs, however, soon disappeared. It is true that even at a later period the altar was reflected in the waves of the fountain; but no fire was lit on it; it remained in its place only as a tradition of former ages. Another memorial of ancient times are the family-portraits (*imagines maiorum*) looking down upon us from the opened wall-presses (*armaria*) surrounding the room. In the atria of old family houses were found masks of wax (*ceræ*), taken from the features of the dead persons, with tablets (*titulus, elogium*) telling of their names, dignities, and deeds attached to them. "The lines of the pedigree" (Pliny, "Nat. Hist.," XXXV. 2) "were drawn to the pictures, and the family archives filled with written and monumental evidence of their deeds. By the doors were seen representations of their valour, and near these were hung the weapons captured from the enemy, which even subsequent owners of the house were not allowed to remove." This custom was abandoned when upstarts bought the old mansions, and placed the marble or bronze busts of fictitious ancestors in their niches. Needy scholars were not wanting to trace back pedigrees to Æneas himself. The craving for portrait-statues is ridiculed by Pliny, who says that the libraries frequently contain sculptural reproductions of features invented for the purpose, as, for instance those of Homer.

The wall-paintings found at Pompeii and Herculaneum, although belonging to provincial towns, afford us sufficient

Fig. 465.

insight to judge approximately of the art of painting as practised amongst the Greeks ; for this art also the Romans had adopted from them. How far the Greeks used this art for wall-decoration of their private houses is difficult to decide, seeing that all such houses have disappeared and that Greek authors only mention the large paintings found in public buildings. Perhaps private wall-painting, although certainly not unknown to the Greeks, was practised amongst the Romans more extensively than amongst their instructors. Most of the better wall-paintings were undoubtedly executed by Greek artists living in Italy. In most cities there were guilds of painters, presided over by a master, perhaps of Greek birth, who himself made the designs of the better pictures, leaving the mechanical part of the work to his assistant. Many of the imperfect designs, however, found at Pompeii are evidently the work of inexperienced mechanics ; but even in these a certain grace of workmanship betrays the influence of Greek schools. The same influence is displayed still more distinctly in those fantastic arabesques, which Vitruvius (" Arch.," VII. 3) considers as the excrescences of a degenerated taste. With this censure we are unable to agree fully ; for these compositions, although frequently bizarre, surprise us by the boldness and accuracy of their designs, which, at any rate, betray a thorough artistic training.

Whether the remaining wall-paintings are originals or copies is in most cases impossible to decide : four monochromes at Herculaneum have the name of the artist, Alexandros of Athens, added to them. The fact, however, that amongst the numerous paintings found in two neighbouring towns, and frequently treating the same subjects, not two compositions exactly like each other have been discovered, seems to prove that the copying of pictures, barring a few celebrated masterpieces, was not customary ; single features of compositions are, however, frequently repeated, which, like the uniform treatment of colour and design, and the almost unvaried repetition of certain figures, tends to prove the existence of schools of decorative painters.

All the different classes of wall-paintings specified by Vitruvius—viz. architectural design, landscapes, still lives, scenes from daily life, tragic and satirical representations, and renderings of mythical subjects—are specified by one or more examples amongst the wall-pictures of Pompeii and Herculaneum. Imitations of architectural materials, particularly of marble, occur frequently, as do also fanciful architectural designs, used mostly as frames of large surfaces adorned with pictures (Fig. 465); lofty buildings resting on thin columns, with winding staircases, windows, doors, and roofs of fantastic, almost Chinese, shape, throughout adorned with statuettes, garlands, and small animal pictures, are drawn in white or light yellow contours on a dark background. Small views of the sea, with ships on it, of harbours, temples, villas (see Figs. 375, 394), halls, forests, and rocks, with figures in the foreground, painted generally on friezes and bases of columns, give us an idea of Greek landscape-painting. The painter Tadius, in the reign of Augustus, was, according to Pliny, the inventor of this style of painting. Still life is represented by numerous culinary subjects, such as game, fish and other marine creatures, fruits, and pastry (see Fig. 479). Amongst *genre* pictures we count numerous scenes from daily life, such as interiors of workshops

Fig. 466.

with genii as carpenters and cobblers, a fullonica with (Figs. 472, 473) workmen, vintners carting home their grapes (Fig. 459), symposia, sales of Cupids, &c.; also representations connected with the theatre, both on the stage and behind the scenes, dancing-girls and floating figures, the latter particularly being amongst the highest achievements of antique painting. We, moreover, refer to the above-described charming picture of a young lady with a pencil and writing-tablet in her hands, as also to that of a female painter (Fig. 466). The artist dips her brush into a colour-box standing on a piece of column; in her left she holds her palette; her eye rests on the herme of a bearded Bacchus, which she has been copying; a boy kneeling by the base of the herme holds the canvas, with the picture of the god nearly finished. We mention in connection with this picture the name of Iaia of Kyzikos, who, according to Pliny, lived in Rome when Marcus Varro was a young man: she painted with the brush and also engraved on ivory, chiefly female portraits; in Naples she painted on a large tablet the portrait of an old woman, and also. her own likeness from a looking-glass.

Of mythological subjects we see specimens in all the more important houses at Pompeii, as, for instance, in the Casa delle Pareti Nere, Casa delle Baccanti, Casa degli Scienziati, Casa delle Sonatrici (with life-size figures), Casa di Adone, di Meleagro, del Poeta Tragico: consisting of larger compositions or of single figures, these pictures occupy the centre spaces of the walls, either in square or round frames. Amongst single figures, we frequently meet with those of Jupiter and Ceres. Of subjects we mention the finding of Ariadne by Bacchus, Adonis bleeding himself to death in the arms of Venus, Mars and Venus, Luna and Endymion, not to mention numerous other amorous adventures of the gods, with which the lascivious taste of the time was wont to adorn bedrooms and triclinia. The same preference for erotic and sentimental subjects appears in many pictures representing the mythical adventures of heroes; others are treated in a purely artistic spirit without sensuous admixture. Amongst the latter we refer to the graceful picture of Leda, holding in her hand the nest containing Helen and the Dioscuri; also to the pictures of the sacrifice of Iphigenia, Chiron giving a music-lesson to the youthful Achilles, the discovery of the same hero amongst the daughters of Lykomedes, and the abduction of Briseis from Achilles's tent. The backgrounds of these pictures are black, reddish brown, deep yellow, or dark blue; particularly on black and dark blue backgrounds the figures appear with a distinctness rivalling plastic art. This contrast of colours, no less than the effects of light and shade, and the grace and truth of many of the compositions, more than fully make up for occasional inaccuracies of drawing.

In order to preserve the pictures, the most important ones amongst them have been sawed from out of the walls and removed to the Museum of Naples, where, after many of them have been partly destroyed by unskilful treatment, the remainder are now placed in a favourable position. Many of those not removed have partly or entirely been destroyed by the influences of daylight and weather; only in cases where the pictures had been protected in time by roofs has the process of decay been, at least, retarded. Two Germans, Zahn and Ternite,* deserve our gratitude for having copied and published a number of the chief pictures at a time when they were still in a good state of preservation. The accurate reproduction of designs and colours leaves nothing to be desired, which is more than can be said of the much more numerous copies which have appeared in the " Museo Borbonico." † The latter reproductions are without colours. In judging of the effects of colour in these pictures it ought to be remembered that they were intended to be seen by the subdued light of the atria and peristylia, or of the adjoining chambers, which had no windows of their own.

A few words ought to be added about the mechanical method of painting amongst the ancients. Many authors speak about the gradual development of the art from the first silhouettes (*linearis pictura*) attempted at Korinth and Sikyon, to the painting of the outlines in monochrome. Darker lines were added to express the various parts of the body and drapery; and this led ultimately to a perspective, life-like conception of the human figure, in exactly the same gradual manner which we observed in vase-painting. About the time of Polygnotos the use of four colours, viz. white earth of Melos, red earth of Sinope, yellow-ochre of Attika, and black, began to supersede painting in monochrome. The use of these four colours and their mixtures implied the fundamental notions of light and shade, the first introduction of which has been severally ascribed to Apollodoros of Athens, Zeuxis, and Parrhasios, the founder of the Ionic school. The highest degree of artistic skill was attained by the school of Sikyon, founded by Eupompos, and brought to its climax of perfection by Apelles. Unfortunately no pictures of the great

* W. Zahn, "Die schönsten Ornamente und merkwürdigsten Gemälde aus Pompeji, Herculanum und Stabiae." Series 1—3. Berlin, 1827—1859. Ternite, "Wandgemälde aus Pompeji und Herculanum." 11 parts. Berlin, 1839.

† "Real Museo Borbonico," vols. i.—xvi. Napoli, 1824—1857.

Greek artists have come to us. The canvases of the great Greek
masters were either brought to Rome as spoil or they were
imported by the dealers. Even wall-pictures were sawed from
out of the walls, in order to be framed and taken to Italy by the
conquerors; this was done, for instance, in several buildings of
Sparta. All these paintings have been lost in the course of
centuries. Only the burial-places of Etruria, the houses of
Pompeii and Herculaneum, some parts of the imperial thermæ
in Rome, and a few remnants of wall-paintings found in various
other places, bear witness of the great perfection of Greek
technique preserved in Italy even after the decay of Greek art
itself. It has been proved by careful and still-continued investigations that the substances used for the colour were almost
exclusively minerals: of animal substances we only know the
slimy matter of the purple snail mixed with chalk; the only
vegetable substance used was the black of charcoal. As unmixed
colours were used the white of chalk and the yellow of ochre,
the admixture of chalk and minium to the latter producing light
yellow and orange; for blue, was used oxidised copper; for red,
red chalk or minium; and for brown, burnt ochre. Green was
only produced by mixture. Previously to applying the colour (see
Vitruvius, VII. 3, 8) one layer of plaster was laid on the wall, on
the top of which one or more thin layers of fine mortar were added;
over these several layers of mortar mixed with powdered marble or
chalk were laid, the upper one being added before the lower had
quite dried, by means of which the whole surface received a firmness
and consistency almost equalling marble. The upper layers were
finally beaten down and smoothed by means of a wooden instrument called *baculus* (stick), the impressions of which are, according
to Mazois, still recognisable on several walls at Pompeii. The
painting was done either *al fresco* or *a tempera*. In the former
case the colours, moistened with water, were put on the damp
wall; by means of a chemical amalgamation the picture was thus
indelibly affixed to the hardening surface. In *a tempera* painting
the colours, after having received an admixture of size in order
to make them adhesive, were put on the dry surface. Both
methods have been used at Pompeii (see Overbeck, " Pompeji,"
2nd edition, vol. ii. p. 182 *et seq.*). The backgrounds were
always painted *al fresco*, as were also generally the architectural

ornaments, imitations of coloured stones; and, in a few cases, the subject pictures in the centre. As a rule, the latter, however, were painted *a tempera* on the *al fresco* background or immediately on the wall, a space being in that case left free for them; the latter pictures may be removed from the wall in thin layers, while a removal of the *al fresco* paintings implies the destruction of the surface underneath.

Encaustic colours were never applied in wall-decorations, although frequently in pictures painted on tablets or canvas. Colours prepared with a resinous substance have been found in the shop of a colourman belonging to the Casa del Arciduca, at Pompeii. In order to preserve them from the influence of the open air the pictures were frequently coated over with varnish made of wax or resinous matter.

94. The floors of the rooms consisted originally of clay, stamped or beaten to make it smooth, and mixed with potsherds to add to its firmness (*pavimentum testaceum*). Soon, however, this primitive method was superseded by a pavement consisting of slabs of white or party-coloured marble, placed together in geo-metrical figures of three, four, or six angles (*pavimentum sectile*); sometimes also square tablets were composed into checkered patterns (*pavimentum tessellatum*). The latter kind of pavement was common in Italy even before the Cimbrian war; it was applied, for the first time on a large scale, in the temple of the Capitoline Jupiter, after the beginning of the third Carthaginian war (see Pliny, "Nat. Hist.," XXXVI. 25, 61). From this kind of pavement (which remained in use down to late Roman times) the mosaic proper was developed, the larger tablets being changed for small parti-coloured pieces of marble, valuable stones (such as onyx or agate), and glass, placed together in various patterns. The art of working in mosaic had been practised in the East from a very early period. The method of surrounding the centre pictures with decorative designs was adopted for these pavements from wall-painting. The dark stripes of the geometrical figures thus form, in a manner, the frames of the pictures themselves. Sometimes the whole floor of a room was occupied by one design, at other times by several smaller medallion-like pictures. Work of this kind received the name of mosaic (*pavimentum musivum*). Before the mosaic was placed, the ground underneath was

firmly stamped down, or received a foundation of slabs of stone; to this foundation a layer of plaster, slow in drying and very adhesive, was added, into which the above-mentioned small pieces were inserted after a certain pattern ; the whole formed a compact mass, impenetrable to dust and rain.

The mosaic floors found in almost every Roman house have mostly been well preserved under the rubbish of centuries. In the various Roman temples, baths, and dwelling-houses we see numerous specimens of mosaic, varying from rude attempts to the highest perfection of workmanship. Remains of Greek mosaic preserved in Greece have not as yet been discovered, barring a rather rude composition of coloured stones in the pronaos and peristylos of the temple of Zeus at Olympia.

The compositions of the mosaic pictures are of the most varied kind, not to speak of the numerous decorative patterns of generally black lines on a white ground. Masks and scenic representations (mosaic of Palestrina), races in the circus (mosaic found at Lyons, see § 104), mythological representations (fight of Theseus with Minotauros, found amongst the ruins of Iuvavia, the modern Salzburg), historical battles (battle of Alexander in the Casa del Fauno, at Pompeii), musical instruments (mosaic pavement in the villa at Nennig, Fig. 245),—such are the subjects chosen, and executed with admirable neatness, by antique artists. Amongst the most celebrated mosaics no more in existence we mention the pavement of the dining-hall of the royal palace of Pergamum, executed by Sosus. It imitated a floor with the remains of a dinner lying on it; the name applied to this hall was "the unswept" (οἶκος ἀσάρωτος), afterwards transferred to all mosaic-work of a similar kind (opus asarotum). Pliny also mentions another mosaic in the same palace representing a dove sitting on the rim of a fountain, with the shadow of its head thrown on to the water. Perhaps the two mosaics seen in the villa of Hadrian and at Naples were imitations of those of Pergamum. Amongst mosaics still preserved, we mention particularly the large battle-scene found, in 1831, in the Casa del Fauno, at present to be seen in the Royal Museum, Naples. With regard to both size and beauty of composition it ranks amongst the finest works of antique art. It represents, most likely, the final victory of Alexander over Darius at Issos : both kings appear in the mêlée, the former piercing with his spear a noble Persian, the latter standing on his chariot surrounded by a few faithful followers; a horse is kept ready for his flight. From the left the Greek cavalry are making an irresistible attack on the wavering lines of the Persians. Helen, the daughter of Timon the Egyptian, is said to have painted a picture of this battle, which Vespasian brought to Rome; perhaps our mosaic is a copy of it. The accuracy of the details

Fig. 467.

may be concluded from the fact that each square inch is composed of one hundred and fifty pieces of glass or marble. Fig. 467 represents a mosaic found in the house of the Poeta Tragico at Pompeii.

Before leaving the house, we must cast a passing glance at the *viridarium*. Homer already mentions a large garden belonging to the palace of Alkinoos, king of the Phaiakai. Enclosed by a quadrangular wall, it contained the choicest kinds of pears, figs, pomegranates, olives, apples, and grapes, not to speak of beautiful beds of flowers. The water supply was plentiful. Horticulture, however, limited itself to the indigenous productions of the soil: the importation of tropical plants was unknown both to Greeks and Romans. We quote a letter of the younger Pliny to give some idea of Roman horticultural art; it somewhat reminds us of the style of the time of Louis XIV., as displayed in the gardens of Versailles. " In front of the portico of the house," Pliny says, speaking of his Tuscan villa, " lies a terrace cut into all kinds of shapes, and edged with box; it is adjoined by a sloping lawn, at the side of which the box is cut into the forms of various animals looking at each other. In the plain stands a cluster of delicate acanthus-plants, round which there is a walk, the latter being inclosed by a hedge of evergreen cut into different shapes and always kept under the shears. By the side of it an avenue resembling a race-course winds round clusters of box cut into various shapes, and trees not allowed to grow high. The whole is inclosed by a wall hidden from sight by box planted in a terrace-like manner. Behind the wall follows a meadow, pleasing by its natural beauties no less than the garden by its artificial charms. Fields and many other meadows and groves lie around." After this follows a glowing description of the villa itself, and the summer-house with its beautiful view of garden, fields, and woods. " In front of this building," he continues, " lies a roomy *manége*, open in the centre and surrounded by maple-trees; ivy encircles their stems and branches, winding from one tree to another. Here you see a small meadow, there clusters of box cut into a thousand shapes, sometimes in the form of letters indicating the name of the owner or that of the gardener. You next come to a grove with a bench of white marble, overshadowed by a grape-vine propped by four small columns of Carystian marble. A small waterspout issues from the bench, as if caused by the pressure of those sitting on it; the water falls into a hollowed stone, from whence it flows unnoticeably into another marble basin. In case people want to dine here, the heavy dishes are put on the rim of the basin, while the lighter ones, shaped like birds or fish, are set afloat on the water." Pliny, of course, is describing one of those large gardens belonging to the country-residences of the rich. In large cities, particularly in Rome, where every square foot of ground was of great value, gardens even of very moderate dimensions could be indulged in only at great expense. Such *viridaria*, deprived of the charms of living trees and flowers, but still showing the remains of verandahs, statuettes, and fountains (compare "Pitture antiche d'Ercolano," vol. ii., Tav. 21), ponds, and borders of flower-beds, have been discovered amongst the ruins of Pompeii; for instance, in connection with the houses of Diomedes, of Sallustius (see Fig. 390), of Meleager, of the Small Fountain, and of the Centaur. The existence of glass houses to protect tender plants from the cold of the winter is proved by the verses of Martial (VIII. 14).

95. The art of arranging in a picturesque manner the few pieces of clothing required by the southern climate of Italy, or by their feeling of propriety, the Romans had adopted at an early period from their Greek neighbours, aided in this respect by their own sense of the picturesque. The old republican type of the Roman dress, although to some extent modified with regard to shape and colour by the luxurious habits of later times, still remained essentially unaltered.

The Greek distinction between epiblemata and endymata reappears in the *amictus* and *indutus* of the Romans; the former class being chiefly represented by the *toga*, the latter by the *tunica*.

The toga, the specifically national dress of the Romans, was
originally put on the naked body, fitting much more tightly than
the rich folds of the togas of later times. About the shape of this
toga, which is described as a semicircular cloak (περιβόλαιον
ἡμικύκλιον), many different opinions prevail. Some scholars consider it to have been an oblong piece of woven cloth like the
Greek epiblemata described by us (§ 42) ; others construct it of one
or even two pieces cut into segments of a circle. Here again we
shall adopt in the main the results arrived at through practical
trials by Weiss (" Costümkunde," p. 956 *et seq.*). The Roman toga
therefore was not, like the Greek epiblemata, a quadrangular
oblong, but "had the shape of an oblong edged off into the form of
an oval, the middle length being equal to about three times the
height of a grown-up man (exclusive of the head), and its middle
breadth equal to twice the same length. In putting it on, the toga
was at first folded lengthwise, and the double dress thus originated
was laid in folds on the straight edge and thrown over the left
shoulder in the simple manner of the Greek or Tuscan cloak ; the
toga, however, covered the whole left side and even dragged on
the ground to a considerable extent. The cloak was then pulled
across the back and through the right arm, the ends being again
thrown over the left shoulder backwards. The part of the
drapery covering the back was once more pulled towards the right
shoulder, so as to add to the richness of the folds." Counting the
whole length of the toga at three lengths of a full-grown man,
the first third of the toga would go to the front part of the
drapery up to the height of the left shoulder, the second third
to the part pulled across the back and under the right arm, the
remaining third being occupied by the part pulled across the
chest and again thrown over the left arm. If the toga is folded
so that the two half-ovals are not congruent to each other, and that
therefore the lower edges of the cloak do not fall together, the
result will be that in putting on the toga two layers of clothing
will appear, the longer one reaching down to the calves (*media
crura*), the shorter one only to the knee (see Fig. 468). The
former part of the cloak touches the body, the latter one lying
outside.

The simpler, that is narrower, toga of earlier times naturally
clung more tightly to the body ; a wide bend of the part reaching

from the right arm across the chest to the left shoulder was
therefore impossible. This rich fold in the later toga is compared
by an author to the belt of a sword (*qui sub humero dextro ad
sinistrum oblique ducitur, velut balteus.* Quinctil., XI. 3, 137). The
same author adds, that the old Roman toga had no such fold
(*sinus*), which in the later toga was large enough to hide objects

Fig. 468.

in. The part of the toga
touching the ground was
pulled across the sinus and
arranged in large folds, as
appears, for instance, from
the statue of the emperor
Lucius Severus (Fig. 468).
Whether the part thus ar-
ranged was called *umbo* we
will not venture to decide.
Although the older toga
impeded comparatively
little the motions of the
body, soldiers thought it
necessary to tie the end
thrown over the left shoulder round their waists, so
as to keep their arms free.
This sort of belt (*cinctus
Gabinus*) remained the military costume till the *sagum*
was introduced: even after
that time the belted toga
used to be worn at certain
religious rites, such as the
founding of cities or the
opening of the temple of
Janus; also by the consul when performing certain religious ceremonies previously to setting out on a campaign. The Romans
had undoubtedly adopted this costume from the inhabitants
of the neighbouring Gabii, who on their part received it from
the Etruscans. The later toga, with its rich folds covering the
whole body, prevented each rapid motion which might have

disturbed their careful arrangement. In order to produce, and give a certain consistency to, these folds, they were arranged by slaves on the preceding evening; sometimes small pieces of wood were put between the single folds, so as to form them more distinctly. Pins or clasps to fasten the toga seem not to have been used. Small pieces of lead sewed into the ends, hidden by tassels, served to preserve the drapery : a similar practice we noticed amongst the Greeks.

The toga as the Roman national dress was allowed to be worn by free citizens only. A stranger not in full possession of the rights of a Roman citizen could not venture to appear in it. Even banished Romans were in imperial times precluded from wearing it. The appearance in public in a foreign dress was considered as contempt of the majesty of the Roman people. Even boys appeared in the toga, called, owing to the purple edge attached to it (a custom adopted from the Etruscans), *toga prætexta.* On completing his sixteenth, afterwards his fifteenth, year (*tirocinium fori*) the boy exchanged the toga prætexta for the *toga virilis, pura,* or *libera*—a white cloak without the purple edge. Roman ladies (for these also wore the toga) abandoned the purple edge on being married. The toga prætexta was the official dress of all magistrates who had a right to the curulean chair and the fasces; the censors, although not entitled to the latter, also wore the toga prætexta. Amongst priests, the Flamen Dialis, the pontifices, augures, septemviri, quindecimviri, and arvales wore the prætexta, while acting in their official capacity; tribunes and ædiles of the people, quæstors and other lower magistrates were prohibited from wearing it. The *toga picta* and the *toga palmata* (the latter called so from the palm branches embroidered on it) were worn by victorious commanders at their triumphs; also (in imperial times) by consuls on entering on their office, by the prætors at the *pompa circensis,* and by tribunes of the people at the Augustalia. Being originally the festal dress of the Capitoline Jupiter, this toga was also called *Capitolina;* it was presented by the senate to foreign potentates. Masinissa, for instance, received a golden crown, the *sella curulis,* an ivory sceptre, the *toga picta,* and the *tunica palmata.*

Besides the somewhat unwieldly toga, there were other kinds of cloaks both warmer and more comfortable. In imperial times the toga was indispensable only in the law courts, the theatre, the circus, and at court ; under the Republic it was considered improper to appear in public without it. Amongst other coverings we mention the *pænula*, a cloak reaching down to the knees, adopted most likely from the Celts. It was without sleeves and fastened together at the back (*vestimentum clausum*), a round opening being left to put the head through. It was open at both sides, and had a seam in front at least two-thirds of its length from the neck downwards. It consisted of thick wool or leather, and was worn by both men and women, over the toga or tunica, during journeys or in bad weather. At first it used to be made of a sort of foreign linen (*gausapa*), the outer side being rough, the inner smooth; the woollen cloak (*pænula gausapina*) was an introduction of later date. The pænula was, most likely, worn by soldiers sent to a rough climate. Another kind of cloak, also worn over the toga or tunica, was the *lacerna*. Its cut resembles that of the Greek chlamys, being an oblong open piece of cloth, fastened on the shoulder by means of a fibula. Although introduced much later than the pænula, it had become the common costume of imperial times, in which Romans appeared even on festive occasions. Being made of thinner material than the pænula, the lacerna gave more opportunity for the artistic arrangment of the folds. Large sums were spent on well-made and particularly well-dyed lacernæ. As a further protection from wind and weather a hood (*cucullus*) was affixed to both pænula and lacerna; to this we shall have to return.

Similar in cut to the lacerna was the warrior's cloak, called originally *trabea*, later *paludamentum* and *sagum ;* it is essentially identical with the Greek chlamys. The *paludamentum*, always red in colour, was in republican times the exclusive privilege of the general-in-chief, who, on leaving for the war, was invested with it in the Capitol, and on his return changed it for the toga (*togam paludamento mutare*). In imperial times, when the military commandership was concentrated in the person of the emperor, the paludamentum became the sign of imperial dignity. It was laid round the body in rich, picturesque folds. The *sagum* or *sagulum* was a shorter military cloak, also fastened across the shoulder like a chlamys; it was worn by both officers and private soldiers in time of war. The sagum of imperial times was longer

than that of the Republic. In the representations of "Allocu-
tions," frequently occurring on monuments (for instance, on the
arch of Septimius Severus and the Columna Antoniniana, Fig. 530),
both officers and privates appear in richly draped saga, reaching
down to the knees. The name sagulum most likely applies to
the short mantle reaching hardly lower than the hips which
is worn by the barbarian soldiers in the bas-relief of the arch of
Severus.

About the form of an article of dress called by the Greek
name of *synthesis* we are entirely uncertain; we do not even
know whether to class it as *amictus* or *indumentum*. Out of doors
it was only worn by the highest classes of society at the Saturnalia; indoors it was usually worn at dinner (*vestes cenatoriæ*).
Nevertheless the synthesis never appears in the numerous representations of festive meals. An epigram of Martial, in which
Zoïlus is made fun of for changing his synthesis eleven times,
owing to its being saturated with perspiration, seems to indicate
that it must have been a close-fitting dress like the tunica.

The *tunica* was put on in the same way as the Greek chiton.
Its cut was the same for men and women, and its simple original
type was never essentially modified by the additions of later
fashion. It was light and comfortable, and was worn especially at
home; out of doors the toga was arranged over it. Like the
chiton, it could be worn with or without sleeves, and reached down
to the calves; underneath the chest it was fastened round the body
with a girdle (*cinctura*), across which it was pulled and arranged
in folds in the Greek fashion. The persons carrying the temple-
treasure of Jerusalem on the arch of Titus (see Figs. 536
and 537) wear the simple tunica arranged in this manner. In
statues clad with the toga, the dress covering the upper part of the
body to the neck must be designated as tunica (Fig. 468, compare
the statues of Julius Cæsar, Augustus, Tiberius, and Claudius in
Clarac, "Musée de Sculpture," Nos. 916, 924, 912 *A*, 936 *B*).
The soldiers on the monuments of imperial times wear the tunica
underneath their armour or sagum. About the time of Commodus
sleeves were added to both male and female tunics (*tunica
manicata*), covering the arm almost to the wrist; in a late Roman
bas-relief we even see a prolongation of the sleeve resembling
a cuff; this kind of tunica is also called *dalmatica*. At a later

date two or three tunics were put on in cold weather: Augustus
is said to have worn four in the winter. The tunic nearest to the
body was called *subucula;* the one over this, *intusium* or *supparus.*
A tunic with a purple edge was the privilege of senators and
knights, the sign of the *ordo senatorius* being one broad stripe,
that of the *ordo equester* two narrower ones; the former ornament
was called *clavus latus,* the latter *clavus angustus,* whence the
distinction between *tunica laticlavia* and *tunica angusticlavia.*

Fig. 469.

Women also used to wear a double tunica, the one nearest to
the body (*tunica interior*) being a close-fitting sleeveless chemise
reaching down over the knee. No girdle was required for it;
a thin band (*mammillare, strophium*) served to support the bosom.
Above the lower tunica the long *stola* fell in many folds: as to its
cut and the way of putting it on we refer the reader to our
remarks about the simple Doric chiton of Greek women. Like

this, the stola was an oblong chemise, cut open on the two upper
sides, the open ends being fastened on both shoulders by means of
clasps (compare the statue of Livia in "Mus. Borbon.," vol. iii.
Tav. 37). Underneath the bosom the stola was fastened to the
body by means of a girdle, through which it was pulled, so that
its lower edge just touched the ground.
In case the tunica had sleeves, the stola
worn over it had none, and *vice versâ*.
The sleeves of the tunica or stola were
cut open, and the ends fastened together
by means of buttons or clasps, in the
same manner as described by us in
speaking of Greek dress (see the celebrated marble statue of the younger
Faustina, Fig. 469; also Fig. 471). An
essential part of the stola is the furbelow
(*instita*) or ornamental border attached to
the bottom of the dress (see Fig. 471).

Out of doors women wore a cloak
(*palla*), appearing frequently on statues.
Its cut resembled either that of the toga
or that of the Greek *himation*, arranged
in graceful folds according to the taste
of the wearer, unrestricted by the laws
of fashion, which exactly prescribed the
folds of the male toga. A third kind of
palla seems to have consisted of two
pieces of cloth fastened over the shoulders
with fibulæ, and either falling down in
loose folds or fastened round the body
by means of a girdle. These three
kinds of the palla occur on monuments,
the first-mentioned being seen most frequently on the statues of matrons of the

Fig. 470.

imperial family, or other portrait-statues of imperial times. Sometimes the back part of the palla is drawn over the back of the head
in the manner of a veil (see the statue of the younger Agrippina,
Fig. 470). Other graceful arrangements of the palla appear in Fig.
469, and on a seated statue of Agrippina, the wife of Germanicus,

in the museum of Florence. Before the introduction of the palla
Roman ladies used to wear a shorter and tighter square cloak,
called *ricinium*, which afterwards seems to have been worn only
at certain religious ceremonies. Similar articles of dress were
the *rica* and *suffibulum*, the former worn by the Flaminica, the latter
by the Vestals in the manner of a veil. Fig. 471 reproduces a

Fig. 471.

graceful picture found in a room at Herculaneum (1761), with
several others, leaning against the wall. It is generally
designated as the "Toilette of the Bride." On a throne is
seated the still youthful mother of the bride, dressed in the stola,
tied round the body with the strophium. The lower part of the
body is covered by the folds of the palla; down her back floats a

long veil fastened to the back of her head. Her right arm tenderly embraces the neck of her daughter; both are gazing at the bride standing in the middle of the room. The stola of this, her second, daughter shows the broad instita already mentioned; its open sleeves, or those of the tunica underneath, are fastened to the upper arm by means of buttons. She wears a palla of the toga kind over her other garments. A maid-servant, standing behind her, is clad in a stola (with sleeves reaching down to the wrists) and a palla.

Up to the end of the Republic the only materials used for these dresses were wool (*lanea*) and linen (*lintea*). The togæ were made of various kinds of wool, those of Apulia and Tarentum being considered the best amongst Italian, and those of Attica, Laconica, Miletus, Laodicea, and Bætica, the finest of foreign materials. Women's underclothing was made of linen, the materials of Spain, Syria, and Egypt being preferred to those of Italian origin. Both materials were worked into lighter dresses for the summer, and warmer ones for the winter. Silk dresses (*holoserica*) and half-silk dresses (*subserica*) began to be worn by ladies about the end of the Republic; under the Empire they were even adopted by men, notwithstanding the prohibitory law of Titus. About the importation of raw silk from Asia into Greece, and thence into Italy, we have spoken before. We only add that the transparent sea-green veils, made principally in the isle of Kos, occur repeatedly in wall-pictures (see " Mus. Borbon.," vol. viii., Tav. 5, III. 36, VII. 20). Goat's-hair was used only for coarse cloaks, blankets, and shoes.

The usual colour of the dress was originally white (for the toga this was prescribed by law): only poor people, slaves, and freedmen wore dresses of the natural brown or black colour of the wool, most likely for economical reasons. Only the mourning dresses of the upper classes showed dark colours (*toga pulla, sordida*). In imperial times, however, even men adopted dresses of scarlet, violet, or purple, colours formerly worn only by women. Fig. 471 may serve to illustrate the different colours of the dresses. The veil of the mother is blue, her stola of a transparent white, through which one sees the flesh-colour of the bosom; her palla is reddish white, with a bluish-white border. The stola of the daughter nearest the mother is also reddish white, her palla being yellow, with a bluish-white border. Yellow was, according to Pliny, a favourite colour with women, particularly for brides' veils. The bride wears a reddish-violet stola, adorned with an embroidered *instita* of darker hue ; her palla is light blue. The servant wears a blue upper dress with white underclothing. Frequently the inside of dresses appears in the pictures of another colour than the outside. In a picture, for instance, representing Perseus and Andromeda (Zahn, " Die schön. Orn.," Series 3, Taf. 24), the outside of Perseus's dress is reddish brown, the inside white; while Andromeda's dress is yellow outside and blue inside. Perhaps these dresses were lined with material of a different colour.

Particularly interesting are the purple-coloured silk or woollen dresses of the Romans ; the raw materials were subjected to the dyeing process. Two kinds of snails, the trumpet-snail (*buccinum, murex*) and the purple snail proper (*purpura, pelagia*), yielded the colour; the exudations of the latter were, in reality, of a yellowish-white colour, but by the combined influence of the sun and of dampness they turned into a rich violet colour. The scarlet juice of the buccinum was generally mixed with purple colour in order to prevent its fading. The purple colour proper had two shades, a black and a red one ; it was applied either pure or mixed with other substances. By means of these mixtures, and by dipping the cloth into the colour more than once, the ancients contrived to produce no less than thirteen different shades and *nuances* of colour. By mixing blackish purple with the buccinum juice the favourite amethyst-violet and hyacinth-purple colours were produced (*ianthinum, violaceum*). In order to gain brightness and intensity of colour the dress was dyed twice (*bis tinctus*, δίβαφος), being dipped first into the purple juice and afterwards into that of the buccinum. Looked at straight, the blood-red dress thus prepared had a blackish tint, looked at from underneath it showed a bright red colour. The double-dyed purple dresses, particularly those of Tyrian and Laconic origin, fetched the highest prices, a pound of double-dyed Tyrian wool being sold at 1,000 denarii (about £43), while a pound of the above-mentioned violet-amethyst-purple wool cost only £15.

At first only the broad or narrow hems of togas and tunicas (worn by senators, magistrates, and knights) were coloured with genuine purple (*blatta*); those of private persons being dyed with an imitation purple. The white toga, with a hem of genuine purple, remained the official dress of certain magistrates; but as early as the last years of the Republic it became the fashion amongst men to wear entire purple togas. The first to wear one of these as the sign of highest dignity was Julius Cæsar, who, like several successive emperors, tried to stem the luxurious habit by restrictive laws; which, however, became soon disregarded. The wearing of genuine purple, however, remained the exclusive privilege of the emperors. Even women were punished for infringing this law, as were also merchants for trafficking in the genuine article.

After being woven the materials of the dresses were further prepared with needle and scissors, as is sufficiently proved by the cut of most of the underdresses, particularly of the pænula and tunica. Most of the Greek dresses were worn unsewed. In Rome each wealthy household counted amongst its slaves several tailors (*vestiarii, pænularii*). The existence of guilds of professional tailors is established beyond doubt. The guilds of fullers and dyers carried on two important trades connected with clothing. The old Greek custom for kings' daughters to superintend personally the cleaning of clothes was, if ever imitated by the Roman ladies of noble families, soon abandoned by them. The cleaning, moreover, of the white woollen materials chiefly worn amongst the Romans required artificial means. For this purpose the guild of the fullers (*fullones*) was established at an early period; like that of the cloth-weavers (*collegium textorum panni*), it did a large and profitable business. The shop and the work of a fuller are illustrated by the remains of a fullery (*fullonica*) found at Pompeii, and also by several paintings on its walls

Fig. 472.

(see Figs. 472 and 473). Near the back wall are four large tanks consisting of masonry, and connected with each other, but on a different level, in order to let the water run from the highest to the lowest. A raised platform runs along these tanks, which one ascends on several steps. To the right of it lie six small compartments destined, most likely, to receive the washing-tubs. To the right of the peristylium there is, moreover, a vaulted chamber containing a large tub and a stone table to beat the clothes on. Large quantities of soap have been found in this apartment, which was the washing-room proper. On one of the corner pillars of the peristylium four wall-paintings have been discovered illustrative of the work of a fuller. In the first (Fig. 472) we see, standing in niches, several tubs filled with water, in the centre one of which a fuller is treading on the clothes, for the purpose of cleaning them; in the tubs on both sides (we only reproduce part of the picture) two other men are occupied in pulling the clothes out of the water, and in rubbing off such stains as may remain on them. After this the clothes were once more rinsed with pure water, to remove the nitre or urine frequently used in fulling. The other picture (Fig. 473) introduces us to a different part of the fullery. In the background a workman is brushing a white dress with a purple hem which hangs over a pole; on the right another workman approaches with a frame resembling a hen-coop, across which the clothes were drawn for the purpose of sulphuration; the vessel carried by the man most likely contains the necessary sulphur. On the top of the frame the bird of Athene Ergane, the goddess of industry, has appropriately been placed. In the foreground is the seated figure of a richly dressed woman, who seems to examine a piece of cloth given to her by a young work-girl. The third picture, not here reproduced, shows the drying-chamber, with pieces of cloth hung on poles for drying. A fourth picture shows a press with two screws, for the final preparation of the cloth.

Fig. 473.

96. With regard to Roman head-coverings of men we have

little to add to our remarks about Greek hats (see § 43, Fig. 222). Most of the forms there shown also occur amongst the Romans. The Roman, like the Greek, generally wore his head uncovered, the toga pulled over the back part of the head being sufficient shelter in case of need. The pileus and petasus, however, were worn by the poorer working-classes continually exposed to the weather, and by rich people on journeys or at public games as a protection from the sun. The pileus was occasionally replaced by the hood (*cucullus, cucullio*), introduced into Rome from northern countries, most likely from Gaul, North Italy, and Dalmatia. The cucullus was either fastened to the pænula or lacerna like the cowl of a monk, or it was worn as a separate article of dress. A cucullus of the latter kind, covering head and body down to the knees, is worn in a bas-relief by a traveller who is just settling his bill with the hostess of his inn ("Bullet. Napoletano," VI. 1) ; the smaller cucullus is worn in a wall-painting by several persons at a rural feast (Fig. 474).

Fig. 474.

The custom of leaving the head uncovered naturally led to a careful treatment of the hair. According to Varro, Romans used to wear long hair and long floating beards covering chin and cheeks till the year 454 of the city. At that time the first barbers (*tonsores*) came to Rome from Sicily ; Scipio Africanus is said to have been the first Roman who had himself shaved (*radere*) with a razor (*novacula*) every day. The fashion of wearing the hair cropped short seems to have made slow progress, and only amongst the higher classes. The hair was either worn in wavy locks, or it was arranged in short curls (*cincinni*) by means of a curling-iron resembling a reed, and for that reason called *calamistrum ;* the slaves charged with this manipulation were called *ciniflones.* The different ways of wearing the hair become apparent from a comparison of the numerous male portrait-heads occurring on coins and statues. "Swells" of the period of moral decline managed to twist their hair into all kinds of unnatural shapes. A common fashion was, for example, to wear curls arranged in several steps (*coma in gradus formata*), such as found on the head of M. Antonius at Venice. Of the Emperor

Gallienus it is told that he had his hair powdered with gold-dust.
About the beginning of the Empire it was a common custom,
both amongst men and women, to wear false hair (*capillamentum*),
either to hide bald places or to give a fuller appearance to the
natural hair. Sometimes also hair was painted on the bald head,
so as to produce the semblance of short hair, at least at a distance
(compare Martial's Epigram, VI. 57). The close-cropped hair
seems to have been the fashion from the time of the Emperor
Macrinus to that of Constantine.

Full beards became again the fashion about the time of
Hadrian. Up to the time of Constantine an uninterrupted series
of portrait-heads of emperors on coins yields excellent information
with regard to these matters ; afterwards the type of the coins
degenerates. Between the reigns of the two above-mentioned
emperors the heads appear with full beards, with only a few
exceptions, as, for instance, the heads of Elagabalus, Balbinus,
Philippus the younger, and Hostilianus, which are always
represented with smooth chins. Barber-shops (*tonstrina*) were
naturally of frequent occurrence amongst the Romans. They
were the gathering-places of all idlers and the centres of town-
gossip in Italy, as well as in Greece. They were well furnished
with razors (*novacula*), tongs (*volsella*) to pull out the hairs of the
beard, scissors (*axisia*), several pomatums to destroy the hair in
certain places, combs (*pecten*), curling-irons (*calamistrum*), mirrors
(*speculum*), towels, &c. The small so-called barber's shop in the
street of Mercury at Pompeii, next to the fullonica, can, it is
true, not have accommodated many persons at a time; but, most
likely, the establishments in the capital were on a larger and
more splendid scale.

Women do not seem to have worn hats; they generally pulled
their palla over the back of their heads (see Fig. 470). Still
more picturesque was the veil fastened to the top of the head
(Fig. 471), and dropping over neck and back in graceful folds.
The *mitra* was a cloth wound round the head in the manner of a
cap ; it resembled the Greek sakkos, and served to keep the hair
in its position (see the servant, Fig. 471; and Fig. 232, where
the woman sacrificing in front of the bridal chamber wears the
sakkos). This cap frequently consisted of the bladder of an
animal; it never reached higher than the top of the head;

the front hair was always arranged in graceful wavy lines. A more handsome head-covering was the net made of gold thread (*reticulum*), also worn by Greek and indeed by our modern ladies (see Fig. 473, where the seated female wears it).

More variegated were the ways of dressing the hair as illustrated by the numerous female statues of imperial times. Ovid remarks "that the different ways of dressing the hair in Rome were equal in number to the acorns of a many-branched oak, to the bees of the Hybla, to the game on the Alps, every new day adding to the number." Compared with this variety even the numerous hair-dresses appearing on coins, representing empresses, ladies of the imperial court, or private persons, seem few in number. At the same time they are representative of the leading fashions. In the first centuries of the Republic the hair was arranged in a simple graceful manner, in accordance with the general character of the dress. The long hair, either parted or unparted, was combed back in wavy lines, and plaited or tied in a knot (*crines in nodum vincti, crines ligati*), sometimes arranged round the top of the head like a crown, at others fastened low down the neck by means of ribbons or clasps (see the daughter standing by the mother's side, Fig. 471). Another fashion was to arrange the hair round the head in long curls, or to arrange the front hair in thick plaits, connecting it with the back hair, &c. The form of the face and the taste of the lady naturally were decisive in this matter (compare Ovid, "Ars Amat.," III. 137 *et seq.*). Married ladies were, at least in earlier times, excluded from this licence; they always used to arrange their hair in a high *toupé*, called *tutulus*, fastened on the top of the head by means of ribbons. This, at least, seems to us the right explanation of the description of the tutulus by Varro (VII. 44) : " *Tutulus appellatur ab eo quod matres familias crines convolutos ad verticem capitis quos habent vitta velatos, dicebantur tutuli, sive ab eo quod id tuendi causa capilli fiebat, sive ab eo quod altissimum in urbe quod est, arx, tutissimum vocatur.*" Perhaps the arrangement of the mother's hair in Fig. 471 ought to be described as a tutulus fastened with gold rings instead of ribbons. The original simple and beautiful arrangement of the hair was soon superseded by fantastic structures of natural and artificial hair, justly described by Juvenal (VI. 502) as "towers of many stories." Hairdressing became a science, and occupied a considerable part of a fashionable lady's time. Special maid-servants were employed for the purpose, whose naked arms frequently had to suffer the pricks of the needle of the fastidious beauty, who perhaps all the while seemed to listen to the speeches of philosophers and rhetoricians. Amongst the numerous heads illustrating the hair-fashions of imperial times we have chosen the portraits of three empresses (Fig. 475), viz., those of Sabina, wife of Hadrian (*a*), of Annia Galeria Faustina, wife of Antoninus Pius (*b*), and of

a   *b*   *c*

Fig. 475.

Julia Domna, wife of Septimius Severus (*c*). The natural hair was frequently insufficient for the tower-like *coiffures*, and the want had to be supplied either by false plaits or by complete wigs. Even plastic art imitated this custom by adding to the head a removable marble hair-dress, which could be replaced by a new one according to fashion. In the Royal Collection of Antiques, Berlin, there is a bust with movable hair, ascribed to Lucilla. The custom of dyeing their hair became common amongst Roman ladies at an early period. As early as Cato's time the Greek custom of dyeing the hair a reddish-yellow colour had been introduced in Rome; caustic soap (*spuma caustica*, also called *spuma Batava*), made of tallow and ashes, was imported from Gaul for the purpose. The long wars of the Romans with the Germans engendered amongst Roman ladies a predilection for the blond hair of German women (*flavæ comæ*); this hair became, in consequence, a valuable merchandise: Roman ladies used to hide their own hair under fair wigs of German growth.

We have already mentioned the numerous pomatums and balsams used for dressing and scenting the hair, by both men and women. Cicero speaks of the demoralised companions of Catilina as shining with ointments. Kriton, the body-physician of the Empress Plotina, gives in his work on "Cosmetics" the receipts of twenty-five different pomatums and scents.

Ribbons and pins served at once to fasten and adorn the hair. These ribbons (worn, for instance, by the daughter standing by the mother's side, Fig. 471) were adorned with pearls and jewels; frequently they were replaced by a ring of thin gold or gold thread (see the hair of the mother and the bride, Fig. 471). Strings of pearls also were tied up with the hair (see the hair-dress of the Empress Sabina, Fig. 475, *a*), with the addition of a stephane studded with jewels (Fig. 475, *a*, *b*). Not the least graceful adornment of the hair were the wreaths, consisting either of leaves of flowers joined together (*coronæ sutiles*) or of branches with leaves and blossoms (*coronæ plexiles*). In a wall-painting of Pompeii ("Mus. Borb.," vol. iv., Tav. 47) we see four Cupids sitting round a table, occupied in arranging wreaths and garlands.

Hair-pins, made of metal or ivory, have been found in great numbers and varieties. We reproduce (Fig. 476, *a*, *b*, *c*, *h*, *i*, *k*) some of the more grace-ful ones worked in ivory, one of which (*c*) shows Venus rising from the sea and strok-ing back her wet hair, a common subject of antique sculpture. Fig. 476, *e*, shows a poma-tum-box with a reclin-ing Cupid in bas-relief

Fig. 476.

represented on it; *f*, a bronze comb (*pecten*), which was used (as by the Greeks) only to comb, never to fasten, the hair. A very elegant bronze comb adorned with coloured stones was found some time ago near Aigle, and is at present in the museum of Lausanne. Combs made of box or ivory are preserved in many of our museums.

We have given (§ 46) a comprehensive account of the sandals, the boots, and the shoes used amongst the Greeks. The same remarks apply essentially also to Roman foot-coverings; little remains to be added. The equivalent of the Greek sandal is the Roman *solea* (worn by the mother, Fig. 471). They were worn by men and women at home, and on all occasions where the official toga did not require a corresponding foot-dress. At table the soles were taken off, for which reason the two expressions, *demere soleas* and *poscere soleas*, are synonymous with lying down to, and getting up from, table. It is, however, unlikely that even in older times the Romans ever appeared in public with naked feet, as is told of the Greeks. The solea, like the tunica and lacernæ, belonged to private life; the official toga required the corresponding *calceus*, a closed high shoe resembling our ladies' boots. Calcei are frequently worn by male and female statues. Official distinctions were, however, made. The calceus fastened to the ankle and calf with four strings (*corrigiæ*), and, moreover, adorned with a crescent-shaped piece of ivory (*lunula*) on the top of the foot, was most likely worn by senators, being, in that case, identical with the black *calceus senatorius*, as distinguished from the *calceus patricius* or *mulleus*. The mulleus, made of red leather, and with a high sole like a cothurnus, was originally worn by the kings of Alba, but afterwards adopted by the patricians: it reached up to the calf; little hooks (*malleoli*) were attached to its back leather for the purpose of fastening the laces. The calceus was cleaned with a sponge, as is proved by the bronze statuette (in the late Hertz collection) of an Ethiopian slave occupied in that manner.*

Besides the calceus, we find on statues numerous varieties of the sandal, and also a sort of stocking tied with laces from the instep to the calf; the name of the latter is entirely unknown to us; it appears frequently on the warlike statues of emperors, the upper borders, made of cloth or leather, being adorned with the heads of lions and other animals, worked most likely in metal (see, for instance, the statues of Cæsar, Tiberius, Caligula, Vitellius, Hadrian, and others, in Clarac, "Musée," pl. 891 *et seq.*). The just-mentioned combination of toga and calceus has, however, not always been preserved by the artists: the statues, for instance, of Cicero in the museum of Venice, of Sulla at Florence, and of M. Claudius Marcellus in the Museo Chiaramonti, wear sandals; while, on the other hand, the statue of Balbus in the Museo Borbonico, and many other portrait-statues, correctly wear calcei with the toga.

The *caliga* was a sort of military boot of imperial times.

---

* "Catalogue of the Collection of Assyrian, &c., Antiquities formed by Hertz." Revised by W. Koner. London, 1851. Tab. III.

Caius Cæsar received his nickname Caligula from this boot. The caliga was most likely a boot with a short top, turned over at the upper edge, resembling the Spanish boots of the middle ages (compare Fig. 523).

Sandals and shoes were fastened to the foot by means of straps tied round the foot and the leg, from the ankle upwards. These straps mostly covered about half of the calf (*fasciæ crurales, tibiales*), extending, however, sometimes up to the thigh (*fasciæ feminales*) ; the latter mode of wearing them was considered to be effeminate. On historic monuments of imperial times we see Roman legionaries clad in socks reaching up to the middle of the calf, and fastened with straps covering the heel, foot (with the exception of the toes), and the leg, up to some inches above the ankle ; they were, most likely, part of the military dress, and very convenient for marching.

Breeches (*braccæ*) were originally worn by barbarous nations, but adopted by Roman soldiers exposed to northern climes. The trumpeters opening the procession, and the soldiers carrying Victories (Figs. 532, 533), are clad in trunk-hose, similar to those worn by the barbarians following the triumphal chariot (Fig. 538, compare Fig. 526). The Persian warriors in the Pompeian mosaic of the "Battle of Alexander" wear close-fitting breeches similar to the tights in which Amazons are generally depicted (see Fig. 272).

97. We add a few remarks with regard to the numerous ornaments made of precious metals, ivory, jewels, and pearls, some of them of artistic value, which have been found at Pompeii and other places, particularly in graves. Hair-pins, earrings, necklaces, bracelets, girdles, and agraffes compose what was collectively called *ornamenta muliebria.** Most of these objects have already been mentioned as worn by Greek ladies (compare § 47, Figs. 225 and 226) ; the specimens found in Italy distinctly betray Greek workmanship.

---

* A complete set of a lady's ornaments, consisting of bracelets, necklaces, rings, earrings, brooches, and pins, has been found near Lyons in 1841 (see Comarmond, "Description de l'Ecrin d'une dame Romaine trouvé à Lyon en 1841," Paris et Lyon, 1844). Of particular value are the seven necklaces, consisting of emeralds, garnets, sapphires, amethysts, and corals. Pliny, "N. H.," ix. 117, relates that Lollia Paulina, the wife of Caligula, used on ordinary occasions to wear ornaments to the value of 40 millions sestertii (about £450,000).

About hair-pins (*crinales*) we have spoken above (see Fig. 476). Simpler specimens, about seven-eighths of an inch long, with round or angular heads, or with eyes for the fastening of the strings of pearls, are found in most collections. The bride (Fig. 471) has her hair fastened with elastic gold *bandeaux*, open in front.

The neck and bosom were adorned with necklaces (*monilia*) or chains (*catellæ*, see mother and daughter, Fig. 471) of gold, studded with jewels and pearls. A necklace of beautiful workmanship, consisting of elastic gold threads twisted together, has been found at Pompeii ("Mus. Borbon.," vol. ii. Tav. 14); attached to it is a lock adorned with frogs. A gold chain for the neck, 5 feet 6 inches in length, and equal in weight to

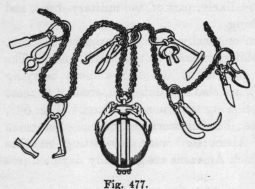

203 ducats, has been found near the Magura mountain in Siebenbürgen (Austria), and is at present in the Münz- und Antiken - Cabinet, Vienna: fifty different instruments, *en miniature*, such as scissors, keys, anchors, saws, tongs, hammers, &c., are attached to it by means of

Fig. 477.

thirty rings (Fig. 477; compare the description of the necklace found at Lyons in Marquardt, "Römische Privatalterthümer," 2nd Series, 1867, p. 294). Other chains, wound several times round the neck, and falling down to the bosom, had frequently a little case (*bulla*) attached to them. It contained a charm against sickness and the evil eye, and was worn by boys of noble families, afterwards also by the legitimate sons of freedmen, up to the time of their relinquishing the toga prætexta. The custom was of Etruscan origin. At a later period grown-up persons, particularly victorious generals at triumphs, used to wear a protective bulla (*inclusis intra eam remediis, quæ crederent adversus invidiam valentissima*). It appears on several statues of Roman youths, as also on the statue of a young man clad with the toga in the Dresden gallery (Clarac, "Musée," pl. 906). A bulla fastened to an elastic gold thread, found at Pompeii, was evidently meant to be worn by a woman (compare the bulla, Fig. 477).

Bracelets (*armillæ, bracchialia*) in the form of snakes (compare the Greek ὄφεις) or simple ribbons, also of rings or plaited gold thread, adorned the lower and upper parts of women's arms. Bracelets frequently appear on statues ; others, made of bronze or precious metals, have been found in Roman graves. They were used as male ornaments by the Etruscan and other Italian nations, as is proved by the story of Tarpeia's treason, as also by the male figures on Etruscan cinerary boxes. In imperial times massive arm-rings were given to Roman men as the reward of prowess (see the centurion, Fig. 531).

Pendants (*inaures, pendentes*) were worn by Roman as well as by Greek ladies, as is proved by several specimens found at Pompeii ; the form of the segment of a globe was, in the first century of the Empire, used frequently for them. We also hear of pearls and jewels fastened to the ear by means of hooks of gold thread (see Fig. 471). "Two pearls beside each other," Seneca complains, "with a third on the top, now go to a single pendant. The extravagant fools probably think their husbands are not sufficiently plagued without their having two or three heritages hanging down from their ears." Another fashion was to wear a single large pearl (*unio*) as a pendant. White pearls, resembling the colour of alum, fetched the highest prices, their value being proportionate to their size, smoothness, and roundness. Cæsar presented to the mother of Marcus Brutus a pearl which had cost him six million sestertii ; the pearl which Cleopatra drank dissolved in vinegar was worth ten million sestertii.

Enormous sums also were spent on rings adorned with jewels and cameos. According to the simpler custom of old times, adopted from the Etruscans, an iron signet-ring was worn on the right hand : even after the introduction of gold rings old families continued wearing the primitive iron signet-ring. Originally only ambassadors sent to foreign nations were allowed to wear gold rings, and were supplied with such at the public expense as a sign of their dignity ; later, senators and other magistrates of equal rank, and soon afterwards knights, received the *jus annuli aurei*. After the civil war, when many *equites* had to drop their knighthood owing to the loss of the census, the privilege was frequently encroached upon. The first emperors tried to re-enforce the old law, but as many of their freedmen had become entitled to wear gold rings the distinction lost its value. After Hadrian the gold ring ceased to be the sign of rank; Justinian granted it to all citizens, free-born or liberated. This *annulus aureus* most likely was a plain and heavy ring, like our wedding-rings. To distinguish it from other rings adorned with stones, &c., the wearing of which was free to men or women of all classes, the gold ring retained its original shape unimpaired by fashion. The passion for rings adorned with jewels and cameos (compare our remarks about Greek rings, p. 182) seems to have been common to all classes. Almost every excavation adds new specimens to our collections of cameos, the number and variety of which enable us to follow the history of the art of engraving from its rise in the time of Alexander the Great to its deepest decline. It is true, however, that a strictly historic basis cannot be established, seeing that the names of artists occasionally found on their works can be fixed historically only in the fewest cases; while, on the other hand, the portrait-heads occurring on cameos give but an approximate indication of the time of their origin. Moreover, the work of incompetent beginners occurs but too frequently contemporaneously with the highest achievements of the art, the general passion for cameos making cheapness appear an almost more important consideration than perfection of workmanship. In this art, also, the Romans were seldom creative, as appears from the Greek names of most of the artists found in the inscriptions, or mentioned by ancient authors. Roman men and women used to cover their fingers with rings of this kind, used partly for sealing, partly as ornaments; small boxes of a peculiar kind (*dactyliothecæ*) served to keep the rings. "At first," Pliny says, "it was the custom to wear rings on the fourth finger only; later, the little and second fingers also were covered with them, the middle finger only remaining free. Some people put all the rings on their smallest finger; others put on it only one ring, to distinguish that which they use for sealing." Rich people had several sets of rings; lighter ones for the summer, heavier ones for the winter. Large public and private dactyliothecæ existed in Rome, where the cameos brought home from foreign wars were exhibited. The well-known Scaurus, for instance, owned a collection of cameos amongst his Greek art-treasures ; Pompey placed a rich collection of cameos, taken from Mithridates, in the Capitol as a votive offering; Cæsar gave six collections of the same kind to the temple of Venus Genetrix.

To conclude, we mention the buckles and brooches (*fibulæ*) destined to fasten the palla of women, and the ends of the toga and paludamentum of men, on the right shoulder; they stood the ancients in the stead of our buttons, hooks, and pins, and are frequently found on the sites of habitations or on battle-fields. At first they consisted of bronze, afterwards of silver and gold, frequently studded with jewels and cameos, *fibulæ gemmatæ.* Aurelian permitted the wearing of gold instead of silver buckles, even to common soldiers. The most common forms of the buckle are shown, Fig. 478.

Fig. 478.

Mirrors of glass were unknown to the Romans : their mirrors were made of polished metal, either square or round in form. The handle attached to it served to hold the mirror in the hand, or to suspend it by, if not used (Fig. 476, *g*, compare Fig. 228). Mirrors hanging on the wall appear in numerous vase-paintings; valuable specimens were kept in cases. Other mirrors could be placed upright (Fig. 476, *d*). The handle and the back and border of the mirror afforded opportunities for engraved or bas-relief ornamentation. At first mirrors were made of a composition of tin and copper; Pasiteles, a contemporary of Pompey, is said to have introduced silver mirrors. In Pliny's time the back of the mirror used to be gilt, which was thought to add to the power of the reflecting surface. Seneca (" Quæst. Nat.," I. 17) complains that for one of the large upright gold or silver mirrors, equal in size to a grown-up person (*specula totis corporibus paria*), larger sums were expended than were given by the State as dowry to the daughters of poor generals. The poorer classes had to be satisfied with a composition of copper and lead, imitating, or plated with, silver. Numerous specimens of a peculiar kind of mirror have been found amongst the ruins of the old Præneste,

and in several burial-places of Etruria. Their form and ornamentation distinguishes them from other mirrors. They are
known by the name of Etruscan metal mirrors, and have been
described by Gerhard in his work, " Die etruskischen Spiegel"
(4 vols., Berlin, 1838—1869). They are either perfectly round or
have the shape of a pear ; their backs show engravings of mythological or realistic scenes, for the greater part slovenly imitations
of Greek originals ; the treatment of the figures is repulsively soft
and sensuous ; only few of them have artistic value. Many of
these mirrors, particularly those found at Præneste, have been
discovered together with other toilette articles in cylindrical boxes
with curved lids, made of wood covered with leather and studded
with metal, or consisting entirely of metal. These boxes, owing
to their resemblance to the holy snake-baskets, frequently occurring on monuments, have been called mystic boxes (*cista mystica*).
Owing to the engravings on the back of the mirrors (resembling
those on the *cista*), and to the slightly bent borders of the
reflecting surface, these mirrors have been for a long time
mistaken for pateræ, which they somewhat resemble in form.
Gerhard's opinion, however, of their being nothing but mirrors
of early Etruscan make has, at present, been generally adopted.

About the mysteries of the toilette of Roman ladies, merci-
lessly laid bare by the authors of imperial times, we shall say
little. Great care was particularly bestowed on the complexion,
and on the artificial reproduction of other charms, lost too soon in
the exciting atmosphere of imperial court-life. During the night
a mask (*tectorium*) of dough and ass's milk was laid on the face,
to preserve the complexion ; this mask was an invention of
Poppæa, the wife of Nero, hence its name *Poppæana*. Another
mask, composed of rice and bean-flour, served to remove the
wrinkles from the face. It was washed off in the morning with
tepid ass's milk (Juvenal, VI. 467), and the face afterwards
bathed in fresh ass's milk several times in the course of the day.
Poppæa was, for the purpose, always accompanied in her travels
by herds of she-asses (Pliny, " Nat. Hist.," XXVIII. 12). The
two chief paints used for the face were a white (*creta, cerussa*) and
a red substance (*fucus minium, purpurissum*), moistened with
spittle. Brows and eyelashes were dyed black, or painted over ;
even the veins on the temples were marked with lines of a tender

blue colour. Many different pastes and powders were used to preserve and clean the teeth. Artificial teeth made of ivory and fastened with gold thread were known to the Romans at the time when the laws of the twelve tablets were made, one of which laws prohibits the deposition of gold in the graves of the dead, excepting the material required for the fastening of false teeth.

98. In order somewhat to illustrate our remarks on the Roman *cuisine*, we reproduce (Fig. 479) one of the numerous wall-paintings at Pompeii and Herculaneum, illustrative of the various dainties of the table, such as grapes, apples, pears, quinces, figs, mushrooms, sometimes kept in transparent glass vessels; also game, fish, and shell-fish; the composition of these groups

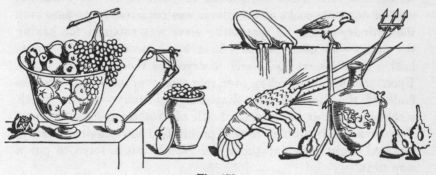

Fig. 479.

reminds us somewhat of the still-lives of the older Dutch school.*

The breakfast (*ientaculum, iantaculum*) of the Romans, taken earlier or later according to the hour of rising, consisted of bread, dipped in wine or flavoured with salt, grapes, olives, cheese, milk, and eggs. Luncheon (*prandium*), consisting of more solid dishes, both hot and cold, was taken about the middle of the day, or at the sixth hour, according to Roman nomenclature. The chief meal, or dinner (*cena*), was taken about the ninth hour, between noon and sunset. The poorer classes at all periods chiefly fed on porridge (*puls*) made of a farinaceous substance (*far, ador*), which served them as bread, besides vegetables, such as cabbage

* Compare "Mus. Borb.," VIII., Tavs. 20, 57. "Pitture antiche d'Ercolano," vol. ii. Tavs. 56 *et seq.*; iii. Tav. 55.

(*brassica*), turnips and radishes (*napus*, *beta*, *pastinaca*), leak (*porrum*), garlic (*allium*), onions (*cepa*), pulse (*legumina*), cucumber (*cucumis*), pumpkins (*cucurbita*), melons (*melo*), &c. Meat was eaten only on festive occasions. In early times the arrangements of the kitchen were in harmony with the simplicity of the dishes prepared there; slaves and masters partook, according to Pliny, of the same fare. On particular occasions professional cooks were hired, who offered their services in the *macellum* or market. After the Roman conquests in Greece and Asia the diet of the richer classes, with regard to both the number and quality of the dishes, became essentially altered. Simple vegetables sufficed no longer; various kinds of meat and fish, delicately flavoured, salads, and rare fruits were found in their stead. A numerous staff of domestic cooks and scullions was required to prepare even the ordinary meals. A particular slave was retained for baking the pastry—an office formerly held by the women of the household. Experienced cooks and pastrycooks received high wages. Upon the whole, however, over-refinement of taste was less the fault of the Romans than disgusting gluttony—a vice which reached its climax between the battle of Actium and the reign of Vespasian, during which period prohibitive laws against luxury, repeated eight different times, were vainly put in force to put a stop to it.

The smaller kind of fish, such as *lacertus*, *mæna*, and *mullus* (mullet), were eaten chiefly by the poorer and middle classes; the larger mullus, on the contrary, was one of the most expensive dainties. Its price increased with its size, one of 4 lbs. being paid with 1,000 sestertii, one of 6 lbs. with 6,000 sestertii, and so forth in increasing proportion. Other fish much appreciated were the *muræna* (a sort of salt-water eel, caught particularly in the Straits of Sicily and Tartessus), the *rhombus* (flounder, generally imported from Ravenna), the *aurata*, the *lupus* (pike, kept in ponds), also the various kinds of salt and preserved fish (collectively called τάριχος), which were imported from the Pontine, Sardinian, and Spanish coasts. Various sauces (*garum*, *muria alec*) served to flavour the fish. Amongst shell-fish or mussels we mention the eatable purple snail (*murex*), the *echinus*, different slugs (*cochlea*), and, most important of all, the oyster (*ostrea*), called by Pliny (" Nat. Hist.," XXXII. 6, 21) *palma*

mensarum divitum. In order to have the fish always ready at
hand the Romans constructed fish-ponds (Lucinius Muræna is
said to have set the example), filled with salt or fresh water
(*dulces* or *salsæ*), according to the nature of the fish kept in them.
These *piscinæ*, or *vivaria piscium*, were connected with canals, to
renew the water, the openings of which were closed with iron
grates. Lucullus had a canal dug through a ridge of mountains
by the sea in order to supply his piscinæ with salt water. Other
celebrated piscinæ were those of the orator Hortensius at Bauli,
near Baiæ; according to Pliny (IX., 55, 81), he shed tears at the
death of one of his muræna. Antonina, the wife of Drusus, is
said to have adorned a favourite fish of the same kind with earrings. The breeding and taming of fish was a favourite occupation with fashionable idlers. The invention of oyster-banks
(*vivaria ostrearum*) is ascribed to the gourmand, Sergius Orata (his
second name was given him from his preference for the fish
called *orata*). Snail-preserves were first kept by Fulvius Lupinus,
in the neighbourhood of Tarquinii. The different kinds of snails
(Illyrian, African, &c.) were carefully kept apart, and fed on
flour mixed with thickened must. The Romans also had preserves
of birds (*vivaria avium*, or *aviaria*), as, for instance, of ordinary
poultry, fig-thrushes, guinea-fowls, pheasants, peacocks, and of
the favourite fieldfare. As the inventor of the aviaries M.
Lænius Strato, of Brundusium, is mentioned. Hortensius was the
first to treat his guests to roast peacock, having imported the bird
from Samos. Peacocks, like pheasants (introduced from Asia)
and fieldfare, were kept in great numbers in the aviaries; the two
latter birds, and the eggs of the former, being considered great
delicacies. For many of the wealthy Romans their ponds and
aviaries were, moreover, a considerable source of income, derived
from the sale of fish and birds.

Hares and rabbits were favourite dainties, the former being
kept in so-called *leporaria*. In the Balearic Islands the rabbits
repeatedly destroyed the harvest, and the inhabitants had to
apply to Augustus for military assistance, in order to diminish
their number. We also mention kids (of which the finest were
imported from Ambracia), pigs, and boars. Pliny ("Nat. Hist.,"
VIII. 51, 77) remarks that, while other animals are only partly
eatable, the pig furnishes no less than fifty different dainties.

The parts eaten in preference were the udder (*sumen*), the womb (*vulva*), and the liver, the latter being artificially enlarged by a diet invented by the *chef* Marcus Apicius. Pork ham (*perna*) and sausages (*botulus, tomaculum*) also were much liked, the latter being carried about the streets in portable ovens, and cried out by the sausage-vendors (*botularii*).

Amongst plants used for the excellent salads of the Romans we mention rue (*ruta*), lettuce (*lactuca*), cress (*lepidium*), mallows, (*malva*), and sorrel (*lapathum*). To these indigenous plants others, brought from the kitchen-gardens of the provinces, were added.

Italy was particularly rich in fruit-trees, both indigenous and acclimatised. Varro calls the Peninsula one large orchard. Apples, particularly honey-apples (*melimela*), pears, plums, cherries, quinces, peaches, pomegranates, figs, nuts, chestnuts, grapes, olives, &c., were found on all good tables. Other fruits and cereals, however, now commonly found in Italy and most parts of Southern Europe, were unknown to the Romans. Melons, oranges, lemons, citrons, and bitter oranges (*Pomeranzen*) were not grown in Italy in Pliny's time. Melons and citrons began to be cultivated in the first century after Christ. Lemons and bitter oranges came to Europe in the time of the Crusades; while the orange was imported from China by the Portuguese as late as the sixteenth century. Of corn the Romans only knew wheat and barley; oats, rye, maize, and rice were unknown to them.

Of particular importance from a culinary point of view was naturally the *cena*. In older times it consisted of two—later of three—courses, the entrées (*gustus, gustatio*) being composed of such dishes as were supposed to excite the appetite, for instance, mussels, light kinds of fish, soft eggs, salad, cabbage, &c. With these was drunk a mixture of honey and wine or must (the proportions being four-fifths wine to one-fifth honey, or ten-eleventh must to one-eleventh honey), so as to prepare the stomach for the richer wines. This mixture was called *mulsum*, whence this part of the meal also received the name *promulsis*. After these entrées the cena proper was put on the table. It consisted of three courses (*ferculum*), called respectively *prima*, *altera*, and *tertia cena*. The dishes of each of these courses were brought in simultaneously on a tray (*repositorium*). The dessert (*mensæ*

secundæ) consisted of confectionery, preserves, and dried and fresh
fruits. We subjoin the *menu* of a *cena pontificalis* given by
Lentulus about the middle of the last century of the Republic,
in celebration of his entering on his priestly office. We give the
original words of Macrobius, leaving it to the reader to find
or imagine approximate modern equivalents for the dainties specified : " *Cœna*," Macrobius says ("Saturn.," III. 13), " *hæc fuit :*
Ante cœnam *echinos, ostreas crudas, quantum vellent, peloridas,
sphondylos, turdum asparagos subtus, gallinam altilem, patinam
ostrearum peloridum, balanos nigros, balanos albos : iterum sphondylos,
glycomaridas urticas ficedulas, lumbos capraginos, aprugnos, altilia,
ex farina involuta, ficedulas murices et purpuras.* In cœna *sumina,
sinciput aprugnum, patinam piscium, patinam suminis, anates,
querquedulas elixas, lepores, altilia assa, amulum, panes Picentes.*"
We also refer the reader to the amusing description of Trimalchio's
feast in Petronius.

Of drinks we have already mentioned the *mulsum* and the
various kinds of wine. Like the Greeks, the Romans used to
mix the wine with water ; as to the strength of the mixture
we are not informed accurately. To drink unmixed wine (*merum
bibere*) was considered a sign of intemperance ; even the adding
of but little water (*meracius bibere*) did not escape reproof ; a
rather weak mixture was considered proper for a sober man
(*homo frugi*). The strength of the mixture, however, was left
to the decision of every individual ; youthful slaves (*pueri ad
cyathos, ministri vini, pocillatores*) prepared the mixture, adding
either hot water or snow, according to taste and season. The
hot beverage was called *calda*, and we still possess a beautiful
chiselled bronze vessel destined for its preparation. It has two
handles, and rests on three lions' claws ; the cover, fastened to it
with a hinge, is of conical shape (see the picture of the vessel in
Overbeck's " Pompeii," p. 312). In the middle of the vessel
is a cylindrical case for the hot coal, with a receptacle for the
ashes at the bottom. A separate cover closes the space round this
cylinder, containing the calda. A tap, about the middle of the
vessel, served to emit the fluid, which was poured in by means of
a pipe let into the upper rim on the opposite side. During the
cena the drinking was moderate ; but after, it not seldom followed
a drinking-bout (*comissatio*), at which the customs and jokes of

the Greek symposion were frequently imitated (*Græco more bibere*).
With their heads and lower limbs crowned with flowers, the
topers reclined round the table after the dishes had been removed.
A master or king of the feast (*magister*, or *rex convivii, arbiter bibendi*)
was chosen by a cast of the dice, the cast of Venus being decisive,
as in the case of the βασιλεύς. The healths were drunk of
present persons (who had then to drain the goblet), with the
words, *bene tibi, vivas*, or of absent friends; in later times,
particularly of the emperor and the army. In case a lady was
the object of the toast, the number of cyathi (wine-glasses of
moderate size) to be drained consecutively was equal in number
to the letters of her name (*nomen bibere;* compare Martial, I. 72).
Cicero compares the end of a convivium given by Verres
(Verr., V. 11) to the end of the battle of Cannæ, where some
were carried away disabled, while others remained in an uncon-
scious state on the field of battle.

Besides witty conversation, many games of hazard and bets
tended to enliven and excite the guests. Particularly games of
dice (*alea*), although prohibited by the law, were often secretly
indulged in (compare our description of this game, p. 270).
Prohibitive laws, and the legal determination that complaints
of cheating or misconduct at gambling-places were not admissible
in courts of justice, were unable to check the passion for
gambling, which was carried on on an enormous scale in private
houses and *popinæ*. Games at dice were permitted only when no
money was staked, as were also the various more intellectual games
played on a board, such as the *ludus latrunculorum*, resembling
our chess, played on a *tabula latrunculoria* divided in squares;
the purpose was, by means of clever drawing (*ciere*), to take away
or block up (*ligare, alligare, obligare*) the men of the adversary,
so as to checkmate him (*ad incitas redigitur*). The men (*latrones*)
consisted of pieces (*calculi*) of glass, ivory, or metal, coloured in
different ways, and used in a different manner; the *mandræ*, for
instance, were a particular kind of men in one game. Another
game of this class was the *ludus duodecim scriptorum*, played on a
board divided into twenty-four parts by means of twelve parallel
lines and one transverse line. Each move (*dare calculum*) of
the fifteen men, black and white in colour, was determined by a
previous cast of the dice. Augustus diverted his guests by a

lottery with valuable prizes, such as pictures of Greek masters, turned with their backs to those partaking in the game. Cultivated people used to amuse their guests with reading or vocal and instrumental music, to which, however, objection was occasionally taken (compare Martial, IX. 77). Less innocent were the dances and scenic representations performed at these feasts by actors and dancers of both sexes since the time of Sulla; even fights of gladiators are said to have taken place at meals on a few occasions.

99. Public bathing-establishments have already been mentioned (§ 80). Originally bathing was with the Roman a matter of health and cleanliness only, in consequence of which the older bathing-establishments were undoubtedly of a very simple kind. Of these older buildings no traces remain; all the splendid buildings described by us (compare Figs. 419—423) belong to a later and more refined period. The chief additions made to the simple cold and tepid baths of older times were the sudatory bath, and the numerous accommodations for walks, conversation, and gymnastic exercises found in all later establishments.

The usual time of taking a bath was the eighth or ninth hour, or indeed any time shortly before the hour of the cena, which greatly varied according to the occupation or convenience of individuals. For that reason the public baths were open during the greater part of the day till sunset. In imperial times they continued open during part of the night, as is proved by numerous lamps found in thermæ, and by the marks of lamp-soot on the walls of the baths of Pompeii. The opening and closing of the establishment was announced by the sound of a bell. Each visitor had first to pay an entrance-fee, which differed according to the accommodation offered, but amounted on the average to a *quadrans* for men. The janitor threw the money into a box (as has been concluded from a box of this kind found in the portico of the thermæ of Pompeii), and returned to the bather a ticket to be delivered to the bathing-master. Sometimes this entrance-fee was remitted to the people by the ædiles desirous to gain popularity. The ædile Agrippa, while in office, built one hundred and seventy bathing-chambers, to which everybody was admitted gratis for the space of one year; on his death, he left his magnificent private thermæ to the people. In the

apodyteria of the Pompeian thermæ we still see the holes in the
walls into which the pegs for suspending the clothes were
inserted. The bather next entered the tepidarium (sudatory
bath), where the dry rubbing (*destringere*) also took place, whence
he proceeded to the *caldarium* to take a hot bath originally in a
tub (*alveus*), in later times in a large reservoir; in a niche of this
room stood the flat *labrum* with cold water. A cold plunge in the
cisterna or *piscina* of the *frigidarium* terminated the bath proper.
Afterwards the bather went into the *unctorium* to be rubbed, or
rub himself, with oil; sometimes this took place in the tepidarium. Even before, and in the intervals of, the bath the
bather was frequently anointed, a slave carrying the oil-bottles
(*ampulla olearia*), the scraper (*strigilis*), to remove oil and perspi-

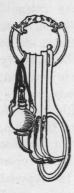

ration from the skin, and the linen towels (*lintea*)
after his master to the bath (compare the bathing-
apparatus Fig. 480). Soap became known only in
imperial times; in its stead were previously used
by the poorer classes a sort of paste made of the
fruit of the lupine (*lomentum*), by wealthy people
different ointments. After the bath the hair and
skin were again rubbed with odoriferous ointment;
even the clothes were scented. For these scented
ointments were used native flowers, and shrubs like
the rose, crocus, myrtle, cypress, or Oriental ingredients, which, if genuine, were bought at enormous
prices. Amongst the most valuable of these Oriental

Fig. 480.

ointments was the *nardium oleum*, made of Indian or Arabian nard.
It was kept in bottles of precious metals or stone, such as the
alabastron mentioned by us on a former occasion. Scented
powders (*diapasmata*) were strewn over the body; the water was
mixed with saffron and other scents, in addition to which the limbs
after the bath were stretched, and the whole body rubbed with
swan's-down or purple sponges. The laconicum above described
was the place for sudatory cures frequently repaired to by the
gourmands of imperial times.

The increasing luxury of Roman manners became particularly
visible in the interior arrangements of the baths. Seneca speaks
of the decorations of private bath-chambers with the most
valuable kinds of marble or with glass; even the taps of the

water-pipes had to be made of silver. The elder Pliny says, that many Roman ladies would not think of entering a bath without silver fittings. This luxury of private baths was far surpassed by the enormous public thermæ of imperial times, where fashionable Romans passed a great part of their day in luxurious idleness or animating conversation. The large thermæ of Agrippa, in the Campus Martius, have already been mentioned; near them lay (between the modern Piazza Navona and the Pantheon) the thermæ Neronianæ, called, after their enlargement by Alexander Severus, thermæ Alexandrinæ. After these follow in chronological order the thermæ of Titus, Trajan, Commodus, the thermæ Antoninianæ built by Caracalla, the thermæ of Decius, Diocletian, and of Constantine. The ruins of other thermæ, although smaller in size than those of the metropolis, are found in provincial towns, almost every year adding a new discovery of substructures, which, by their hypocausta, can be recognised as Roman baths. Besides these common baths, the Romans knew and used the medicinal powers of mineral springs. From the waters of the Rhenish country, such as the *aquæ Mattiacæ* (Wiesbaden) or *aquæ Aureliæ* (Baden-Baden), to the numerous springs on the slope of the Atlas, the *aquæ Tibilitanæ*, and other *aquæ calidæ*—from the "Baths of Hercules," near Mehadia, in Siebenbürgen, to the waters of Bagnères in the Pyrenees—few medicinal wells had escaped the notice of the Romans; many votive inscriptions tell of successful cures in these places, which frequently also show the remains of old bathing-houses. The watering-places of the Romans, like those of modern times, were frequented by both sick and healthy; some, indeed, Baiæ foremost amongst them, became centres of fashionable life and amusement. The beautiful air and scenery, and the vicinity of Naples, Puteoli, Cumæ, and Misenum, the chief station of the navy, not to speak of the hot sulphur wells, the steam of which led by means of pipes into the sudatoria was considered a remedy of various illnesses,—all this tended to make Baiæ a fashionable watering-place. The dance, the chase, gambling and other vices, were the order of the day, and indulged in with even greater freedom than in Rome. Seneca calls Baiæ the seat of vice ("diversorium vitiorum"), a term which, in a modified sense, may have applied to many of the smaller watering-places.

Of the accommodations for games, walks, and conversation connected with the thermæ we have spoken before. *H* in the plan of the Pompeian thermæ (Fig. 420) signifies a court surrounded on two sides by colonnades, while a third is occupied by a vaulted hall receiving its light through large windows. This court was the *ambulatio* (walk), the hall (Fig. 420, *I*) being destined for conversation. For gymnastic exercise previous to the bath no separate space is assigned; in the thermæ of Caracalla (Fig. 422) we find, on the contrary, ephebea, conisteria, and places for the spectators at wrestling competitions. Together with the youths, men of riper years took part in these exercises, the abstaining from which was a matter of reproof except in cases where bodily infirmities or a learned occupation (as in Cicero's case) were considered as sufficient excuse. These gymnastic exercises, however, never attained amongst the Romans the high development of Greek agonistic games. In Rome these exercises were chiefly considered as a preparatory school for actual warfare : the principal ones amongst them were the throwing of the disc, the use of dumb-bells, fencing with a wooden sword against a pole (*palus, stipes*, frequently practised by grown-up people before their bath), wrestling, and running. Although the Greek scheme was thus essentially adopted by the Romans, their public games took an entirely different character from those of the Greeks : instead of the καλοκαγαθία, the chief aim of the Romans was enjoyment. They merely assembled to witness the agonistic prowess and skill of professional athletes, notwithstanding the attempts made in imperial times at introducing the Greek agones in their full significance. The same was the case in the thermæ : members of the guilds of professional wrestlers showed their skill, the wealthy Roman looking on and preferring for himself some easier means of exercise. For this purpose a sphæristerium was added to most larger private houses, consisting, like those of the thermæ, of open or covered halls, in which young and old previously to taking a bath practised some easy kind of gymnastic exercise, as, particularly, the game at ball.

We have described at some length (p. 228) this game as played by the Greeks : we therefore add only a few remarks with regard to Roman peculiarities. Three kinds of balls were

used, viz. the *follis* (a large ball filled with air), *pila*, and *paganica*.
The ball was thrown up, and caught, and thrown back again
by the different players—a game described in the words *datatim
ludere*. Another kind of game at ball is described by the words
expulsim ludere : as to its nature we know nothing; it is, perhaps,
identical with an exciting game played by modern Italians, in
which the ball before touching the ground has to be caught, and
thrown back with a wooden ring round the under part of the
right arm. The *paganica* was a ball stuffed with feathers, as to
the use of which we have no means of information. The game at
ball could be played by two or more persons; the name *trigon* or
pila trigonalis indicates three players, who, if skilful, threw and
caught the ball with the left hand. The *harpastum*, according to
Athenæus originally called φαινίνδα, admitted of any number of
players; it was a rough exciting game: one or more balls were
thrown up into the air by one person, whereat the players standing next tried to catch them. The interior of a sphæristerium or
tennis-court is shown in Fig. 260, taken from a wall-painting in
the thermæ of Titus. Boys, however, used to improvise sphæri-
steria in the streets and squares of Rome, particularly in front of
the butchers' booths in the Forum Romanum.

100. Trades and handicrafts were, according to the aristo-
cratic notions of the Romans, somewhat beneath the dignity of a
free citizen; even commerce, particularly retail traffic, was little
esteemed. Landed property on a large scale was the only source
of income not unworthy of a free Roman of good position in
society. Cicero in his " De Officiis " expounds this view at some
length; he, however, makes a distinction between the trades
according to their usefulness and to the intellectual faculties
required by them. Commerce, if carried on honestly and on a
large scale, is to some extent approved of, particularly if its
proceeds are invested in landed property, the only source of
income quite worthy of the Roman gentleman.

Slaves and freedmen were the chief tradesmen and mechanics,
the former supplying the various requirements of the household,
the latter working for payment and selling their wares in shops.
The list of slaves attached to a wealthy Roman household
comprises handicraftsmen of almost every kind. For the present
we omit the slaves employed in agriculture and horticulture : we

mention a complete staff of architects, &c. (*architecti, fabri, tectores, pictores*), tailors and hairdressers (*vestiarii, pænularii, cosmetæ, tonsores*), cooks, pastrycooks, &c. (*pistores, coqui, dulciarii, fartores, placentarii*), together with slaves employed in the triclinium (*triclinarii,* with the triclinarchus at their head, *structores, scissores*) ; also musicians and troops of mimics and jugglers. Physicians and surgeons were mostly slaves or freedmen; the important post of private secretary of the master of the house also was occupied by a slave.

The numerous class of the slaves was recruited by the children of slaves, captives taken on the field of battle or in conquered cities, and sold at once by the quæstor accompanying the army,* and by slaves continually imported from other slave-holding countries.   Slave-traders (*mangones, venalicii*) always followed the armies, or bought their human wares in the chief markets of Rome and Delos, &c.   Ordinary slaves were exhibited on a scaffolding (*catasta*) erected for the purpose : a tablet (*titulus*) fastened to the neck of the captive indicated his country, age, corporal and intellectual achievements or debilities, as also his guiltlessness of crime.   Accomplished slaves, particularly of Greek origin, were kept in separate rooms of taverns, and shown only to wealthy customers.   To distinguish them from free-born captives, the children of slave parents or of a slave mother were called *vernæ* or home-slaves, in reference to the masters to whom they belonged by birth.

All the slaves belonging to a master were collectively called *familia*.   In older times their number was small, the work of the simple town household or of the farm (the latter, for the greater part, performed by the owner himself) not requiring many hands. As town and country houses grew larger and more splendid, the number of slaves had to be increased accordingly.   For almost every one of the many services required by the luxurious owner and his family a separate slave was kept, this perfect division of labour being considered characteristic of a grand house.   The slaves employed in the town house were called *familia urbana,* those attached to the villa *familia rustica,* a distinction which, however, was not always strictly kept, the same slaves often serving both

---

* Such captives where crowned with a wreath to show their being for sale whence the expression—*sub corona venire.*

purposes, at least amongst the less wealthy classes. Some of the slaves even of rich people occasionally followed their master from the *villa urbana* to the *villa rustica*.

The *latifundia* taking the place of the old farms naturally required a much larger staff of labourers. Besides the agricultural slaves proper, employed in ploughing, sowing, reaping, or attending to olive-trees and vines, gardeners for orchard, kitchen, and flower gardens were required ; not to speak of those who had to take care of the poultry-yard, the fish-pond, the beehive, and the game cover. Sometimes several thousands of slaves were required for these various purposes.

Another class of slaves were those employed in the household, or waiting upon the master and his family. Amongst the lower domestic slaves (*vulgares*) we mention first the *ostiarius* or *janitor*, who, from his box (*ostiaria*), had to watch the entrance of the house, and the *cubicularii*, who had to keep bedrooms and sitting-rooms in order, and also to announce visitors. In the houses of rich people a particular *nomenclator* was appointed for the latter purpose, whose office it was to call out the names of clients who came to say their matutinal *Ave* (*salutatio*) to their *patronus*, and of numerous other visitors thronging the vestibule in the early hours of the day. The same nomenclator had often to accompany his master in his walks, to recall to his memory the names and circumstances of persons met in the street whose vote or assistance were required for a particular purpose.

The wealthy Roman was always accompanied by one or more slaves (*pedisequus*), who had to carry any object that might be required at the bath or a party, and also to act as torch-bearers on returning at night. Another class of slaves were the *lectiarii*, or carriers of sedan-chairs, which, about the end of the Republic, had become the usual means of conveyance in travelling. In town only senators and ladies were allowed to be carried in them, a law which, most likely, was often infringed. We have to distinguish the litter (*lectica*), a frame with straps to support a mattrass and pillow, and the sedan-chair (*lectica operta*) with a canopy (*arcus*), and curtains (*vela*, *plagœ*, *plagulœ*) that could be pulled up or down. The latter means of conveyance was always used by modest women ; it resembled the modern Oriental palankeen, and is said to have been introduced from the East, together with numerous other Oriental customs, after the defeat of Antiochus by the Romans. Strong slaves, in rich red liveries, carried the litter on their shoulders by means of poles (*asseres*) passed under its bottom.* Syrians, Germans, Celts, Liburnians, and Mœsians, in later times particularly Cappadocians, were employed as carriers, their number varying with the size of the litter. A portable chair (*sella gestatoria* or *portatoria*) was introduced by Claudius, and used chiefly by emperors and consulares; it was covered at the top, and could be closed with curtains. One or several litters, with slaves to carry them, were found in every good Roman household; there were, however, in Rome litters on hire, the stand (*castra lecticariorum*) of which was in the "XIV. regio trans Tiberim."

Besides litters, carriages were employed on travels; their use in Rome, and most likely also in the colonies and municipia, was restricted by law. Under the Republic respectable women were allowed to drive in town, a privilege taken away from them in imperial times. Vestals, Flamines, and the Rex sacrorum in certain sacred processions, as also the triumphing general, and the magistrates in the procession preceding the festive *ludi circenses*, were allowed to drive in carriages. Even carts with merchandise, &c., were forbidden to appear in the streets of Rome during the ten hours from sunrise to sunset (by the *lex Julia*, passed 45 B.C.), with the exception of those destined to transport the materials of the large buildings. With the beginning of the third century carriages became more frequent in the cities, although their use remained the privilege of the highest imperial officials. We possess many representations of carts and carriages, the classification of which according to the expressions found in the authors is not always possible. The body of the carriage is generally clumsy, while the wheels, with spokes (*rota radiata*), are almost always of a graceful shape. On the monument of Igel (Fig. 414) we see a small open carriage on two wheels drawn by mules, in which two persons are seated; perhaps we may recognise in it a *cisium* or *essedum*. Another richly decorated carriage (*carpentum*), also on two wheels, but with an awning to it, appears on the coins of Julia, daughter of Titus, and on those of Agrippina,

---

* A small terra-cotta, not yet reproduced, in the Museo Borbonico at Naples shows two men carrying a litter in the manner described.

daughter of Germanicus. Fig. 481 shows a two-wheeled travelling carriage (*covinus?*) with an awning. *Reda* and *curruca*, mentioned by the authors as large travelling-carriages for several persons, do not appear on the monuments; where, on the other hand, we frequently meet with carts and waggons loaded with rural produce, merchandise, armour, &c.; the generic term for these is *plaustrum*, the expressions *sarracum*, *carrus*, and *arcera* marking subdivisions no longer definable by us. Fig. 450 shows a four-wheeled market-cart with a wineskin on it; Fig. 482 (from a mosaic found at Orbe, in Switzerland), a cart, drawn by two oxen, the load of which is secured

Fig. 481.

against rain by a blanket; even the step to mount the cart has not been omitted. On the arch of Severus (compare Fig. 535) and the column of Antoninus we see a number of baggage-carts, some of them on two wheels with spokes, others on massive round discs of wood (*tympanum*), all laden with pieces of armour and provisions in sacks and barrels. Bronze rings attached to the collars of horses, bits, and other parts of the harness, as well as the ends of poles shaped like animals' heads, exist in numerous specimens.*

Numerous slaves followed the travelling-carriage or litter of the wealthy Roman, the scnty accommodation of the inns making a complete travelling apparatus a matter of necessity. The members of the imperial family and other wealthy Romans took a pride in their travelling equipment, and the precious plate and carpets carried after them by a numerous train of pack-horses. Numidian horsemen, forerunners, negroes, &c., saddle-

Fig. 482.

* See Lindenschmit, "Die Alterthümer unserer heidnischen Vorzeit," vol. i. Part II. 5, and vol. ii. Part X. 3, 5.

horses, grooms, domestic and body slaves, preceded the caravan
or brought up the rear.

Amongst the slaves (*vulgares*) we further mention the tailors of
the master and his family, also valets and chambermaids, besides
which lower slaves the Romans used to keep a number of other
menials to amuse them and their guests, particularly at table, such
as bands of musicians (*pueri symphoniaci*), mimics, dancers of both
sexes, gladiators (who frequently accompanied the master in his
walks), jugglers, and rope-dancers (compare our description of the

Fig. 483.

Greek symposion, p. 269, Figs. 305—
307). About the arts of these acrobats
and rope-dancers (*funambuli, schœnobatæ*)
we hear astonishing accounts from the
ancient authors. Even elephants were
trained to mount the rope (Pliny, VIII.
2, 3). Fig. 483 shows the reverse of a
coin of Cyzicus (a city celebrated for its
acrobatic feats) illustrating the mounting
of a rope. We also hear of *petauristæ*
amongst the domestic slaves, *i.e.* flying

men, who rose into the air by means of the *petauron* or flying-
machine, the construction of which, in the absence of monumental
evidence, cannot be sufficiently understood from the meagre
accounts of the authors.

Amongst domestic slaves we also mention the unfortunate
beings whose bodily or intellectual frailties were the laughing-stock
of their master (*moriones, fatui*, and *fatuæ*). Dwarfs of both sexes
(*nani, nanæ*), who were taught to fight and dance, were particular
favourites with ladies. A pet dwarf of Julia, the granddaughter
of Augustus, was only two feet one palm high; his name was
Canopas. Two bronze statuettes found at Pompeii represent two
crippled, misshapen forms with large heads, one of them dancing
and beating the castanets, the other clad in a toga, with a
bulla fastened to a chain round his neck, and holding a writing-
tablet in his hand (compare also "Pitture d'Ercol.," vol. ii.,
Tavs. 91, 92).

Several overseers were employed in keeping the numerous
slaves in order; the higher officials of this kind had also to
superintend the management of the house, the stores, &c. The

procurator, the first person amongst the *familia* of slaves, managed the income and domestic expense of his master. The agent of the landed property was called *actor*, to whom, in case he had no agricultural knowledge, a practical farmer (*vilicus*) was given as assistant. At the villa urbana the *atriensis*, or steward, kept the accounts, at least in older times; afterwards this became the business of a separate official, *dispensator*, the atriensis being limited to the superintendence of domestic arrangements. The *cellarius* or *promus* had the keys to store-room and wine-cellar. The higher slaves of the last-mentioned kind were collectively called *ordinarii*.

An important position was held by the *lectores* or *anagnostæ*, slaves who had to read out to their master while at table or in the bath, and to write from dictation, copy documents, or take care of the library.

We finally mention the physicians and surgeons, who, at least in republican times, belonged for the greater part to the classes of slaves and freedmen.

The position of the slave amongst the Romans was widely different from that of his fellow-sufferer in Greece. In the latter country the mutual positions of master and slave were legally defined, the right of punishing or even killing a slave being considerably limited by the law. Different in Rome: here the slave was the absolute property of the master, unprotected by the law against his cruelty. The harshness of this relation was, of course, in individual cases, modified by the humanity of the master or the usefulness of the slave; but as many of his numerous slaves were hardly known to the master, they were, particularly in the country, at the mercy of overseers. This, of course, was not to be feared in earlier times, when the slaves sat down to their meals on lower benches (*subsellia*) at the foot of their master's couch, or when the latter shared the labour of the field with his servants. But the attachment thus engendered disappeared with the increasing luxury of later times, which banished most of the slaves from any familiar intercourse with their owners. They now had their rations (*demensum*) dealt out to them by the day or month, and with the savings out of these (*peculium*), to which the master had no right, the slaves frequently bought their liberty; unless they tried the shorter way of theft and defraudation, undaunted by the cruel punishment to which their slightest misdemeanours were liable. The pride of a freeman made captive on the field of battle could ill brook such treatment, whence the furious determination with which the death-struggle of the revolted slaves was carried on. Refractory slaves had their legs fettered with *compedes,* so as to make their escape impossible, or, loaded with iron collars (*collare*) and manacles (*manica*), they were imprisoned in dungeons (*ergastulum, pistrinum*) built on most farms for the purpose, or condemned to hard labour in the quarries. Flagellation with a stick, rod, or whip was a common punishment (*fustis, virga, mastix*), as was also the carrying of the *furca,* a fork-like instrument laid round the neck, the arms being tied to the protruding front part of the furca. Runaway slaves, or those found guilty of theft, had the initial letters of the crime branded on their foreheads with a hot iron (*stigma,* whence their name *stigmosi* or *literati*). Their capital punishment was crucifixion (*in crucem ager, figere*), or being thrown into the *vivaria,* or opposed to wild animals in the amphitheatre.

Slaves were, of course, forbidden to wear the toga. Their costume was the tunica, of coarse dark materials, worn in the manner of the Greek exomis, to which workman's costume a pænula or lacerna might be added in bad weather. Other slaves, who had to wait personally on the master and his family, most likely wore a finer tunic of lighter colours.

After his liberation (*manumissio*) had been granted, the slave stood to his patron in the relation of a *libertus.* This manumissio was effected by the patron presenting himself with his slave before the highest magistrate of the city: after having proved his right of possession (*iusta servitus*), he pronounced the words, "Hunc hominem ego volo liberum esse," whereat the *assertor* (without whom the slave could not appear in a legal transaction, not having yet received his liberty) touched the slave with a rod on the top of his head, or, according to a later custom, boxed his ear. After this the patron took his former slave by the hand, turned him round, and ended the ceremony by once more repeating the just-mentioned formula. Besides this liberation, called *manumissio vindicta,* there existed the so-called *manumissio censu,* consisting in the name of *libertus* being entered in the census lists; and the *manumissio testamento, i.e.* the liberation of the slave by the owner's last will. After his liberation the former slave put on the pileus, donned the toga, wore a ring, and shaved his beard—the signs of a freeman.

101. The mechanical or intellectual occupations of the slaves were continued by them as freedmen, in consequence of which the trades were shared by the *plebs* with the *liberti*. The contempt against trades expressed by Cicero is further illustrated by the fact of tradesmen being, with few exceptions, debarred from serving in the legions. Roman tradesmen and mechanics, therefore, were a low, cowardly, and at the same time unruly class of people—*fæx urbana*, as Cicero calls them. Livy mentions particularly that when, in the year 426 of the city, the Gauls threatened Rome, the Consul L. Æmilius Mamercinus was compelled to recruit his legions from the just-mentioned classes, "*minime militiæ idoneum genus.*" The same Livy reproaches the Consul Terentius Varro, known by the battle of Cannæ, with his descent from a butcher's family. Epigrammatists loved to ridicule tradesmen grown wealthy, who, like true *parvenus*, made a show of their riches.

Mechanics' guilds (*collegia opificum*) existed at an early period, their origin being traced back to King Numa : they were nine in number, viz. pipers, carpenters, goldsmiths, dyers, leather-workers, tanners, smiths, and potters, and another guild combining, at first, all the remaining handicrafts, which afterwards developed into new separate societies. Amongst these later guilds, frequently mentioned in inscriptions, we name the goldsmiths, bakers, purple dyers, pig-dealers, sailors, ferrymen, physicians, &c. They had their separate inns (*curia, schola*), their statutes and rules of reception and expulsion of members, their collective and individual privileges, their laws of mutual protection, and their widows' fund, not unlike the medieval guilds. There was, however, no compulsion to join a guild. In consequence, there was much competition from freedmen—foreign, particularly Greek, workmen who settled in Rome, as also from the domestic slaves who supplied the wants of the large families—reasons enough to prevent the trades from acquiring much importance. They had, however, their time-honoured customs, consisting of sacrifices and festive gatherings at their inns ; on which occasions their banners (*vexilla*) and emblems were carried about the streets in procession.

A wall-painting at Pompeii (*Archäol. Zeitg.*, T. XVII., 1850, p. 177 *et seq.*) is most likely intended as an illustration of a carpenters' procession. A large wooden tray (*ferculum*), surmounted by a decorated baldachin, is being carried on the shoulders of young workmen. On the tray stands a carpenter's bench in miniature, with two men at their work, the figure of Dædalus being seen in the foreground.

The shops in which the mechanics worked and exhibited their wares were collectively called *tabernæ*, a name derived from the old booths (*quod ex tabulis olim fiebant*), such as stood in the Forum Romanum in old times. Under Domitian these wooden structures were banished from the streets and Forum of Rome, only the money-changers being allowed to retain their old places. Martial (VII. 61) highly approves of this measure. The shops lay in the ground floors of houses opening towards the street. The shops of a provincial town, as, for instance, of Pompeii, consisted of one large compartment with one or two smaller back rooms, the latter sometimes connected by means of stairs with bedrooms in the upper story (compare the house of Pansa, Fig. 386). The shops are open towards the street (in corner houses even on both sides), so as not to impede the view of the wares. Facing the street stood a stone counter, a narrow passage being left for those who wished to enter the shop; bottles containing the liquids for sale were let into this counter, cases in the back wall of the shop being filled with glasses, bottles, and stores. Shop-signs, mostly hewn in stone, indicated the nature of the objects for sale : the shop of a milkman at Pompeii shows the sign of a goat; that of a wine-merchant exhibits two men carrying an amphora on a stick over their shoulders; that of a baker, a mill put in motion by a donkey.

Private bakeries, as attached to every large household, have been found in several Pompeian houses, as, for instance, in those of Pansa and Sallustius; in an oven belonging to the Casa di Marte e Venere numerous loaves of bread have been found, completely burnt, but still distinctly recognisable. Close to the house of Sallustius lies a large bakery containing four mills made of coarse porous tufa. Fig. 484 serves to illustrate their construction, one half showing the exterior aspect, the other the cross-section of a mill. The stone base, in the form of a disc, is marked *a*; its upper surface shows a rill or groove (*b*), going all round it. On this base stands a massive conical stone (*c, meta, μύλη*), being worked of one piece, with the base or otherwise let into it. This stone is surmounted by a hollow double cone or funnel (*d d, catillus, ὄνος*), the corn being poured into its upper half, whence it dropped through another groove (*e*) into the narrow space between the lower half of the double funnel and the outer surface of the cone (*c*). On the double funnel (*d d*) being whirled round the corn was crushed, the flour dropping into the groove (*b*). The groove (*e*) could be closed by means of an iron plate with five holes, the centre one of which was connected with the top of the cone by means of a strong iron peg, so as to facilitate the action of the double funnel, the four other holes serving to admit the grain. Two bars (*ff*), fastened in the middle of the double funnel, served to work the mill, which was done either by men (*mola versatilis*) or animals (*mola jumentaria, asinaria*). Windmills were unknown to the Romans; not so water-mills (*mola aquaria, hydraleta*), one of which is described by Vitruvius; its principle of action resembled that just explained: water-mills were introduced in Rome about the fourth or fifth century A.D. A Pompeian wall-painting ("Mus. Borbon.," vol. vi., Tav. 51) depicts the *Vestalia*, or millers' feast, celebrated on the 9th of June, genii taking the place of men, as is often the case in these pictures. The day was celebrated by the millers and bakers by a simple family dinner, consisting of bread, salt, vegetables, and fish, served in earthenware. The donkeys had a resting-day, animals and mill being adorned with flowers, and garlands composed of loaves strung together. In the just-mentioned bakery of Pompeii we see also an oven cleverly constructed, and furnished with a contrivance to retain the heat. The act of baking itself is illustrated on a small grave monument in Rome, just outside the Porta Maggiore, where the Via Labicana and Via Praenestina meet at a pointed angle. According to the inscription: EST HOC MONIMENTVM MARCEI VERGILEI EVRYSACIS PISTORIS REDEMPTORIS APPARET, it has been erected by M. Vergilius Eurysaces, baker and bread-dealer,

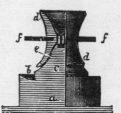

Fig. 484.

for himself and his wife, Atistia. The name of the monument is
panarium (bread-basket), and it is adorned with the emblems of
the trade, amongst which we distinguish heaps of corn, two mills
moved by donkeys, two flour-strainers, and two miller's knives;
also a machine for kneading dough moved by horses. A similar
machine appears in a relief on a sarcophagus of the Lateran
(Gerhard, " Denkm. u. Forsch.," 1861, No. 148). Scales to weigh
large and heavy quantities (a pair of which also appears on the

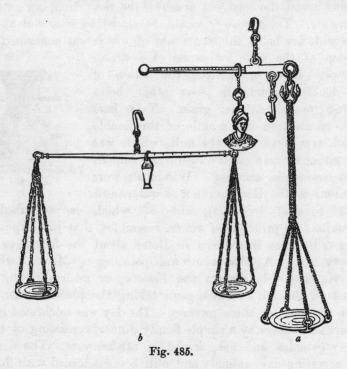

Fig. 485.

monument of Eurysaces) are frequently met with on Roman and
Greek monuments; they resemble those at present in use.

Smaller quantities of dry or liquid substances, such as meat,
fish, oil, or chemicals, were weighed in the *libra* (Fig. 485), two
specimens of which have been found at Pompeii. The object to
be weighed is suspended from the smaller of the two unequal ends
of the beam (*jugum*), while to the longer end is attached a weight
(*æquipondium*), by means of a movable ring. By pushing this
equipoise to and from the point of revolution the weight of the

object could be determined exactly, this part of the beam being divided by means of incised points. Fig. 485, *a*, shows another balance, from the shorter end of whose beam are suspended a hook and a scale (*lanx*), the former for the fastening of bottles or pots with fluids, the latter for the reception of dry objects to be weighed. The longer end of the beam is here divided by a double system of points, the one to determine the weights of solid, the other that of fluid substances. In other balances the beam is divided into two equal parts (Fig. 486, *b*), a scale being suspended from each end. One of these ends, moreover, is marked in the manner described, the equipoise here showing the form of an acorn, while in the former case it was a head of Minerva; the heads or forms of animals occur often. Numerous other weights to be put in one of the scales have been found. They are made of bronze, lead, or stone; some of them have their value marked on them.

After the bakeries we mention cook-shops, low inns (*popinæ*), and wine-shops (*cauponæ*). They were frequented by the poorest classes, and were often the scenes of vice; it was considered disreputable for a gentleman to visit such places. There were, however, taverns, &c., for *roués* of the better classes, where debauchery and games of hazard were the order of the day; the trade of inn-keeper (*caupo*) was, for these reasons, considered disreputable. The interior arrangement of such places most likely resembled that of the modern *osterie*. Signboards (*insignia*), hung out at the door, proclaimed the name of the house: at Pompeii there was an Elephant inn; in Rome, near the Forum, a Cock; at Lyons, a Mercury and Apollo, &c. A wall-painting at Herculaneum ("Pitture d'Ercol.," vol. iii. p. 227) gives a vivid idea of an antique *taberna*. In the foreground of a square, which a colonnade shows to be a forum, mine host is helping a guest to some beverage brewing in a kettle on the fire; in the background a woman is selling pears and vegetables.

With the work of a potter we have already become acquainted (see § 90 and Figs. 193 and 194). In Pompeii a potter's oven has been found to the left of the street of graves. The fireplace has a flat top full of holes, through which the heat enters the baking-oven. A similar arrangement is shown in the tilers' and potters' ovens found near Rheinzabern (in 1858, thirty-six of the former and seventy-seven of the latter kind had been discovered), as also in those found near Waiblingen (Würtemberg) ; at the excavation of the latter, in 1840, the author was present.

The surface of a kylix in the Royal Museum, Berlin (Gerhard, " Trinkschalen des Kgl. Museums," Tafs. XII., XIII.), represents the workshop of a metal-founder ; although taken from Greek life, the picture will serve our present purpose. We there see the large furnace with the cauldron standing on it ; one workman is poking the fire, while another, leaning on his sledge-hammer, seems to wait for the melting of the metal. In another part of the shop the bronze statue of a praying youth lies on the floor. The head has not yet been soldered on to the body ; a man is

working with a hammer at one arm of the figure. On the opposite side is seen, under a scaffolding, the finished colossal statue of a youthful warrior ; two workmen are polishing the legs with a scraper, while two men in long cloaks, most likely the artist and the owner of the foundry, are looking on. Hammers, saws, modelled arms, legs, and heads, and sketches on tablets, cover the walls. Vulcan's smithy has been shown, Fig. 261 : cyclops at their work are frequently met with in bas-reliefs (Millin, "Gallérie Mythol.," No. 383). A cutler's shop and workshop are illustrated by two bas-reliefs on a cippus in the Vatican, the former of which (Fig. 486) shows a rich choice of sickles, pruning-knives, and long carving-knives. The owner of the business seems to be selling a knife to a customer.

Fig. 487, from a bas-relief found at Capua, has, according to its inscription, been let into the proscenium wall of a stage by Lucceius Peculiaris, a builder, in consequence of a dream he had. Near the figure of Athene Ergane we see a sculptor working at a Korinthian capital, while two men are lifting the drums of a

Fig. 486.

column by means of a tread-wheel. Chisels, gravers, files, drills, and half-finished statues have been discovered in a sculptor's studio at Pompeii; pairs of compasses used by stone-masons and carpenters, leads, and folding foot-rules have also been found at Pompeii, the latter divided into twelve *unciæ* (by points on the side surface) and sixteen *digiti* (marked on the edge); * similar instruments appear as emblems on tombstones.

A blacksmith's workshop, recognisable by the axles of carts, fellies, and tools found there, has been discovered at Pompeii outside the Herculaneum gate. A carpenter's workshop appears in a wall-painting at Herculaneum, where two Cupids are sawing a board with a saw exactly resembling those at present in use.

Fig. 487.

The bottom of a glass vessel found in the catacombs of Rome represents the manipulations of a cabinet-maker and cutter of wood in six pictures painted on a gold ground ("Pitture d'Ercol.," vol. i. Tav. XXXIV., and Perret, "Catacombes de Rome," T. IV. 22, 14; see also Jahn, *loc. cit.*, Taf. XI. 1).

Tanneries are represented (Figs. 472 and 473) in Pompeian wall-paintings: the interior of a cobbler's shop appears in a wall-painting at Herculaneum ("Pitture d'Ercol.," vol. i. T. XXXV.), where one of two Cupids sitting by a table seems to beat the leather on a last, while the other is sewing at a shoe; rows of finished shoes stand in an open cupboard and on boards on the wall, which proves that the shop was used both for working and

* See "Mus. Borb.," T. VI., Tav. XV.

selling. In the street leading towards the Odeum at Pompeii there is the shop of an oil-merchant, with eight earthen vessels let into the counter, in which olives and clotted oil have been found; we also mention a perfumer's shop, the signboards of which, now illegible, announced the sale of pomatum, incense, and the ingredients for embalming the dead: in a colourman's shop in the Casa del Arciduca di Toscana, colours, partly in a raw state, partly prepared with resin, have been found. A series of market-scenes appear in a picture at Herculaneum ("Pitture d'Ercol.," vol. iii. Tav. XLII. *et seq.*) representing the colonnade of a forum, where clothes, bronze vessels, ironware, and cakes are sold, while shoemakers take the measure of people sitting on benches.

102. Three classes amongst the slaves and freedmen held a distinguished position by their intellectual accomplishments, viz., the *medici, chirurgi,* and *literari.* About physicians, their first appearance amongst the Romans and their social position, we gather interesting information from Pliny's remarks at the beginning of the twenty-ninth book of his "Natural History." In the first centuries of the Republic slaves and freedmen used to treat their patients according to certain old prescriptions and nostrums. In the year 575 of the city (219 B.C.) a Greek surgeon of the name of Archagathus settled in Rome, whose art was acknowledged by the erection, at the public expense, of a booth for him on the Acilian cross-road. To his passion for burning and cutting he owed the nickname of butcher: altogether he brought discredit on Greek doctors; they were called charlatans, filling their purses and endangering their patients' lives by their ignorance, there being no law to restrict or punish them. Nevertheless, the appearance of Archagathus and other Greek medical men gave rise to the establishment of a medical profession in Rome. Numerous physicians became known, one rejecting the remedies of the other, and seeking renown by the introduction of new methods. "Hence," says Pliny, "those disgraceful squabbles at sick-beds, when all the physicians disagree only in order to avoid the appearance of consent; hence the dreadful inscription on tombs— 'The number of his doctors has killed him.' Medical art is changed every day by new additions; we are sailing before a Greek wind, and the decision of life and death lies with him who has got most to say for himself, &c." The large income of a

physician (for want of chemists, they also sold their drugs, frequently composed of expensive ingredients) may be guessed from the fact that Quintus Stertinius, body-physician to the emperor, considered it highly meritorious on his part to be satisfied with 500,000 sestertii, as his private practice had brought him 600,000 sestertii (£6,450 according to the value of money in Augustus's time). Krinas, a contemporary of Pliny, left at his death ten million sestertii, after having spent almost as much on the building of fortifications at Massilia (his native town) and other cities. Under Nero the medical profession became organized, an upper class of physicians, the *archiatri*, being created, amongst which the body-physicians of the emperors (*archiatri palatini*) and the *archiatri populares* held again distinguished ranks. The former were amongst the most important court-officials,

Fig. 488.

their title being *spectabiles.* After the time of Antoninus Pius a certain number of the archiatri populares were appointed to reside in each town; they were elected by the citizens and examined by the college of *archiatri;* they received a salary from the city, besides being exempted from all *munera,* for which in return they had to attend the poor. Medical men were divided into physicians (*medici*), surgeons (*medici vulnerum, vulnerarii, chirurgi*), and oculists (*ocularii* or *medici ab oculis*); besides these, we hear of dentists, specialists for diseases of the ear, lady-physicians for the diseases of their own sex, midwives, and assistants (*intraliptæ*), whose chief business was to rub patients with medicinal ointment; we also mention the numerous sellers of Oriental salves, &c., who added their share to the grand system of quackery obtaining in Rome. Surgical instruments and medicine-boxes made of bronze with silver inlaid covers have been discovered; little weights, to exactly determine the quantity of the medicine used were also kept in these boxes. Fig. 488 represents a box found in the Rhenish country, at present in the Royal Museum, Berlin. On its sliding cover it shows the inlaid image of Æsculapius placed in a small temple. In Pompeii two chemists' shops have been found, the signboards of which show the snake of the same God, with a

pineapple in its mouth; solid medical substances, liquids dried
up in glasses, and a surgical apparatus of bronze (now in the
Museum of Naples) have been discovered there. Fig. 489
represents a number of surgical instruments found in the house
of a surgeon in the Strada Consolare at Pompeii: *a* is a bronze
box containing probes (*specillum*), such as appear separately in
n, o, p. Pincers (*forceps*) are seen *e, g, i ; f* is a scalpel (*scalpellum*) ;
l, a *spatula* ; *m*, a sound ; *q*, a straight pin ; *k*, pincers to remove
splinters of bones ; *h*, a *speculum magnum matricis* ; *d*, a chopper of
unknown use.

Frequent diseases of the eyes occurring from about the end of
the Republic, as the results of vice or exaggerated hot bathing,
necessitated a separate class of oculists. The names of the
oculists of the Empress Livia are found in her columbarium.

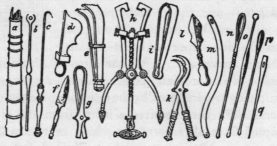

Fig. 489.

Many small vases, previously taken for children's toys, have turned
out to be receptacles of drops and salves for diseases of the eye :
one of them shows the inscription "*Lycium Iasonis*," *i.e.* the
prescription of the Greek oculist Iason. Particularly in the
occidental provinces of the empire small tablets of slate are found
in great numbers, indicating the names of oculists, their prescriptions, and the way of applying them : these were advertisements
of Roman oculists. The quackeries of medical men were favourite
subjects with both Athenian and Roman playwrights. A Greek
vase-painting (Panofka, "Bild. antik. Leb.," Taf. VII. 5) represents a travelling quack practising his art in a booth standing in
a market-place ; he is feeling the head of a patient, whom, with the
assistance of his servant, he is pulling up the stairs of his booth.

Numerous *tabernæ* were, by the advertisements on the door-posts or porticoes of the houses, marked as booksellers' shops. Such shops were found in Rome, in the Forum near the Curia, in the Vicus Sandalarius, and in many other much-frequented quarters. Several names of celebrated publishing firms are known to us. Inside the shops lay in pigeon-holes (*armaria, nidi*), carefully arranged, the book-rolls, in more or less costly bindings. The shops, at the same time, were meeting-places of literary men and persons interested in literature. In reading of the numerous private libraries, and the enormous quantities of books required by the reading public of the Empire, we naturally ask how this demand could be supplied without the printing-press. We answer this question in the words of Schmidt ("Geschichte der Denk- und Glaubensfreiheit im ersten Jahrhundert der Kaiser-herrschaft," p. 119) : "the place of the press in our literature was taken by the slaves." We have already mentioned the *literati*, cultivated slaves, generally of Greek origin, who had to copy books or write from dictation. By these slaves manuscripts were copied with astounding celerity, with the aid of abbreviations called, from their inventor, Tiro, a freedman of Cicero, Tironian notes. These copies, sometimes full of mistakes, went to the shops of the booksellers (*bibliopola*), unless these kept copyists in their own shops. Numerous copies were thus produced in little time. The satirical writings of Ovidius, Propertius, and Martialis were in everybody's hands, as were also the works of Homer and Virgil, the odes of Horace, and the speeches of Cicero; grammars, anthologies, &c., for schools, were reproduced in the same manner ; indeed, the antique book-trade was carried on on a scale hardly surpassed by modern times. Augustus confiscated, for instance, in Rome alone, 2,000 copies of the pseudo-Sibylline books—by no means a recent work. Pomponius Atticus, the friend and publisher of Cicero, possessed a large number of slaves for the manufacturing of writing materials and the copying and correcting of manuscripts ; besides which he carried on a lucrative publishing business (see Cicero's speech "Pro Ligario"). More-over, authors used (according to a custom introduced by Asinius Polio in Augustus's time) to read their unpublished productions either to their friends or (after due advertisement) to public audiences in the Forum, at theatres, baths, &c. Hardly a day passed without an exhibition of this kind ; the younger Pliny, in one of his letters (I., 13) graphically describes the difficulties of attracting, and still more of retaining, the *blasé* audiences of the metropolis.

About the writing materials of the Greeks we have spoken before. The Romans also used wax tablets (Fig. 490, *c, d*), called *tabellæ, pugillares,* or simply *ceræ,* for writing letters, notes, first drafts, or school exercises. Only the inner side was written on, a raised wooden border serving to protect the writing when two or more tablets were joined together or made into a book (*duplices,* δίπτυχα, *triplices,* τρίπτυχα, *multiplices,* πολύπτυχα). The outer surface or cover was generally adorned with ivory carvings, jewels, or precious metals. Several of these diptycha, which, in imperial times, the new-appointed consuls and prætors used to present to each other, have been preserved. Several wax tablets, most of them with Roman, and a few with Greek, documents written on them, have been discovered at various times since 1786 in the old Roman mines near the towns of Abrudbanya (Gross Schlatte) and Vöröspatak, in Siebenbürgen ; most of them are at present in the Hungarian National Museum, Pesth, a few others in private collections.*

a   b   c   d

Fig. 490.

The pencil (*stilus, graphium*), used for incising or erasing the letters (*stilum vertere*), we have mentioned before. Fig. 490 shows a pencil lying on an open book (*c*). The tablets were also used for writing letters, separate slaves or freedmen being occasionally employed as *librarii ab epistulis.* On sending the letter the *tabellæ* were fastened together with a thread tied into a knot, on which the wax seal was pressed. The outside of the letter bore the address. Another kind of writing was done with ink (*atramentum librarium*), made of a solution of soot and gum, on papyrus or parchment (see Fig. 490, the inkstand, *a*, with the *calamus* lying on it, and the half-opened writing-scroll, *b*). Of the materials and manufactory of the papyrus

---

* The chronological enumeration of these discoveries from 1786 to 1856 is found in Erdy, "De Tabulis ceratis in Transsilvania repertis." Pesth, 1856. See Massmann, "Libellus aurarius sive Tabulæ ceratæ," Leipsic, 1840 ; and Detlefsen's Contributions to the Sitzungsberichte of the Wiener Akademie der Wissenschaften, Hist. Cl. vols. xxiii. and xxvii.

we have already spoken. The height of the scroll varied, according to the quality of the paper, from 6 to 13 inches; as to its length, no rule can be given. A papyrus found in 1821, containing a fragment of the twenty-fourth book of the Iliad, is 8 feet long by 10 inches high. One end of the papyrus was fitted into the hollow part of a cane, and rolled round the cane, the ends of which, slightly protruding, were adorned with buttons of ivory or metal (*cornua, umbilici*). To secure it against moths and dust the papyrus was put in a purple or yellow case (*membrana*): to it, or (as appears from several wall-paintings) to the umbilici, the title of the book was tied. Several scrolls together were put into a cylindrical case (*scrinium*, compare Fig. 235) with a cover to it; books or documents could thus be conveniently carried. Several statues, clad in the toga ("Augusteum," Tafs. 117, 119), have a scrinium standing at their feet; and in a bas-relief (Micali, "Monumenti per servire alla Storia degli ant. Popoli Italiani," Atlas, Tav. 112), a scrinium, together with the sella curulis and several books, is carried by the attendants (*apparitores*) in front of a procession of magistrates. Most houses had a library, which, according to Vitruvius, ought to face the east in order to admit the light of the morning, and to prevent the books from becoming mouldy. At Herculaneum a library with book-cases containing 1,700 scrolls has been discovered. The grammarian Epaphroditus possessed a library of 30,000, and Sammanicus Serenus, the tutor of the younger Gordian, one of 62,000 books. Seneca ridicules the fashionable folly of illiterate men who adorned their walls with thousands of books, the titles of which were the delight of the yawning owner. According to Publius Victor, Rome possessed twenty-nine public libraries, the first of which was opened by Asinius Polio in the forecourt of the Temple of Peace; two others were founded during the reign of Augustus, viz. the Octavian and the Palatine libraries. Tiberius, Vespasian, Domitian, and Trajan added to their number; the Ulpian library, founded by the last-mentioned emperor, being the most important of all.

Of agricultural implements we first mention the plough (*aratrum*). Originally the land was turned up by means of a long hoe, which soon was developed into the wooden plough, consisting of a strong wooden hook pointed at the bottom like a ploughshare, or cased with iron, the back part forming the plough handle. This plough, of Etruscan origin, but adopted by the Romans, is shown, Fig. 491, from an Etruscan bronze group; it naturally could only dig into the earth, without turning up the furrows. The later Roman plough consisted of a share-beam (*dentale*), with the ploughshare (*vomer*) at one end, and the *stiva* (plough-handle) with a cross-bar (*manicula*) at the other; beam and handle might be made of one piece, or the latter inserted into the former; the manicula served to direct the plough by being either raised or pressed down by the ploughman. About the middle of the share-beam was fastened the *buris* or *bura* (plough-tail), about eight feet long and slightly bent; in the Roman plough it served at the same time as pole (*temo*), to the further end of which the oxen were yoked (see Fig. 491, where the yoke itself is also

shown separately, above the animals). To even the furrows two mould-boards (*aures*) were fastened behind the plough-share. A particular kind of plough was the *plaustraratrum*, used in Gallic Rhetia and in the north of Italy. In it the plough-tail rested on two low

Fig. 491.

wheels, into the axle-tree of which the pole was inserted. The plough was drawn by two or more oxen, according to the nature of the soil. We next mention the harrow (*occa, crater*) and the *irpex*, an instrument consisting of iron hooks. It was drawn by oxen, and served to tear up roots and weeds. We further name the *bidens*, an instrument with two prongs, the rake (*rastrum*), the *ligo* (a hoe used in gardens and vineyards), and the spade (*pala, rutrum*). The *falx vinitoria* and *falx arboraria* were used for pruning vines and trees. The former had a curved blade and a spike, the latter a bent blade. Sickles were used to cut grass or corn, not too near the root; the ears were gathered in baskets and trodden out by oxen on an open piece of ground, which had previously been made firm by being stamped upon; a custom still obtaining in southern countries. Another way of thrashing the corn was by means of the *tribulum*—according to Varro, a board, portions of which were raised by means of inserted stones or pieces of iron. It was pulled across the ears by oxen, the ploughman standing on it. The remaining husks were left to be blown away by the wind, or else removed. The corn was kept in subterraneous caves (*horreum subterraneum*), still in use in southern countries, or in dry, airy granaries resting on columns (*horreum pensile*). In times of famine these granaries were filled at public expense, according to the example set by C. Sempronius Gracchus. The ruins of the large *horrea populi Romani* were still visible in the sixteenth century, between the Aventine hill and the Monte Testaceo; at present they have entirely disappeared, as have also the granaries called by the names of their founders, *horrea Aniceti, Vargunteii, Seiani, Augusti Domitiani*.

The culture of the olive-tree in Italy dates from the times of the kings. Venafrum, Casinum, and the Sabine country were celebrated for their oils. The culture of the vine is of later date. It became of importance only when the growing of grain began to cease. The shoots were planted in furrows or holes, and the vines were trailed (*maritare*) on trees, chiefly elms, planted at distances of twenty feet; their distance apart was doubled in case the ground lying between was used for the growing of grain, as is still the case in modern Italy. The custom of trailing the vine on poles or trellis-work was equally known to the Romans. Hedges of briars, fences made of osiers, or walls protected the vineyards against the cattle. Numerous sculptural groups of reapers and herds of cattle illustrate the agricultural pursuits of the Roman people.

103. We propose in the following pages to give a short sketch of the priestly colleges, the sacrificial rites, and the festive games connected with them, always availing ourselves of monumental evidence. All religious acts performed in holy places (*locus sacer*) were called *sacra :* in case they were performed by individuals or by the head of a family in honour of the domestic gods, the Lares, Penates, &c., or by a priest in the name of a community (*gens*), they were called *sacra privata ; sacra publica*, on the other hand, were performed at the public expense by public priests (*sacerdotes populi Romani*) for the people (*pro populo*), or by certain societies (*sodalitates*) which were charged by the State with the veneration of certain deities, as, for instance, the Gens

Nautia with that of Minerva, the Gens Julia with that of Apollo, and the Gens Aurelia with that of Sol. The public priests (*sacerdotes*) were divided into three classes : the first class, that of the *sacerdotes publici populi Romani*, formed the great *collegia* of the *pontifices*, comprising the subdivisions of the *VII viri epulones*, the *XV viri sacris faciundis*, the *augures*, *Salii* and *Fetiales;* the second class comprised the *sodalitates*, which had to perform the *sacra popularia;* the third, those officiating at the *sacra gentilitia.*

The priests of the first class enjoyed many privileges; they were allowed to wear the toga prætexta, they were exempt from military or civil service, and had seats of honour at feasts and games. They were also in possession of public land (*ager publicus*), the rental of which covered the expenses of the sacra ; moreover, the State kept for them a number of subaltern officials, partly slaves (*servi publici*), partly freemen. Amongst these we mention the *lictores*, mostly freedmen, who preceded priests and priestesses (just like the lictores of civil magistrates), in order to make room for them through a crowd; also the *pullarii* (keepers of the fowls), the *victimarii* (sacrificial butchers), the *tibicines* and *fidicines* (musicians), the *calatores* (messengers to announce meetings), and the *camilli* and *camillæ*, boys and girls partly officiating at the sacrifices, partly aspirants for the priestly dignity. For the last-mentioned class originally free-born children alone were eligible with parents still alive (*pueri patrimi et matrimi* and *puellæ patrimæ et matrimæ*).

The pontifices formed, in the time of the kings, a college of four priests, with the king himself as high priest at their head. When (300 B.C.) the tribunes of the people Q. and Cn. Ogulnius carried a plebiscite granting the plebeians admittance to the priestly offices, previously held by patricians only, four plebeians were added to the original four pontifices, the high priest (*pontifex maximus*) being chosen from amongst them. Sulla, the reformer of many priestly colleges, increased the pontifices to fifteen. In imperial times the dignity of pontifex maximus was, by the senate, conferred on, or on his own authority assumed by, the emperor. We possess, for instance, a statue of Hadrian in pontificals, with a sacrificial vase in his hand (Clarac, " Musée," Tom. II. pl. 945). Saturnus, Ops, and Vesta were the chief gods whose worship was committed to the pontifices. The high priest had his dwelling in the Regia, near the temple of Vesta in the Forum. The atrium of Vesta was the hearth of the State house-hold, where the priests, as heads of the Roman family, and the Vestals, like the maidens in private families, performed sacrificial rites. The college of pontifices, therefore, formed the centre of Roman public worship, and to them was confided the keeping of the religious State-archive, where the religious annals (*annales maximi*), written by the high priest himself, the *leges regiæ* (the oldest customary laws referring to sacred matters), the *libri pontificii*, and the minutes and decisions of the meetings of pontifices (*commentarii pontificum*), were deposited. By this college was pronounced every year the *sollemnis votorum nuncupatio* (the vows of the State), and its advice was asked by the magistrates with regard to religious ceremonies, the pontifices alone being supposed to know the sacrifices agreeable to the gods. Previous to devoting a place or object (statue, vase, &c.) to the gods, men had to solicit the approbation of the pontifices, who also performed the *consecratio* preceding the act of devotion itself. They were consulted about the mode of *expiatio*, when faults had been committed against the sacred precepts, or at burials (where the *manes* had to be pacified), &c.

Amongst other offices connected with this college we mention that of "sacrificial king" (*rex sacrorum* or *rex sacrificulus*), a dignity held at first by the Roman kings, and, after their expulsion, by a priest, who had to perform certain acts of worship, particularly the *sacra* of Janus. Although his functions were of comparatively little importance, the sacrificial king occupied nominally a higher rank than the pontifices themselves, at whose festive meals the place of honour was granted to him. His wife, the *regina sacrorum*, shared the honour of his priesthood.

The pontifices, like several other priestly brotherhoods (*e.g.* the *fratres Arvales* and *sodales Augustales*), had sacrificial priests (*flamines*) attached to them, whose name was derived from *flare* (to blow the fire). The number of flamines attached to the pontifices was fifteen, the three highest of whom (*flamines maiores*), viz. the *flamen Dialis*, *Martialis*, and *Quirinalis*, were always chosen from old patrician families; the remaining twelve were called *flamines minores*. Free from all civil duties, the Flamen Dialis, with his wife and children, exclusively devoted himself to the service of the deity. His house (*domus flaminia*) lay on the Palatine hill. His marriage was dissoluble by death only; he was not allowed to take an oath, mount a horse, or look at an army. He was forbidden to remain a night away from his house, and his hand touched nothing unclean, for which reason he never approached a corpse or a burial-place. He always appeared in his official dress, consisting of a toga prætexta, woven by his wife of thick wool (*læna*), which was not allowed to be tied in a knot, but had to be fastened by means of fibulæ, the sight of fetters being forbidden to him. For the same reason the ring he wore on his finger had to be a broken one; neither was he allowed to approach

Fig. 492.

a trailed vine or touch ivy: a prisoner on entering his house was freed from his fetters, which were thrown through the impluvium into the street. His head-dress was the *albogalerus*, a sort of pileus, to the top (*apex*) of which was tied an olive branch with a white woollen thread (*filum*). This head-dress appears on several coins, of which we mention one of Julius Cæsar, bearing the inscriptions PONT. MAX. and AVGVR. The albogalerus, Fig. 492, *k*, resembles that seen in a bas-relief of the temple of Vespasian in Rome,* but for its apex, which is a little lower. The adornment of the albogalerus with a flash of lightning shows its being destined for a Flamen Dialis. In the daytime the Flamen Dialis was not allowed to take off his head-dress, and he was obliged to resign his office in case it fell off by

* Reber, "Die Ruinen Roms." 1863, p. 82.

accident. In his belt he carried the sacrificial knife (*secespita*), and in his hand he held a rod (*commetacula*), in order to keep off the people on his way to the sacrifice. For the same purpose he was preceded by a lictor, who compelled everybody on the way to lay down his work, the flamen not being allowed to see the business of daily life. The wife of the flamen (*flaminica*) had to submit to an equally strict etiquette; she also appeared always in long woollen robes, her hair was tied in a tutulus with a woollen ribbon of purple colour, over which a kerchief (*rica*) was fastened with the bough of a lucky tree (*arbor felix*) attached to it. She wore a purple veil (*flammeum*), and her shoes had to be made of the leather of sacrificed animals. She also carried the sacrificial knife. Fig. 492 shows a bas-relief illustrative of all the utensils used at sacrificial acts by the upper priests, such as the sacrificial vase (*culullus, e*), the vessels for drawing liquids (*simpulum, f*), the sacrificial knife (*secespita*) in a case (*g*), and the albogalerus (*k*).*

Besides the flamines, the Vestals (*virgines Vestales, virgines Vestæ*) were closely connected with the college of pontifices. They are said to have come from Alba soon after the foundation of Rome: at first there were two Vestals for each of the two tribes Ramnes and Tities; afterwards two others were added for the Luceres, and the number of six was exceeded at no period. The vestal, on being chosen, was not allowed to be younger than six or older than ten years; she was to be *patrima et matrima*, and free from bodily defects. After having been examined she was clad in white garments and devoted to the service of Vesta for thirty years; during the first ten years she was a novice, during the second ten an active priestess, and for the remaining period a teacher of novices. After this period she was at liberty either to remain in the service of the goddess (which was generally done) or to return to her family and get married. Her dress was always white; round her forehead she wore a broad band like a diadem (*infula*), with ribbons (*vittæ*) attached to it. During the sacrifice, or at processions, she was covered with a white veil (*suffibulum*), fastened under her chin with a fibula (see Gerhard, "Antike Bildwerke," Taf. XXIV., and the Vestal Claudia Quinta, Fig. 493,

* Sacrificial utensils appear frequently on cameos and coins; for instance, on the denarii of the families, Antestia, Antonia, Cassia, Cornelia, Domitia, Iulia, Hirtia, Sulpicia, &c.

from a bas-relief). She was carefully guarded against insult or temptation; an offence offered to her was punished with death: no man was allowed to enter her dwelling or approach the temple by night; in public every one, even the consul, made way to the lictor preceding the maiden. At public games and pontifical banquets she had the seat of honour; and a convicted criminal accidentally meeting her was released. Amongst her priestly functions was the keeping of the eternal fire in the temple of Vesta, each Vestal taking her turn at watching; in case the fire went out the negligent maiden was liable to corporal punishment at the hands of the Pontifex Maximus. The temple of Vesta had, moreover, to be sprinkled every day with the water of the fountain of Egeria; on the 1st of March of every year it was decorated anew with purifying laurel (see the laurel-branch lying on a censer, Fig. 492, *a*). The sprinkling with water was done with an *aspergillum*, sometimes in the form of a horse's leg with a horse's tail attached to it (see Fig. 492, *h*), sometimes with a spiral handle. In accordance with the simple offerings at the domestic hearth, the gift of the vestals consisted of different preparations of salt (*muries* and *mola salsa*), offered in earthen vessels. The sacrifice was accompanied by prayers for the people. Breach of chastity on the part of the Vestal was punished with death; the culprit was carried on a bier to the *campus sceleratus*, outside the Porta Collina, beaten with rods, and afterwards immured alive, the violent killing of a Vestal being considered *nefas;* only miraculous intercession of the goddess could save the culprit. We know of twelve cases of Vestals being punished in this manner.

We now come to the colleges independent of the pontifices, mentioning first the *VII viri epulones.* Their origin dates from the year 196 B.C., when, owing to the pontifices being overworked, a separate college of seven members was founded, chiefly in order to perform the rites of the sacrificial meal (*epulum Jovis*), taken in the temple of the Capitoline Jupiter, in the presence of the whole senate; the *ludi plebeii* always followed on the next day. In later times such meals were arranged on many public occasions, the *viri epulones* always presiding.

The colleges hitherto mentioned had the care of the worship of the old Roman gods (*dii patrii*); the *XV viri sacris faciundis,*

on the other hand, presided over the religious rites of strange
gods (*dii peregrini*) introduced in Rome. The number of these
priests was, under Tarquinius Superbus, two; since the year 367 B.C.
the college consisted of five patrician and five plebeian members,
to whom five further priests were added, most likely by Sulla.
They had to keep and expound the Sibylline books, and to choose
the new decisions of oracles to be recorded in them. As is well
known, nine books of oracular sayings were offered to Tarquinius
Superbus by the sibyl of Cumæ, three of which the king bought,
while the others were thrown into the flames by the sibyl. These
three books were kept in the temple of the Capitoline Jupiter,
together with which they were destroyed by fire (83 B.C.). A
new collection of oracles was made in Asia Minor (the most fertile
soil for such sayings) and other countries, which again was
deposited in the rebuilt Capitol. The *XV viri* were charged by
Augustus with the critical selection of these oracular sayings,
many corrections and additions being made under subsequent
emperors. Stilicho is said to have burnt these books. In times
of plagues, earthquakes, and the like, these books were consulted
by the priests, and the proper mode of expiation expounded from
them. One of the expiatory acts was the introduction of new
gods. The worship of Apollo, Artemis, Ceres, Dis pater, Venus,
Salus, Mercury, Æsculapius, and Magna Mater (Cybele) were thus
transferred to Rome on the authority of the Sibylline books,
public games being at the same time introduced in honour of
many of these gods, as, for instance, the Apollinaria and Secular
games in honour of Apollo, the *ludi
Cereris*, in honour of Ceres and the
Megalenses to celebrate the Magna
Mater. Fig. 493 refers to the worship
of the latter goddess. The figure
of the vestal drawing with her girdle
the vessel on whose deck Cybele is
seated, is Claudia Quinta. A late
Roman bas-relief on a sarcophagus

Fig. 493.

represents a scene from the grand procession preceding the
ludi circenses during the festive days of the Megalenses (see
Gerhard, "Ant. Denkm.," Taf. CXX. 1). The image of Cybele
in her chariot drawn by lions is carried on the shoulders

of seventeen persons. The two figures clad with the toga, opening the procession, are most likely two of the *XV viri*.

The *augures* also were fifteen in number. Their institution coincided with the foundation of the city, Romulus himself being mentioned as the first augur. No public act or ceremony in peace or war, no inauguration or exauguration could be performed without the augurs' assistance, who, according to certain rules, derived the will of the gods from the appearance, non-appearance, or manner of appearance of the sign. Only the magistrate had a right to consult the augurs about the auspices with reference to public affairs (*spectio*); his questions only were answered by the augur (*nuntiatio*). The important political position of these priests is sufficiently explained by these facts. Standing in the centre of the temple, or temple-enclosure, under a tent (*tabernaculum*) the augur (after having divided the holy precinct into regions with a smooth stick slightly bent at the top, *lituus*, see Fig. 494) turned towards the south, and, offering prayers, expected the divine message. Lightning (*servare de cœlo*) and the flight of birds were the

Fig. 494.

principal signs. The lightnings coming from the left (*fulmina sinistra*) were considered favourable, those from the right unfavourable. The Etruscans had no less than eleven categories of lightnings, according to their direction, colour, &c.: the Roman theory was less elaborate, the lightnings being classified only according to their occurring in the night or daytime; in imperial times, however, the Etruscan theories were more generally adopted, which

had previously been the case only in a few instances, such as the purification of places struck by the lightning. For, like the body of the dead, the lightning had to be buried, which was done by building a shaft with walls of masonry, which protruded from the ground like the rim of a fountain (whence the name *puteal*); this tomb of the lightning was inscribed, *Fulgus conditum;* another name, *bidental*, was derived from the circumstance of an animal two years old being sacrificed on the spot. A puteal consisting of a round structure resting on eight Doric columns has been found at Pompeii. Fig. 493 represents a puteal from a denarius of L. Scribonius Libo, with the inscription, PVTEAL

Fig. 495.

SCRIBON.* We observe laurel-wreaths, lyres, and a pair of pincers on the puteal, which has the form of an altar. Scribonius had been commissioned by the Senate to find the spot struck by lightning, and had, in consequence, erected a puteal in the temple of Minerva.

The birds of omen (*signa ex avibus*) were divided by the augur into such whose cry (*oscines*) and into such whose flight (*alites*) signified the divine will. To the former class belonged the raven, the crow, the owl, the woodpecker, and the cock; to the latter, the eagle (*Jovis ales*), hawk, and vulture. These auspices were in later times (particularly during campaigns, or on other occasions when no augur was present) supplied by the signs derived from the manner of eating observed in the sacred hens (*auspicia pullaria* or *auspicia ex tripudiis*). Hens were kept in a cage for the purpose; in case the animals devoured their dumplings (*offa pultis*) as soon as the hen-keeper (*pullarius*) opened the hen-coop, the omen was favourable, particularly if they dropped little pieces while eating (*tripudium sollistimum*); in case they refused to eat or to leave the cage, evil might be anticipated.

Fig. 496.

Sometimes the pullarii or augurs used undoubtedly artificial means in bringing about the desired omen. Fig. 496 shows a hen-coop with two chickens eating, from a cameo (several cameos with similar representations are in the Berlin Museum; compare Toelken, "Verzeichniss der antik vertieft geschnittenen Steine der kgl. Preuss. Gemmensammlung," p. 77, No. 175, and p. 250, No. 1484 *et seq.*). We finally mention the two less important auguria *ex quadrupedibus* and *ex diris*. To meet certain animals, such as a wolf, a fox, a snake, &c., was considered an evil augury.

The *haruspices*, nearly related to the augures, were of Etruscan origin: under the Republic they were consulted only in a few individual cases; under the emperors they gained more importance, remaining, however, inferior to the other priestly colleges.

* On the puteal depicted on a gold coin of Æmilia Scribonia we see a hammer instead of these pincers; see Cohen, "Descr. gén. des Monnaies de la Répubi. Rom.," pl. I.

They also expounded and procured lightnings and "prodigies," and moreover examined the intestines of sacrificed animals ; their more developed Etruscan method competing successfully with that of their Roman colleagues. Besides drawing down the lightning by their art, &c., the haruspices had made a speciality of the inspection of the intestines of animals. Heart, liver, and lungs were carefully examined, every anomaly being explained in a favourable or unfavourable sense. Although on solemn occasions the haruspices were officially invited to Rome for consultation, their art was never much esteemed by the more enlightened classes. Cato's saying, that no haruspex could look at his fellow without laughing, is significant in this respect.

The fifth college of priests, that of the *Salii*, was traced back to Numa. In his time a shield of peculiar form (*ancile*) is said to have dropped from the sky. To prevent it from being stolen the king ordered eleven other shields exactly like it to be made by the artist Mamurius. In order to keep these shields a college of twelve priests, the Salii, was instituted on the Palatine. Unfortunately for the story, however, there was another college of Salii, of Sabine origin, on the Quirinal hill, the former being devoted to the worship of Mars, the latter to that of Quirinus ; both were undoubtedly representatives of the oldest worship of Mars, whose name is also connected with the above-mentioned tradition of the shield. In the month of March, devoted to that god, the feast in his honour was celebrated. Clad in the toga picta and in full armour, the toga prætexta, worn above them, being tied in a Gabine knot, the head covered with the helmet (resembling the above-mentioned apex), armed with sword and lance, and carrying (on the left arm or fastened round the neck) the ancile, the Salii walked through the streets in solemn procession, dancing a warlike dance (whence their name) before every sanctuary, and beating their shields with their lances or staffs to the measure of an old song, the words of which (*axamenta, assamenta, carmina saliaria*) had, at a later period, become incomprehensible to the priests themselves. These songs celebrated Janus, Jupiter, Juno, Minerva, and Mars, the names of departed citizens being added to these as a mark of highest distinction. During the greater part of March these processions were repeated daily, and returned every evening to the quarters (*mansiones*) of the Salii, several of which existed in Rome.

The ancilia were carried into the house by servants on poles (they were not allowed to touch them), a festive meal, celebrated for its sumptuousness, ending the proceedings. Fig. 497, from a cameo in the Florentine collection, shows several of these ancilia being carried by servants in the manner described. A silver coin of the Gens Licinia (Cohen, " Desc. gén. des Monnaies de la Républ. Rom.," pl. XXIV.) shows two ancilia and an apex with the inscription, PVBL. STOLO III VIR.

Fig. 497.

The next college of priests, that of the *Fetiales,* also dates back from the time of the first kings. They had to perform the sacred rites accompanying declarations of war and treaties of peace or alliance. Usually four Fetiales, with a speaker (*pater patratus*), were sent by the king, and afterwards by the senate, to foreign nations to demand satisfaction for injuries received. They were clad in priestly robes, and in front of them were carried holy herbs (*sagmina*), which the consul or prætor delivered to them in the Capitol, after having touched with them the forehead of the pater patratus. Thus equipped they demanded satisfaction from the foreign nation, calling down the wrath of the gods upon their own heads in case their requests were unjust. On this demand being refused they returned to Rome, and after an interval of from ten to thirty days the pater patratus declared war by throwing a bloody spear across the frontier into the enemy's country in the presence of three witnesses. When the Roman territory began to extend more and more this ceremony was performed in Rome itself, a piece of ground near the temple of Bellona being considered as the enemy's country (*terra hostilis*), on which a *columna bellica* was erected at a later period. At least two Fetiales had to be present at the conclusion of treaties of alliance, viz. the pater patratus and the herald carrying the holy herbs (*verbenarius*). After the words of the treaty had been read, a pig was killed with a pebble (*silex*) kept in the temple of Jupiter Feretrius, whence the expression *fœdus ferire.* This ceremony is represented on a silver coin of the Gens Antistia, and on a number of coins of the cities of Capua and Atella.

The only remaining priestly college, that of the *Curiones* and the religious sodalities of the *Luperci, Titii,* and *Fratres Arvales,*

we refrain from noticing for want of monumental evidence. The
head-dress of the last-mentioned sodality consisted of a crown of
wheat-ears.

The dress of those going to pray or sacrifice was usually
white, a symbol of guiltlessness and chastity. The sacrificial
utensils and the offering itself had to be free from stain ; profane
interruption by word or deed was considered a bad omen, whence
the exclamation *favete linguis*, pronounced at the beginning of
the sacrifice. A flute-player accompanied the holy act on his
instrument, as appears from the representation of a sacrifice on
an earthen lamp (Passerius, "Lucernæ Fict.," I. 35). To the
right of the altar stands the priest, and an assistant carrying a
box of incense ; to the left we see the butcher with his axe ; in
the foreground several fettered bulls lie on the ground, and behind
the altar a tibicen is playing on the double-flute.

Prayers to the celestial gods were offered standing and with
hands held up to the eastern sky (see the bas-relief of a praying
woman, Zoega, "Bassiril," vol. i. Tav. 18). The gods of the
nether world were propitiated by touching the earth with the
hands, and the *supplicationes* were offered kneeling; at the suppli-
cations for the averting of threatening evil, women appeared with
loosened hair. Unlike the Greek, the Roman sacrificed with the
toga pulled over the back of his head in the manner of a veil ;
only the sacrifices imported from Greece were performed (*Græco
ritu*) bareheaded.

In the oldest time the offerings were bloodless: first fruits,
mola salsa, milk, honey, wine, and cakes were offered. The
animals (which began to be sacrificed under the last kings) were
divided by the Romans into *victimæ* and *hostiæ*, *i.e.* heifers and
smaller animals, offered to different gods according to holy custom.
After having been examined, and found without blemish, the
animal was led by the attendant (*popa*) to the flower-crowned
altar, the resistance, and still more the flight, of the animal being
looked upon as a bad omen. The horns of oxen and wethers were
frequently gilt, and the animals always adorned with ribbons and
ties (*vittæ, infulæ*), partly wound round the horns, partly spread
over the back (compare Figs. 498, 539, and 492, *b*, *l*). The
question "*agone ?*" of the sacrificial butcher (*victimarius*) was
answered by the officiating priest with "*hoc age*," after which the

priest strewed mola salsa and incense on the head of the animal, and burnt a bunch of hair cut from between its horns; he also drew with a knife a line on the back of the animal from the forehead to the tail. The victim thus prepared (*macta est*) was killed by the victimarius with an axe (*securis, bipennis*, Fig. 492, *e*) or mallet (*malleus*, Fig. 492, *f*), provided it was a large animal: pigs, sheep, and birds had their throats pierced with a knife by the *cultrarius*, who caught the blood in a vase (Fig. 492, *e*); it was then poured over and round the altar. After this the body was opened with the *secespita* (Fig. 492, *g*), and the intestines taken out with smaller knives (*cultri*, Fig. 492, *d*), and examined by the haruspices. In case of an unfavourable omen the sacrifice had to be renewed; otherwise the intestines were sprinkled with wine and burnt on the altar amidst prayers. A libation of wine and incense, the former poured from an amphora (*præfericulum*, Fig. 492, *c*), the latter taken from a box (*acerra, turibulum*, Fig. 492, *i*), concluded the sacrifice, after which the priest dismissed those present with the word "*Ilicet.*" A meal followed; prepared by the priests in case the sacrifice

Fig. 498.

had been public, by the family in case it had been private.

To conclude we mention the expiatory sacrifice performed at the end of a lustrum and after the triumph; in the latter case by the triumphator in honour of the Capitoline Jupiter: the technical name was *suovetaurilia, i.e.* sacrifices of pigs, sheep, and oxen. The first-mentioned sacrifice is illustrated by a bas-relief (Clarac, "Musée," pl. 221, No. 751) composed of twenty-one figures. On the left we see the censor inserting the names of citizens and soldiers in the census lists; two musicians play on the cithara and flute respectively. To the right three crowned animals are brought forward by the servants, while another attendant carries a box of incense on his shoulders. The priest

is pouring the libation into a vase presented to him by a *camillus*.
Fig. 498, taken from the arch of Constantine, represents the
sacrifice of the emperor, surrounded by his army, in honour of
Jupiter after his triumph. The emperor pours a libation on the
burning altar. Suovetaurilia are led forward by crowned servants.
A camillus offers a box of incense to the emperor, while the tibicen
plays on his instrument.

104. Public games were, from the earliest times, connected
with religious acts, the Roman custom tallying in this respect
with the Greek. Such games were promised to the gods to gain
their favour, and afterwards carried out as a sign of gratitude for
their assistance. Such vows (*vota pro salute rei publicæ*) were
made on the 1st of January of every year by the new-elected
consuls, according to a formula first pronounced by the Pontifex
Maximus; after Cæsar's time special *vota pro salute principis* were
added to these. The expenses of the games thus promised
(whether the vow was made in Rome by the highest magistrate
or in the field by the general) were at once guaranteed, either
from the public treasury or from the booty. These *ludi votivi* were
either performed only once, or repeated annually (*ludi annui,
solemnes, stati, ordinarii*) on a certain day appointed for the
purpose. During the first years of the Republic the consuls had
to arrange the games; but after the creation of ædiles (494 B.C.)
this duty devolved upon them, the higher magistrates only
superintending. The expense was, at least for the greater part,
covered by the State; in later times, however, the public money
by no means sufficed for the splendid preparations required, and
the ædiles, and later on the imperial officials appointed for the
arrangement of the ludi circensis, had frequently to waste their
private property in the service of the multitude. The admission
to the games arranged by the State was gratis; private persons
who arranged games at their own expense (*editor ludi*) were
allowed to raise entrance-fees. In imperial times the number of
annual games increased enormously, the birthday of the emperor,
the anniversary of his accession, the delivery of the empress, the
memorial days of the dead members of the family, becoming
occasions for the ruler to gain the favour of the multitude by the
institution of splendid games. Augustus charged the prætors
with the arrangement of public games, but on the onerous offer

proving too much for them alone, the consuls and quæstors were conjointly made responsible; the arrangement of the most expensive games, however, the emperor reserved to himself, a court official (*curator ludorum*) being appointed for the purpose.

As early as the times of the kings horse and chariot races are said to have taken place in the circus; in 364 B.C. scenic representations introduced from Etruria were added to them. Both were performed either separately or on one and the same occasion, in which latter case the beginning was always made with the scenic representations. Fights of gladiators, at first arranged only by private individuals, soon became an equally important feature of the public games. The agon of gymnastic and musical arts, so highly developed amongst the Greeks, never became popular amongst the Romans. Augustus initiated one of these in memory of the battle of Actium. Nero instituted an agon consisting of horse-races and gymnastic and musical competitions, in the latter of which he took part himself; his agon was a *certamen quinquennale*. The agones were renewed for the last time by Gordianus III.

The nature of the games necessitated different local arrangements. Horse and chariot races took place in the circus, fights of gladiators and wild animals in the amphitheatre, and scenic representations in the theatre (compare §§ 83-85). The two earliest amongst the ludi circenses were the *consualia* and *equiria*, said to have been founded by Romulus; both were celebrated twice a year, the former on the 21st of August and the 15th of December, the latter on February 27th and March 14th; they consisted of chariot-races in the Campus Martius. The *ludi Romani*, also dating from the time of the kings, were celebrated in honour of the three Capitoline deities; they lasted at first only a few days: Augustus extended their duration from September 4th to 19th. The *ludi plebei* were instituted in memory of the confirmation of popular power after the secession on the Aventine; their duration was afterwards extended to a fortnight (November 4th to 17th), the final days being in this, as in the just-mentioned games, reserved for the ludi circenses. The *Cereales* were celebrated from April 12th to April 19th; their institution seems connected with the building, by the dictator Postumius, of a temple for Ceres, Liber, and Libera; at first they were *ludi votivi*, having to be decreed each time by the senate, afterwards they became annual: Cæsar appointed separate *ædiles Cereales*. The *ludi Apollinares* were instituted in consequence of an oracle contained in the *carmina Marciana* to the effect that the expulsion of the Carthaginians would be impossible till games in honour of Apollo were instituted. Ludi circenses took place on the final day, being preceded by dramatic representations. They dated from 212 B.C., being at first *ludi votivi*, afterwards *ludi stati*, celebrated on the 5th July; still later, from the 5th or 6th till the 13th of July. The prætor urbanus was charged with the arrangements. The *ludi Megalenses* (also comprising ludi circenses) were instituted to celebrate the arrival in Rome of the Magna Mater, on April 12th, 204 B.C. In order not to interfere with the Cerealia (April 12th to 19th), these games were celebrated from April 4th to 10th, it being always the custom to add new days not after, but before the day first appointed. We finally mention the *Floralia* (April 28th to May 3rd), the last day of which was occupied with the hunting of tame deer in the Circus Maximus; also the temporary games in honour of Cæsar Augustus (*ludi victoriæ Cæsaris, Augustalia*), &c., always ending in ludi circenses.

About the Circus Maximus we have spoken before (see Fig. 431). A second circus, that of Flaminius, was built 220 B.C. by the censor C. Flaminius in the meadows called after his name. Other buildings of the same kind, partly still recognisable by their ruins, were the results of later times; we mention the circus built by Caligula in the gardens of Agrippina, commonly called the Circus of Nero, also the circus near the grave of Cæcilia Metella (erroneously called Circo di Caracalla), built by Romulus, son of Maxentius, not to speak of numerous racecourses in provincial towns (compare Fig. 430). From circumstantial evidence (such as the plan of the circus of Bovillæ, Fig. 430, sculptural representations, and descriptions by the authors) we are able to give an accurate account of the arrangements of the Circus Maximus, which itself has disappeared almost entirely.

On entering through the festive entrance-gate (to both sides of which lay the cages, *carceres*, for the racing-chariots) one observed, in the centre of the course, the spina, with three conical columns (*metæ*, *i.e.* goals) at each end. The spina itself was adorned with columns, small sanctuaries, statues of gods, and a tall mast, instead of which Augustus erected the obelisk now in

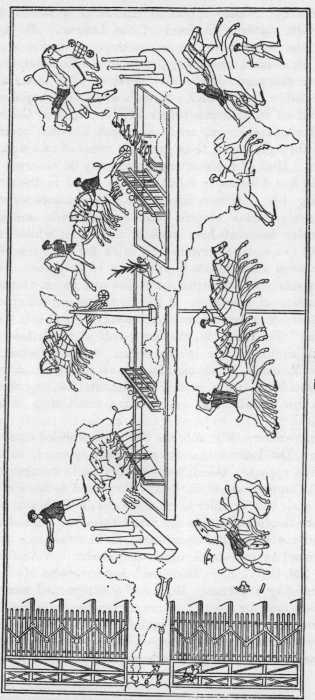

Fig. 499.

the Piazza del Popolo. Constantine added a second higher obelisk, now standing in front of the Lateran. M. Agrippa adorned the spina with seven water-spouts in the shape of dolphins, in allusion, most likely, to Neptunus Equester, to whom races were dedicated. Here also stood an altar (see Gerhard, " Antike Bildw.," Taf. CXX., 2) with seven egg-shaped objects (*ova*) lying on it, in remembrance of the origin of Castor and Pollux, horse-breakers *par excellence*. Each time the course had been run through, one of these eggs was removed as a sign to the spectators. Most of these arrangements may be observed in the mosaic, 15 feet 6 inches by 9 feet 6 inches, found in the circus of Lyons, Fig. 499. On both sides of the chief entrance we see four carceres; we further observe three conical metæ standing on semircircular bases at both ends of the spina, which is here formed by two water-reservoirs with brick facings, each of them filled by seven water-spouts in the shape of dolphins. Between the two ponds rises an obelisk, while the ova lie on two rows of poles standing in the water. A different arrangement appears in a bas-relief on a late Roman sarcophagus (Gerhard, " Antike Bildwerke," Taf. CXX., 2), the lower half of which most likely represents a chariot race in the circus, in the presence of the Emperor Maximus. The spina there is adorned with an obelisk, two Korinthian columns, and a Korinthian base, on which the dolphins are placed. The ova lie on a small altar at a little distance.

We have shown, Fig. 258, the light two-wheeled chariot used at races. The Roman charioteers (*auriga, agitator*), unlike the Greek who appeared naked, wore a short tunic strapped tightly round the upper part of the body; they used to have a curved knife in their belt, in order to cut the traces on the horses running away; the thighs had straps tied round them (see the statue of an auriga in the Museo Pio Clementino), or else the arms and legs were dressed in reticulated tights (see Gerhard, " Antike Bild-werke," Taf. CXX., 2). Their head-dress consisted of a leathern cap resembling a helmet. Bigæ and quadrigæ, and more rarely trigæ, were used for racing; an inscription mentions the victor of a race won with seven horses running in a row. In the biga the two horses were yoked together, in the quadriga only the two wheel-horses carried the yoke. Favourite charioteers and horses

were received by the public with loud applause. Sicily, Spain,
Africa, Cappadocia, &c., were celebrated for their race-horses,
whose pedigree, age, and name were recorded with the utmost
accuracy. The left wheel horse was watched with particular
anxiety, because it had the most difficult task in doubling the
meta ; its running against, or being frightened at, the meta
exposed chariot and charioteer to the danger of destruction. In
inscriptions the name of the victorious horse is frequently mentioned together with that of the charioteer.

The umpire, sitting on a balcony above the chief entrance-
portal, gave the sign for beginning the race by throwing a white
cloth (*mappa*) into the arena (compare Fig. 499). On the towers
or *oppida* mentioned by us stood musicians, who played in the
intervals between the races. The chariots began the race from
the right hand side of the entrance-portal, keeping on the right
side of the spina, and returning on the left after doubling the
meta ; in this way the course was measured seven times without
stopping. After the last time they left the circus through the
carceres on the left side of the chief entrance. The whole race of
seven courses was called *missus*, a single course being denominated
curriculum or *spatium*. Usually four chariots ran at a time ;
the first arrival after the missus at a line marked with chalk
in front of the carceres on the left being decisive as to the victory.
In republican times about ten or twelve races were run in a
day ; after Caligula the usual number seems to have been twenty-
four, an amount sufficient to fill up the whole day. Counting the
length of the Circus Maximus, which had to be measured fourteen
times, at three stadia, the whole distance run in each missus
amounts to 25,176 feet, Rhenish measure. Making allowance
for preparations, removing of impediments, and smaller intervals
after the completion of six races, &c., and counting the day
at twelve hours in which the twenty-four races were run,
the time for each race may be roughly calculated at twenty-five
minutes.

Sometimes the ordinary number of four chariots must have
been increased to six, as appears from the temporary existence
of six "factions" of the circus (of which more anon), and from
the fact that the circus of Maxentius had twelve carceres.

In republican times already, two parties of the circus

(*factiones*) had been formed, each of which furnished two of the racing-chariots, the charioteers wearing either red or white tunics, according to the party they belonged to. The names of these parties were *factio albata* and *factio russata*. The increased *insania et furor circi* of imperial times called two new parties into life, the *factio prasina* (green) and the *factio veneta* (blue) ; under Domitian two other parties, the *aurea* and *purpurea*, were temporarily added to these. About the end of the third century A.D., the four original factions were combined into two, white joining green, and red blue, the *prasina* and *veneta* taking the lead, followed by the two other colours, whose separate existence, however, did not entirely cease. These four colours appear in the tunics of the mosaic of Lyons (Fig. 499) : in our illustration the oblique lines signify green, the horizontal ones blue, and the vertical ones red ; while the white tunics are left blank. In Constantinople these parties (δῆμοι) of the circus received a political character, and frequently made the circus the scene of their internecine warfare. In 501 A.D., under Anastasius, 3,000 citizens were thus killed in the hippodrome : during the so-called Nika revolt, A.D. 532, under Justinian, no less than 30,000 people were killed in three days, the throne being saved only by means of the German soldiers under Belisarius.

In older times the charioteers were free citizens ; afterwards this occupation, although never dishonourable, like that of the gladiators, was considered unworthy of a free Roman, and therefore mostly left to slaves and freedmen, who, previous to appearing in public, were trained at schools. Such schools, comprising a complete staff of chariot-makers, tailors, shoemakers, surgeons, teachers, &c., were kept by one or several *domini factionum*, who let out both chariots and charioteers to the highest bidding of the parties of the circus. Victorious charioteers received silver crowns, valuable garments, and money ; the successful ones amongst them frequently made large fortunes, and became *domini factionum* on their own account.

Horse-races were not run in the Roman circus : occasionally a horseman appeared with two horses (*desultores*), who jumped from one on the other while they were running at full speed, a trick learned from the Numidian cavalry (see Bartoli, " Lucerne Antiche," p. 24). The destination of the horsemen seen riding by the side of the chariots (see, for instance, Fig. 499, and Gerhard, *loc. cit.*, Taf. CXX. 2) seems uncertain.

Like the charioteers, the wrestlers and athletes appearing in the circus were, at least in later times, always professional men. Only exceptionally, and by express command of the emperor, Roman noblemen appeared in this capacity. Different in the military games and evolutions, *ludi sevirales* and *ludus Troiæ;* the former, instituted by Augustus in honour of Mars, were performed in the circus by six *turmæ* of Roman knights with three *seviri* at their head, and commanded by the *princeps iuventutis,* a title borne by the imperial princes, and, after Caracalla, claimed by the emperors themselves; the imperial coins with the inscription PRINC. IVV. showing a galloping horseman, refer to the *ludi sevirales.* The *ludus Troiæ* was a military exercise performed by boys of noble families on horseback.

Whether all ludi circenses were opened with a *pompa* seems uncertain; the fact is proved, however, of the *ludi Romani, Megalenses,* and the *ludi votivi;* it may be assumed with tolerable certainty of the *ludi Cereris.* The procession was opened by a band of musicians, followed by the officiating magistrate in a triumphal chariot, clad in the costume of a *triumphator,* and holding in his hand an ivory sceptre adorned with an eagle. A *servus publicus* held a golden crown studded with jewels over his head. His chariot was surrounded by white-robed clients (see Fig. 540), and followed by the images of the gods, with the priestly sodalities and colleges belonging to them, also by the statues of the reigning family, and of those of the deceased members of that family to whom the games were devoted. This splendid procession, starting from the Capitol, traversed the Forum, the Vicus Tuscus, the Velabrum, and Forum Boarium, entering the Circus Maximus through the chief entrance. Accompanied by the applause of the spectators, who rose to their feet, it once walked round the nearest meta, and repaired to the seats reserved for the purpose, whereat the sign for the beginning of the race was given in the manner described.

105. The fights of gladiators and the baiting of wild animals took place in the amphitheatre (see § 85). The former became known in Rome in the third century B.C., and were thence introduced into Athens, where at first they were little relished by

the refined inhabitants. Only after the conquered Greeks had become demoralised they accepted this, with other Roman customs. The origin of the gladiatorial games must, most likely, be looked for in Etruria, where they formed part of the funereal ceremonies, replacing the still older custom of human sacrifices ; they seem to have been connected with the worship of Saturn—an opinion confirmed by the fact that in Rome duels of this kind originally formed part of the Saturnalia—a limitation soon swept away by the growing passion for such exhibitions. It was natural to the warlike spirit of the republican Romans to wish for the continuation of the scenes of war on a smaller scale at home; but the gloating over the sight of the *vilis sanguis* of the slaves, indulged in to an ever-increasing degree, was more apt to breed cruel tyrants than high-minded patriots.

The first *munus gladiatorium* was, according to Valerius Maximus, arranged by the brothers Marcus and Decimus Brutus in the Forum Boarium (264 B.C.) on the occasion of their father's burial. Rome did not possess an amphitheatre at that time. Several other gladiatorial fights are mentioned in connection with funerals. In the year 200 B.C. the sons of Marcus Valerius Lævinus arranged a fight of twenty-five pairs of gladiators at his funeral. In 174 B.C. T. Flaminius arranged a fight lasting three days in honour of his deceased father, seventy-four gladiators being hired for the occasion. The development of gladiatorial games as an established institution belongs to the last years of the Republic. Schools of gladiators (*ludi gladiatorii*), comprising the *familiæ gladiatorum*, owned by the State or private individuals (*lanistæ*), were formed in Rome and many other cities of the empire. They became the rallying-points of many of the most depraved elements of Roman society, and the revolts of the slaves and gladiators more than once endangered the State. Most of the fighters appearing at the public fights came from these schools. Soon these fights became an essential feature of the public games ; the ædiles and other magistrates, and ultimately the emperors themselves, trying to gain popularity by means of them (*ad plebem placandam et mulcendam*). The lex Tullia against gladiatorial extravagance, moved by Cicero less from humane considerations than in order to stay the party intrigues furthered by such exhibitions, was but too soon forgotten. Augustus (22 B.C.) ordered

that fights of gladiators should take place only twice a year after
the consent of the senate had been obtained, the number of the
gladiators being limited to 120 ; but this restriction was cancelled
by Caracalla, who arranged battles of gladiators fighting not only
in couples but *catervatim.* He even compelled twenty-six knights
who had ruined themselves to appear in this dishonourable combat.
Many characteristic incidents of the gladiatorial fights arranged by
Claudius, Nero, and Domitian are recorded by the authors ; even
Trajan, after his return from the victorious campaign on the
Danube, arranged festive gladiatorial games lasting 123 days,
10,000 fighters being engaged for the occasion. Commodus, of
whom Lampridius relates, " *et nomina gladiatorum recepit eo gaudio,
quasi acciperet triumphalia,*" and who designated himself as *primus
palus secutorum,* brought the passion for exhibitions of this kind to
its climax, the income of the State being squandered for this ignoble
purpose. Even the Christian emperors were obliged to buy the
favour of the populace, and divert its attention from political
passions by inhumane spectacles of this kind. Private schools of
gladiators, and gangs of them amongst the *familiæ* of rich Romans,
were of common occurrence during the last years of the Republic.
The emperors often used to establish imperial institutions of the
same kind. Domitian built in Rome four large gladiatorial
schools, viz., the *ludus Gallicus, Dacius, magnus,* and *matutinus.*
Several towns, as Præneste, Ravenna, and Alexandria, were
recommended for the same purpose, owing to their healthy situation. Capua was, from the first, celebrated for its gladiatorial
schools. In Pompeii, barracks of gladiators have been recognised as such by Garrucci by the fittings, by inscriptions, and pictures of gladiators, &c., scribbled on walls and columns, and by
the numerous gladiatorial weapons found there. The structure
consists of an open court (55 by 40·10 metres) surrounded by
colonnades, and adjoined by buildings of two stories, containing
sixty-six separate rooms. Counting two gladiators to each room,
the number of the inmates must have been 132. Captive
Germans, Dacians, Gauls, Æthiopians, &c., as also slaves and
criminals condemned to death, were received as members of the
familia gladiatorum ; even free-born Romans, after having wasted
their property, frequently sold themselves to the *lanistæ,* receiving
sums of money (*auctoramentum gladiatorium*) as the price of their

infamy (*auctorati*). Guided by the fencing-master (*doctores* or *magistri*), and fed on a peculiar diet (*sagina*, chosen with a view to strengthen the muscles), the apprenticed gladiator (*tiro*) practised the technical manipulations of his art at first with light wooden, and afterwards with exceedingly heavy, weapons against a post or a straw puppet. After having got successfully through his public *début*, he received an oblong tablet of ivory (*tessera gladiatoria*) as a reward, and sign of his proficiency, on which were written his name, that of his master, and the day of his first fight and

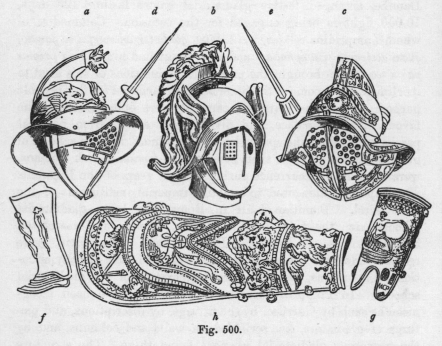

Fig. 500.

victory. The tiro was thus admitted to the rank of the *spectati* (distinguished persons): a certain number of these decorations most likely entitled the gladiator to be received amongst the *veterani*. About sixty genuine *tesseræ* marked SP, in rare cases SPECT or SPECTAT (*spectatus*), have been discovered (compare Fr. Ritschl, "Die Tesseræ gladiatoriæ der Römer." München, 1864).

A number of weapons of gladiators have been found; by means of these, and of numerous specimens seen in pictures and plastic representations, we are enabled to give an accurate account of their form, which essentially differs from that of the weapons used by legionaries. Several gladiatorial helmets are kept in the Museo Borbonico : the one shown Fig. 500, *c*, has a massive crest adorned with sculptures; a broad brim serves to protect neck and forehead. The visor consists of four plates, the two lower ones being massive, the two upper ones pierced with holes like a sieve for the gladiator to look through. The visor in Fig. 500, *b*, consists of two plates, with an opening for the eye in each; the opening on the left being round, while that on the right resembles a sieve. Fig. 500, *a*, shows a helmet of a similar kind also kept in the Museo Borbonico. Many different kinds of the gladiatorial helmet appear on the monuments.

The shield of the gladiator was the square, oval, or circular *parma* (compare Fig. 505), differing from that used in the army by its lighter weight and more graceful form, &c. An oblong shield of a very different form, with rounded edges and a curve at the upper end to ease the movements of the shoulder and upper arm, is kept in the Museo Borbonico. The right hand and arm were protected by straps of leather (compare Fig. 505) or by iron splints (Fig. 500, *g*). The way of protecting the legs seems to have differed amongst the various classes of gladiators. Some appear with straps round their thighs, while their shins are protected by greaves (Fig. 505). Others wear greaves or leather gaiters (resembling the κάλτζα of the modern Greeks) on the right or the left leg only (Fig. 500, *f*, compare Fig. 505) ; others, again, wear the foot-coverings of the legionaries, or appear with naked feet (Fig. 501). Fig. 500, *g*, *h*, shows two richly ornamented, not to say overloaded, coverings for arm and thigh, from originals in the Museo Borbonico.

The aggressive weapons of the gladiators were the lance, the dagger, straight or curved, and the Roman sword, or, in its stead, the rapier (Fig. 500, *d*, *e*, compare Fig. 504). The gladiator's chest was uncovered; his body was dressed in a loose garment fastened with a belt, and hanging down to the knees in front, but pulled up on the hips (Figs. 502, 503).

The different classes of gladiators were distinguished by their weapons and by their mode of fighting. The *Samnites* derived their name from their peculiar equipment, imitated from that nation.* It consisted of a large oblong shield (*scutum*), a helmet with visor, crest, and plume, a greave on the left leg, and a sleeve of leather or metal for the right arm, to which a shoulder-piece (*galerus*) reaching above the shoulder was attached (compare

Fig. 501 *a.*

"Bullet. Napol." New Series, I., Tav. 7). Their sword was short. It is difficult to distinguish the Samnites amongst the numerous statues of gladiators ; neither does it appear from the authors what class of gladiators was usually opposed to them, for the gladiators

Fig. 501 *b.*

fighting with each other never belonged to the same class. A second class of gladiators, much liked in imperial times, were the *secutores*, whose antagonists were the *retiarii*. The latter wore a short tunic or apron (*subligaculum*), fastened round the body with

* It is said that after the defeat of the Samnites by the Dictator Papirius Cursor in the year 444 of the city, their national armour was adopted for the gladiators as a sign of contempt.

a belt, and generally a sleeve on the left arm. Their head was
uncovered. Their weapons of attack were the trident (*fuscina,
tridens*) and the dagger; besides which they
carried a large net (*iaculum*), in which they
tried to entangle the *secutores*, the latter
being armed with helmet, shield, and sword.
Suetonius, in his life of Caligula (cap. 30), tells
of a fight between five gladiators of each class,
in which the retiarii were beaten without
offering resistance; but when by command of
the emperor they were to be killed, one of
them suddenly took a *fuscina* and killed all
the *secutores*. A mosaic (Fig. 501, *a, b*)
illustrates their mode of fighting. In Fig.
501, *a*, the secutor, entangled in the net, attacks

Fig. 502.

the retiarius lying on the ground, while the latter, having dropped
his trident, defends himself with a dagger. In Fig. 501, *b*, the
retiarius attacks his entangled
antagonist with the fuscina,
seemingly with success. According to Isidorus, the secutores
carried a stick with lead bullets
attached to it, with which they
tried to keep off the net.*

The *laquearii* also were light-
armed gladiators. They carried
a sort of lasso, which they threw
over their antagonist in order
to pull him down. They were
of late imperial origin. The
myrmillo and the *Gallus* were
frequently opposed to the retiarius. Their armour was that
of the Gauls, the name *myrmillo*

Fig. 503.

being derived from a fish (μορμύλος) adorning the crest of their
helmet. Fig. 502, taken from a tomb, most likely represents a

---

* " *Gestabat enim cuspidem et massam plumbeam, quæ adversarii iaculum impediret, ut
antequam feriret rete, iste superaret ;* " compare *Revue Archéol.*, IX., p. 80.

myrmillo. A fight between a myrmillo and a retiarius is represented in the mosaic pavement of the Roman villa at Nennig (see
v. Wilmowsky, "Die röm. Villa zu Nennig "). The *torques* round
the neck of the gladiator in our illustration (Fig. 502) indicates the
Gallus, while the crest of the helmet hung on the pole distinctly shows
the fish, characteristic of the myrmillo. Another class of gladiators,
frequently mentioned in imperial times, were the *Thraces*. They
were armed with a small round shield (*parma*), greaves, and a
dagger, either curved like a scythe (*sica*, frequently seen on
imperial monuments in the hands of barbarian warriors) or bent
in a straight-lined angle. The *hoplomachi* were completely armed
with helmet, cuirass, and greaves. Gladiators also fought in chariots
or on horseback. A large bas-relief at Pompeii (Fig. 505) contains
two *equites*, wearing helmets with closed visors; their arms, like

Fig. 504.

those of the scutores, were protected by straps; their offensive
and defensive weapons were the *spiculum* and *parma* respectively.
The gladiators fighting in chariots were called *essedarii*. This
mode of fighting seems to have been introduced by Cæsar, in
imitation of the skilful manœuvres of the chariot-fighters of
Brittany described by him ("De Bello Gall.," IV. 33). We
finally mention the *andabatæ*, who wore helmets with closed visors,
containing no opening for the eyes; and the *dimachæri*, who
fought with two swords, a mode of fighting belonging exclusively
to a later age. Fig. 503 perhaps represents a gladiator of this
kind—a supposition which, however, has been greatly doubted of
late.

The announcement of gladiatorial fights was made by *libelli* sent to the people in the neighbourhood or by advertisements on the walls (*programmata*). An inscription on the Basilica of Pompeii announces the appearance of the "family" of the lanista, N. Festus Ampliatus, in these words: " *N. Festi Ampliati familia gladiatoria pugnabit iterum, pugnabit XVI kal. Iunias, venatio, vela.*" In these advertisements the number and names of the gladiators and the mode of their fighting were announced. On the day of the performance a solemn procession of gladiators, walking in couples, went through the streets to the arena; there the weapons were examined, and a sort of introductory fight (*prolusio*) with blunt weapons (*arma lusoria*) opened the proceedings. The sound of a bugle announced the commencement of the real fight. The words of command were shouted: " *Ponite iam gladios hebetes, pugnatur iam acutis,*" whereat the lanista or *editor muneris gladiatorii* determined the position of the antagonists, and drew the limits within which the battle was to be fought. Fig. 504, from a Pompeian wall-painting, illustrates these preparations. In the centre stands the lanista marking the lines in the sand with a stick. One of the gladiators stands ready for the fight, while an assistant presents his sword to him; his antagonist is blowing the signal-horn, while two attendants cowering in the background hold his helmet and shield in readiness. On one of the gladiators being disabled, the words " *Hoc habet* " were shouted. The wounded man dropped his weapons (*arma submittit*) and, holding up his forefinger, begged his life from the people, or from the lanista or editor muneris in case he was their

Fig. 505.

private property. In imperial times the emperor, of course, had
the decision of life and death. In case the spectators lifted their
clenched fists (*verso pollice*) the fight had to be continued; the
waving of handkerchiefs was the sign of mercy granted. A
gladiator who had behaved in a cowardly manner had no claim
to mercy; he had to take up his weapon (*ferrum recipere*), and
was, if necessary, compelled by whipping or burning with a hot
iron to resume the fight. In case the fight was *sine remissione*
(*i.e.* without quarter asked or given) no appeal to the people
could take place. The victor was rewarded with a palm-branch,
crowns, and, in imperial times, money. The blunt rapier (*rudis*)
given to a gladiator signified his release; he then again became
a slave till the granting of the pileus made him a freedman.

Fig. 505 shows a large bas-relief adorning the wall of the erroneously so-called tomb of Scaurus at Pompeii. The two equites in
the left corner (armed both alike) we have mentioned before.
The curved spike of their helmets is remarkable. The two next
following gladiators are also armed alike, but for the coverings of
their legs. One of them, bleeding from a wound in his chest, is
leaning on his shield, and implores mercy with lifted forefinger,
his unwounded antagonist seeming to wait for the permission to
continue the fight. In the next group one of the gladiators,
wounded in his chest, and sunk on his knee, implores mercy in
the manner just described; he has dropped shield and lance, and
turns his head towards his threatening antagonist. Here we
notice a difference of greaves and shields in the two gladiators.
The third group shows the final execution of a conquered
gladiator by his victor. A figure holding a trident, most likely
an assistant destined to carry off the killed gladiator through the
porta libitinensis to the death-chamber (*spoliarium*), lays hold of
the dying man. Another official of the same kind is seen in the
background. If on arriving in the death-chamber there remained
signs of life in the vanquished gladiator, it was the duty of these
people to kill him.

Another spectacle, no less sanguinary, of which, in imperial
times, the amphitheatre, and in some cases the circus, were the
scene, is the *renatio* of wild animals, the introduction of which
dates back to the year 186 B.C. Like the gladiators, the fighters
with animals (*bestiarii, renatores*) were trained at schools (*familiæ*

venatoriæ). Sometimes they were hirelings, sometimes captives or criminals, compelled to fight the ferocious animals in the arena. In the latter case the spectacle of untrained men imperfectly armed or quite without defence exposed to the fury of the animals must have been horrible. At other times these animals, made furious by hunger or fire, were let loose at each other. The rarest animals from the most distant regions

were brought to Rome for the purpose. Pompeius arranged a fight of 500 or 600 lions, 18 elephants, and 410 other ferocious animals brought from Africa. In a chase arranged by Augustus (A.D. 5), 36 crocodiles were killed in the Flaminian circus, flooded for the purpose. Caligula arranged a

Fig. 506.

fight between 400 bears and an equal number of African wild beasts. The authors are full of horrid descriptions of animal-fights under the later emperors, at which frequently numbers of captives lost their lives. Amongst the numerous plastic representations of such scenes we have chosen (Fig. 506) a bas-relief rendering a fight of armed bestiarii with animals near the theatre of Marcellus,

Fig. 507.

which is seen in the background. The animals (a bear, panther, and lion) wear the leathern girths with rings attached to them, by means of which they were fettered in their cages underneath the arena. Figs. 507 and 508 render subjects of a similar nature; they are taken from the above-mentioned gladiatorial bas-relief on a tomb at Pompeii. The former shows the fight between a bestiarius and a panther or tiger leashed to a bull,

which latter is made to advance by the pricks of the lance of
another bestiarius. This is one of the less dangerous tricks
of professional bestiarii. Fig. 508 shows
a bestiarius with arm and leg protected
by straps, and holding in his hand a
cloth to be thrown over the head of the
attacking bear.

Fig. 508.

A third spectacle produced at some
of the amphitheatres was the *naumachia*,
or naval combat. The arena was flooded by means of a system
of canals, pipes, and locks; in other cases large ponds were
dug for the purpose. Cæsar built the first naumachia in the
Campus Martius (46 B.C.), large enough for the manœuvres of
two fleets manned by 1,000 soldiers and 2,000 rowers. Augustus
(2 B.C.) built a naumachia of stone in the vicinity of the *horti
Cæsaris*, near the Tiber, in which a naval battle between
Athenians and Persians was fought by thirty vessels. Titus
and Domitian used the Coliseum for the same purpose. Of
existing amphitheatres that of Capua shows the flooding apparatus
in the best state of preservation. The largest of all naval fights
was that arranged by Domitian on the Fucine Lake (52 A.D.).
One hundred men-of-war, manned by 19,000 soldiers and rowers,
attacked each other at the signal of a trumpet blown by a Triton,
who suddenly emerged from the water in the centre of the lake.
The number of killed tends to prove that the battle was by no
means a feigned one.

Sometimes mythological scenes were performed in the arena
with cruel accuracy. Condemned criminals had to mount the
pyre like Hercules, or to give their hand to the flames like
Mucius Scævola, or to be crucified like Laureolus the robber;
others were torn by bears, in imitation of the fate of Orpheus.
Mythological scenes of a frivolous kind also were enacted: dwarfs
and women performed sham-fights, &c. Seneca sternly reproves
these levities.

106. The first scenic performances are said to have taken
place in Rome in 364 B.C., when, during a plague, Etruscan
actors performed mimic dances to appease the divine wrath. The
mimic dances thus introduced were soon afterwards accompanied
by the recital of comic verses in changing metres, the result being

the satirical drama (*satura*). The creator of the drama proper
was Livius Andronicus, who first added to the pantomime, accompanied by flute-playing and singing, the dialogue (*diverbium*)
founded on a story or plot (*fabula*). His successors were Nævius,
Ennius, Plautus, Terentius, Pacuvius, Atticus, and others who,
under the influence of Greek models, further developed the
Roman drama. The close relation of Roman to the later Greek
comedy explains the absence of the chorus, which, in its turn,
accounts for the want of the orchestra in Roman theatres, the
space assigned for it in Greek theatres being used for seats of
spectators. The action, therefore, was limited to the stage itself,
which was both wider and deeper than that of the Greeks, to give
space to the numerous actors of the Roman drama,* and to the
gorgeous pageants frequently introduced in imperial times. At
first a temporary wooden stage was erected for the *ludi scenici*,
mostly on the slope of a hill. There were no seats for the public,
neither was a space reserved for the upper classes. The first
distinction of this kind was made in 194 B.C., when the front part
of the cavea was separated from the rest by a barrier, and reserved
for senators. During the next forty years it became the custom
of the rich to have chairs carried after them to the theatre by
slaves; but the original form of the cavea was retained till after
the subjection of Greece, when the first theatre, with semicircular
rows of seats rising in the manner of terraces, was erected; the
seats of the senators were placed immediately in front of the
stage, not without the indignant murmurs of the populace.
Further distinctions soon were made. The fourteen rows behind
the seats of the senators were assigned to the knights, the
priestly colleges received seats of honour; the women were placed
higher up, separated from the men, only the highest steps of
the cavea remaining to the populace. All the theatres built in
the seventh century of the city consisted of wood, and were
pulled down after being used. The first stone theatre was built
by Pompeius in the year 699 of the city (55 B.C.), the second
by Cornelius Balbus, 13 B.C., the third by Augustus in honour of
Marcellus. All the other theatres mentioned in imperial times

---

* In the Greek drama the various parts were divided amongst three actors: not
so in Rome, where each part was performed by a separate actor.

consisted of wood, and were pulled down after having been used once.

About the scenery and mechanical appliances of the Roman theatre nothing certain is known; most likely they resembled those of the Greek stage. The curtain (aulæum), after the performance, did not drop, but was raised. Besides this chief curtain there was a second (siparium) one, closed between the acts; it parted in the middle.

The professional actors were mostly slaves or freedmen, united in troupes (greges, catervæ), and kept by a manager (dominus gregis), frequently by an old principal actor (actor primarum). This manager treated with the magistrate, who had the cura ludorum, and who paid the salary of the actors. Not inconsiderable sums were paid to favourite actors, at least in later times, when the theatre had gained vast popularity : besides this, the actor who had gained the loudest applause was rewarded by the curator ludorum with the palm or crown of victory and honour, in imperial times also with costly robes and money.

Since the time of Terentius actors used to wear masks; up to that time a fair, black, or reddish head-dress (galerus), resembling most likely the onkos of the Greeks, served to mark the actor's age. The costume varied in accordance with the different kinds of masks required for tragedy and comedy (compare Figs. 311 and 312) : in the former long floating garments (syrmata) and the high cothurnus were worn, while comedians appeared in an every-day dress of the loudest possible colours and in low shoes (soccus).

Amongst dramatic representations we also mention the atellanæ, the mimus, and the pantomimus. The atellanæ fabulæ, called after the Oscian city of Atella, were a thoroughly national and thoroughly Italian burlesque, played by young citizens in typical masks. Amongst these types still recognisable in those of the modern commedia dell' arte we mention maccus (arlechino); pappus or casnar, the grave old father of the piece (pantaleone); bucco, the glutton (brighella); and dossennus, the humpbacked charlatan, and soothsayer (dottore). At first these plays, partly improvised, contained only rough parodies of tradesman and peasant life; after the war with Carthage they were developed more regularly by special playwrights, and given on the regular stage as postludes (exodium) of the drama. At the same time the parts were given over to professional actors, the citizens naturally shrinking from an occupation which, even in later times, was at least legally infamous.

The mimus, also, was a sort of burlesque, serving, like the atellanæ, as interlude to the serious drama. The dialogue was witty, frequently coarse, the whole being destined to parody real life in a grotesque, not seldom indecent, manner. The chief actor (*archimimus*) was dressed in the parti-coloured costume of an harlequin (*centunculus*), over which a short cloak (*ricinium*) was worn; he acted before a curtain which divided the front part from the back of the stage. The other characters (amongst which we mention particularly the bald-headed *parasitus* or *stupidus*) played minor parts, mainly seconding, by occasional retorts or gesticulations, the chief actor. Actors of both sexes appeared in the mimus, the grossest obscenities frequently adding to the attractiveness of the play,—at least, at a later period.

The pantomimus was an outgrowth of the *canticum* of the comedy, in which the actor indicated by a dramatic dance or by gesticulations the subject of the song. Already, in republican times, this dance became to be a separate branch of art, brought to its climax of perfection in imperial times by Pylades of Cilicia and Bathyllos of Alexandria. The subjects of the pantomime were taken from the myths of gods and heroes, the actor having to represent male and female characters by turns, while a choir, accompanied by flute-players, sang the corresponding canticum. Sometimes several male and female dancers appeared in the pantomime, which in that case became a sort of dramatic ballet called *pyrrhicha* (not to be mistaken for the Pyrrhic dance of the Dacians).

107. Notwithstanding many descriptions of the Roman army, not to speak of the numerous remaining specimens of weapons, our account of the equipment of the Roman soldier must be in many cases imperfect and conjectural. We shall limit ourselves, in accordance with the aim of our book, to a description of Roman armour as far as it can be illustrated by the remaining monuments. The comparatively small amount of weapons found on the numerous battle-fields is explained by the fact, that a century before our era bronze weapons began to be replaced by iron ones, which latter metal is more liable to destruction by rust.

We first turn to the weapons of defence.   The Roman helmet
(*cassis*, *galea*) differs from the Greek by the absence of a visor.
The simplest form, specified by two helmets found in Etruscan
graves (Fig. 509, *c*, *d*), resembles the pileus, and at the same time
reminds one of the steel cap worn by common soldiers in the
Middle Ages.   A more developed form of the helmet is shown,
Fig. 509, *f*, from an original in the Museo Borbonico.   To the low
semi-globular cap a stripe of metal has been added, surrounding
the head on all sides, and considerably enlarged at the back so as
to protect the neck.   It covers the forehead to about the eyes.
Cheekpieces (*bucculæ*) are added.   The top of the common soldier's
helmet consists of a simple button (see Fig. 509, *e*, from the arch of
Severus); sometimes it is adorned with a short plume: a helmet of
the latter kind is worn by almost all the soldiers on the arch of

a   b   c   d   e   f

Fig. 509.

Constantine.   The helmet of centurions and higher officers are
adorned with three feathers, or with a crest of horsehair (*crista*,
iuba), which was taken off on the march, but put on again in the
battle, so as to distinguish the leaders in the fight (see the two helmets, Fig. 509, *a*, *b*, from the arch of Constantine, where they are
worn by foot-soldiers and horsemen).   The upper part of the body
was protected by an iron cuirass, fashioned according to the lines
of the muscles both in front and at the back, like the old Greek
θώραξ στάδιος.   Servius Tullius re-organized the Roman army of
citizens after the pattern of the Greek phalanx, and adopted the
iron helmet, the oval shield, and the cuirass of the hoplitai for
the two first ranks of the phalanx.   At the later re-organization of
the army the cuirass was dropped by the common soldiers, and
perhaps retained only by the leaders in exceptional cases.   The
Latin name of the cuirass is unknown to us.   The *lorica ferrea*,

which Tacitus (Hist. II. 11) mentions as worn by the Emperor
Otho, was most likely an iron cuirass. Several specimens of the
bronze cuirass are still in existence (Fig. 510, *a*). It was,
perhaps by Camillus, the great reformer of tactics and armour,
exchanged for the *lorica* proper, made of stripes of metal. It was
commonly worn by the legionaries of the empire. From five to
seven stripes of beaten iron or bronze (Fig. 510 *b*), each equal in
width to about three fingers, attached to leather straps, were
fastened round the body with hooks from the
waist up to the armpit, thus forming the breast-
armour (*pectorale*, Fig. 511) proper, while similar
stripes were laid across the shoulders (*humeralia*),
and fastened by means of hooks to the upper
stripes of the pectorale. Several stripes, hanging
down in front, protected the lower part of the
body. Quite as common as the lorica is the tight-
fitting leather jerkin, reaching down a little
lower than the thighs, and worn over the tunic
by the common soldiers on imperial monuments
(see the soldier to the right, Fig. 530). Occasionally (for instance, by a number of soldiers on
the arch of Severus) the lorica, or a portion of
it, is worn over this jerkin. Scale and chain-
armour (*lorica squamata* and *hamata*) was (owing
to its high price) worn in older times only by the hastati and
principes ; at a later period, also, it remained the exclusive dress
of officers and of certain corps of the army (Fig. 512). The Antiquarium of the Royal Museum, Berlin (bronzes, No. 1025), possesses a fragment of a chain-and-scale armour, found near Rome,
in which the scales are put on the meshes of the fine iron mail.

Fig. 510.

Generals, and the emperor himself, wore undoubtedly the
more costly Greek chalkochiton, which, perhaps in an idealised
form, appears on monuments frequently adorned with inlaid or
chiselled ornaments (see, for instance, the military statue of
Caligula, Fig. 510, *c*). The marble statuette of Augustus, found
in 1863 in the villa of the Cæsars, nine miglie from the Porta del
Popolo, is most remarkable, both by the chiselled decoration of the
armour and by the perfect colours in which the marble is painted.

Greaves (*ocrea*) of bronze are found in many of our museums.

They were worn in the time of the Republic by the hastati, principes, and triarii, on the right leg, unprotected by the shield; the cavalry in Polybius's time wore greaves made of leather. In imperial times metal greaves were, at least by the

Fig. 511.   Fig. 512.

legionaries, altogether abandoned for leather or woollen stockings extending over the calf. The foot, to above the ankle, was covered with straps by the whole army (see Figs. 511 and 512).

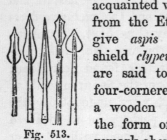

Fig. 513.

According to Diodorus, the Romans, previously to becoming acquainted with the Etruscans, used square shields; from the Etruscans they adopted the common Argive *aspis* (see page 237), or the circular iron shield *clypeus*.* Besides this shield, the Romans are said to have adopted from the Samnites the four-cornered *scutum* (4 feet long by $2\frac{1}{2}$ feet wide), a wooden shield covered with leather, showing the form of a cylinder cut in half (compare our remark about the shield of the gladiators called Samnites, p. 557). The upper and lower edges of the shield were, by

* The Royal Museum, Berlin (bronzes, No. 1008), possesses an Etruscan shield (found in a grave near Corneto) of gilt bronze, richly ornamented. The thinness of the metal in this and other shields found in the graves of Cære and Tarquinii seems to show their purely ornamental character (see Friederichs, "Berlins ant. Bildwerke," II., 1871, p. 218 *et seq.*)

Camillus's order, lined with iron. In the old Roman phalanx the
first class of legionaries carried the clypeus, the second, third, and
fourth classes the scutum; after the Servian re-organization of the army the latter was worn by
hastati, principes, and triarii, while the heavy
iron clypeus disappeared entirely, the light
circular *parma* made of leather being given in
its stead to the light-armed soldier (*velites*).
Of the time when the oval and hexagonal shields
were introduced in the army we have no
certain knowledge. Rectangular, hexagonal,
and oval shields are worn by the Roman soldiers
on the bas-reliefs of one and the same triumphal
gate or column; for instance, on the arch of
Septimius Severus. It therefore may be assumed
with certainty, that the different parts of the
army were distinguished not only by the form,
but also by the painting on their shields
(see Figs. 521, 523, 525, 526) of various signs,
such as appear on the shields of larger or smaller
divisions on the monuments of imperial times.
We there see winged thunderbolts, lightnings
surrounded by wreaths, single and double eagles
("Col. Traian.," 26, 91, 110; "Col. Anton.," 31,
45, 46, 58), rhombic figures, crescents, and crowns
of lilies ("Col. Anton.," 21), laurel crowns round
the umbo of the shield (" Col. Traian.," 71, 72),
and other designs composed of rhomboids, crescents and rays. While marching, the foot-
soldiers frequently hung their shields over their
backs on straps ("Col. Anton."); horsemen
fastened them under the saddle-cloth at the
horse's side ("Col. Traian.," 66).

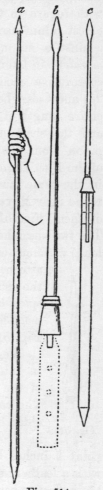

Fig. 514.

The spears used by the different divisions of the Roman army
greatly varied in form; their shape also changed considerably in
the course of centuries (see the different spear-heads, Fig. 513).
The long Etruscan *hasta* (resembling the old Greek lance) is said
to have been introduced by Servius Tullius; Camillus retained
it for the triarii, while to the hastati and principes he gave an

additional javelin (*pilum*), used for throwing. Several heads
of *pila* have been found in the Rhinelands and Switzerland.
Lindenschmit and Köchly * have made careful researches both
with regard to the history and the varieties of the pilum. The
oldest pilum used by the triarii, chiefly for the defence of walls
against a storming enemy, was a long heavy weapon (*pilum
murale*) ; in later times it was used only on rare occasions. The
consecutive modifications of the pilum by Marius (Plutarch,
25) and Cæsar belong to the special history of Roman arms. The
entire length of the Cæsarian pilum was six feet, the iron head
and the shaft being each three feet long. Fig. 514, *a*, shows a
pilum from the tombstone of Q. Petilius Secundus, a private
of the 15th Legion, in the Museum of Bonn. Another tombstone
in the same museum, and two spear-heads (most likely of pila)
found near Mayence, and now in the museum of that city (see one
of them, Fig. 514, *b*), further illustrate the form of the pilum.
The two spear-heads consist of four-edged pieces of iron (two feet
long) with four-edged pyramidal points to them, and with a flat piece
attached to the bottom end, which was let into a split of
the shaft. A four-edged ring was pulled over the
spear-head up the shaft, besides which the iron was
made fast by means of cross nails (see the restored pilum,
Fig. 514, *c*).

Vegetius describes the *spiculum*, a kind of pilum used
in late imperial times. It was 5½ feet long, the size
of the three-edged spear-head being 9 inches to 1 foot.
The soldiers of later imperial times who objected to the
older heavy pilum, frequently used the *vericulum* (called

Fig. 515.

in Vegetius's time *verutum*), 3½ feet long, with an iron
point 5 inches long. About the same time we hear of javelins
with a leathern strap (*amentum*) attached to them, so as to increase
their effect on being thrown (compare our remarks about the ἀγκύλη,
p. 242, as also Clarac, "Musée," II., pl. 148, No. 319). Some
of the troops of late imperial times were armed with arrows to be
thrown (*martiobarbuli, plumbatæ* sc. *sagittæ*), of which every soldier

* "Verhandlungen der 21. Versammlung deutscher Philologen und Schulmänner
in Augsburg." Leipsic, 1863, p. 139 *et seq.* Compare Lindenschmit, "Die vater-
ländischen Alterthümer der F. Hohenzoller'schen Sammlungen zu Sigmaringen."
Mainz, 1860, p. 17 *et seq.*

carried five fastened inside the shield. Their heads were made heavy with lead, and had a barb. Fig. 515 shows an arrow-head of this kind (8 inches long), found near Mayence, at present in the Museum of Wiesbaden.

Of swords (*gladius*) used by Roman soldiers we have to distinguish the older Gallic and the later Spanish swords. The Gallic sword was rather long and heavy; it had no point, and its blade was sharpened on one side only. After the battle of Cannæ, in which the Romans experienced the superiority of the lighter two-edged Spanish sword used by the Carthaginians, the latter weapon was adopted by them. The older sword does not appear on monuments. The two swords shown, Fig. 516, *a* and *b*, are such as were used by common soldiers; of these, numerous specimens are still in existence. Officers undoubtedly used superior weapons, distinguished by the graceful form of the handle (Fig. 516, *c*) or by the valuable material and ornamentation of the scabbard. Fig. 516, *d*, shows a scabbard adorned with gold and silver ornaments; it was found, in 1848, near Mayence, and is, perhaps, a sword of honour presented by Tiberius (whose portrait, *en médaillon*, appears on it) to one of his generals. The Spanish sword was carried in a shoulder-belt (*balteus*, Figs. 511 and 512) or waist-belt (Fig. 523); in the latter way it was worn chiefly by superior officers, and always on the right

Fig. 516.

side, while the old Gallic sword was worn on the left. In close fights the soldiers used to advance the right leg, while in throwing the javelin the left leg was put forward. Besides the sword the soldiers on the imperial monuments frequently have a long narrow dagger on the right side (see the *signifer* in Lersch, "Centralmuseum," II., and the centurio, Clarac, "Musée," II., pl

148, No. 319), which considerably differs from the broad, short dagger, frequently found in the graves of barbarian nations. Longer swords (*spatha*) reappear after the time of Hadrian, used only by certain divisions of the army. Fig. 516, *e*, represents a sabre worn (on arches and columns) only by barbarian soldiers.

Bow (*arcus*) and arrows (*sagitta*) seem to have been first adopted in the time of Marius from the foreign allies, and their

Fig. 517.   Fig. 518.

use always remained limited to these. On imperial monuments we, therefore, see this weapon always in the hands of barbarians or of such soldiers of the Roman army who, by their dress, are marked as auxiliaries (see Figs. 517 and 518). After the wars with Carthage the bow gained greater importance, and troops of Cretan and Balearic bowmen ever since that time formed regular divisions of the Roman infantry. The Asiatic allies sent chiefly bowmen on horseback, covered from head to foot in scale armour (*cataphracti, loricati equites*, Fig. 518). They were renowned for their skill. The bow and arrows used by all these troops exactly resembled those of the Greeks (see two arrow-heads, Fig. 519). Three-edged arrow-heads are frequently found amongst Roman ruins; they were fastened to the shaft with a nail. The crossbow marked amongst the ancients the transition from light to heavy artillery. It was called *arcuballista* (γαστραφέτης), and to bend it the small three-spiked instruments found in our museums were most likely used.

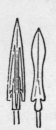

Fig. 519.

Slingers (*fundibalatores*) we find, under the name of *accensi velati*, as a corps of the older Roman army attached to the *rorarii*. Like the bow, the sling gained its real importance after the Carthaginian wars, owing to the skill of the Balearic allies. Dressed in the tunic and sagum, in the folds of which latter thrown over the left arm the ammunition was kept (see Fig. 520), the slinger held his weapon (*funda*, compare p. 248) in the right. The slingers of the Columna Traiana are, moreover, armed with a short sword and a small one-handled shield, while a slinger on the Columna Antonina is without either. The missiles thrown by the slingers were either stones (*lapides missiles*) or pieces of lead in the form of acorns (*glans*); many such, found chiefly at Enna, in Sicily, and at

Fig. 520.

Asculum, are seen in our museums, some with defying inscriptions in Latin or Greek, such as, *pete culum Octaviani, fugitivi peristis, feri Pomp(ejum)*, δέξαι, &c. (see the missiles kept in the Royal Museum, Berlin, Bronzes, No. 1128-42).

Elephants appear in the Roman army for the first time during the war with Philip, after they had been used for many centuries by Asiatic nations, from whom they were adopted by the Greeks. The elephant was conducted by a *rector* riding on the neck of the animal, and pricking it with an instrument called *cuspis*, resembling a *harpe* (Fig. 278, *b*). A bronze coin of the city of Nicæa, with the head of Caracalla, shows on its reverse a *rector* riding on an elephant with the *cuspis* in his hand.

Soldiers on the march had to carry a rather heavy baggage besides their arms. Only a change of arms and the heavy baggage were carried by packhorses and mules (*iumenta sarcinaria*). In imperial times carts on two or four wheels were used for the purpose, as appears from the baggage-trains on the column of Antoninus and the

Fig. 521.

arch of Severus. Amongst the heavy baggage were the tents (*tentorium, tabernaculum*), made of leather or canvas, and the poles and pegs belonging to them. The base of the tent was

about 10 square feet; it had a roof-like cover (see "Col. Anton.,"
Nos. 10 and 26), accommodating about ten men (*contubernium*).
Each *centurio* had, moreover, a separate tent, and each *tribunus*
two for himself and his attendants. The camp of a legion, therefore, consisted of about 500 tents. Poles to mark out the camp,
standards, and tools, and, on large expeditions, stores and hand-
mills, were carried after the army. The legionaries themselves
had, moreover, at least in older times, to carry saws, spades, axes,
hoes, sickles, linen, a cooking apparatus, a change of clothes, and,
on longer expeditions, stores for twelve days, to which list we
have to add, in ante-Cæsarean times, the gabions. The baggage
of the foot-soldier, including arms, weighed about sixty pounds,
or about as much as that of a soldier of the Prussian infantry in
former years. The soldier's knapsack was unknown to the Romans.
Marius greatly eased the burden of the soldiers by the so-called

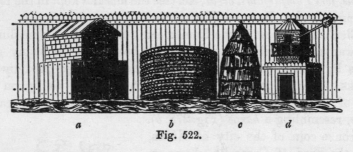

Fig. 522.

Marian mule (*muli Mariani*), that is, a pole with forked ends,
across which a piece of wood was laid; the victuals and dress, being
made into a bundle (*sarcina*) and fastened to the crosspole, were
thus conveniently shouldered, and taken off at the beginning of
the fight. This arrangement seems to have remained unaltered
in imperial times, as appears from a group of marching soldiers on
the column of Trajan (Fig. 521).

To supply the men and horses with food in barren countries
magazines containing corn (*horrea*) and hay (*fœnilia, palearia*) were
instituted on the line of march, places with good communications
by road and water being chosen in preference. Stores of fuel
and wood for gabions, bridges, and besieging engines also were
collected. Such magazines, fortified by palisades, are shown in
the first of the series of bas-reliefs on the columns of both Trajan

and Antoninus (Fig. 522, *a*, *b*, *c*). Fig. 522, *d*, shows one of the fortified sentry-boxes, which were placed at moderate distances from each other. The sentry who had to watch the enemy's movements stood on the gallery surrounding the building, and gave the signal of alarm by lighting a torch.

Fig. 523 shows two *prætoriani* from a bas-relief in the Louvre, restored, it is true, in rather an arbitrary manner.

Augustus instituted an imperial body-guard of nine cohorts (*cohortes prætoriæ* or *prætoriani milites*), stationed in Rome and the neighbouring towns; by Vitellius this guard was increased to sixteen cohorts or 16,000 men, afterwards reduced again to ten cohorts. Their pay was better and their time of service shorter than that of ordinary legionaries, from whom they were also distinguished by their dress. They had barracks (*castra*) assigned to them in Rome by Tiberius; they frequently exercised the most detrimental influence on political affairs, and on the decisions of the emperor himself. Our

Fig. 523.

group distinctly shows the proud, overbearing demeanour of these soldiers.

The standard had the same importance for Roman soldiers as for those of the Middle Ages and of modern times. By it the soldier was sworn; it formed the rallying-point in the battle; its preservation was a point of honour, and its loss brought contempt on the standard-bearer and the legion. In several cases officers threw the colours into the ranks of the enemy or across his fortifications, so as to excite the valour of the troops in its recovery. In the battle on the Trasimenus, the dying standard-bearer buried the eagle (*signum*) with his sword; and at the defeat of Varus the standard-bearer tore the eagle from its pole to hide himself with it in a bog.

The original form of the standard was that of a bunch of hay * fastened to the point of a lance. This hay was changed for

* The bunches of leaves tied together with ribbons frequently seen on the

a cloth (*vexillum*, Fig. 524, *a*) fastened to a transverse piece of
wood; this standard belonged to smaller divisions of infantry or,
more frequently, of cavalry (see "Col. Traian.," Nos. 6, 16, 66;
"Col. Antonin.," Nos. 26, 51, 52). Different from the *vexillum* is
the *signum*, consisting of an animal's form (*insigne*) fastened to
a pole; the animals usually chosen were a she-wolf, horse,
elephant, boar, and capricorn: we also meet with an open hand
(Fig. 524, *c*, *d*, *h*, *i*), usually in the standard of a *maniplus*, while
that of the *cohors* shows the above-mentioned animals. The
common signum of the whole legion was, since Marius, a silver
or golden eagle (*aquila*), always with extended wings, and
frequently holding a thunderbolt in its fangs. Many signa found

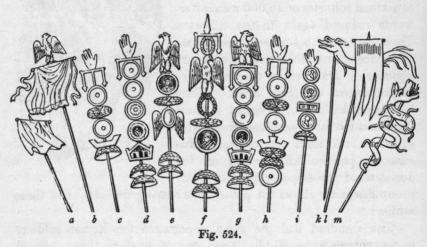

a   b   c   d   e   f   g   h   i   k l   m
Fig. 524.

on coins or bas-reliefs cannot be classified for want of written
evidence. The poles generally showed, besides animals, the images
of generals or emperors (Fig. 524, *d*, *f*, *i*), disks (Fig. 524, *c*, *d*, *g*, *h*),
walls with gates and battlements (Fig. 524, *d*, *g*, *h*), most likely
memorials of conquered cities, *rostra*, and tablets with the number
of the cohors written on them. The eagle-standards, however,
are without these additional decorations (Fig. 541), showing only
occasionally a *vexillum* (Fig. 524, *b*). The chief banner of the
Christian emperors was the so-called *labarum*. Eusebius describes
it as a long lance with a cross-piece; to the latter a square silk flag

standards of later times are perhaps a reminiscence of those primitive ones, Fig.
524, *a*, *c*, *e*, *f*, *h*.

was attached, into which the images of the reigning emperor and his children were woven. To the point of the lance was fastened a golden crown enclosing the monogram of Christ and the sign of the cross. A banner answering this description, save that the monogram of Christ is inscribed on the flag, is seen on the coins of Constantine the Great, Constantius II., Valens, and others; it was considered as the palladium of the army, and always protected by a guard of fifty picked men.

The standards of barbarian nations greatly differ from those of the Romans. Sometimes they resemble mediæval banners (Fig. 524, *l*), but most frequently they appear in the form of dragons with open mouths, showing rows of sharp teeth (Fig. 524, *k, m*); they frequently are seen amongst the trophies on Roman monuments. According to Suidas, these dragons were made of silk; they were inflated with wind through their mouths, emitting it again with a hissing sound through small openings in the tail.

Trumpeters (*tubicines*) and buglers (*cornicines*) formed the military bands. The former had to blow the signals of attack and retreat on their *tuba* or straight trumpet, as also to intone the fanfare at the sacrifice celebrated by the emperor in the presence of the army (see Fig. 498). The signal for the starting of the army was given on the horn (*cornu*), a marching-tune being perhaps played on the same instruments. Buglers, at least, walk in front of the marching army on the column of Antoninus and the arch of Constantine (Fig. 532). The signal of relieving the sentries at night was given on a smaller spiral brass instrument (*bucina*), while the cavalry used a brass instrument (*lituus*) curved like the shaft of an auger (compare Fig. 241, *i*). After the wars with the Germans it seems to have become the custom of the Romans to dress their standard-bearers and buglers in skins of animals (*Wildschur*), after the German fashion (compare Figs. 529, 530).

We now come to the heavy artillery and to the engines destined to protect the storming columns. In case fortifications were attacked without protecting engines, the second rank and those following used to hold their shields horizontally over their heads, while the first rank and the two end men of each rank held theirs vertically in front of them. In this manner a protecting roof resembling the shell of a tortoise (*testudo*) was formed (Fig. 525).

A regular siege of fortified places of course required many preparations. First of all, the besieged city was surrounded by a wall with bastions (*circumvallatio*), so as to cut off supplies. From this circumvallation the further operations were conducted. Sheds (*musculi*) were erected, under cover of which the miners worked and the storming party mounted the breach. Similar engines of protection for bowmen, slingers, and diggers were the *crates* (hurdle), *plutei* (sheds), *vineæ* (literally bowers of vine

Fig. 525.

branches), &c. The besieging wall (*agger*) and the walking towers (*turres ambulatoriæ* or *mobiles*) had to be erected, and the heavy besieging engines (*tormenta*) placed in favourable positions. Of the latter we have descriptions; while, on the other hand, the specimens seen on the columns of Trajan and Antoninus render us but little assistance in forming an idea of their aspect. Accurate descriptions, founded on technical knowledge and scholarly research, we owe to the joint efforts of Rüstow and Köchly.*

* Rüstow and Köchly, "Geschichte des griechischen Kriegswesens," p. 196 *et seq.*, 307 *et seq.*, 378 *et seq.* Rüstow, "Heerwesen and Kriegführung C. Julius Cæsar's," pp. 137—154. "Griechische Kriegsschriftsteller, griechisch und deutsch, mit kritischen und erklärenden Anmerkungen von Köchly und Rüstow."

We mention a few engines occurring on the monuments of the imperial epoch.

After the wall of the beleaguered city had been approached sufficiently, a strong beam, the end of which, cased in iron, had the shape of a ram's head (whence the name *aries, κριός*), was brought into action. The smaller and older battering-ram was knocked against the walls at regular intervals by a number of strong men (see the attack by barbarian soldiers on a Roman fortification on the column of Trajan, Fig. 526). Amongst the smaller battering-rams we also count the *aries subrotatus*, resting on wheels, which were used up to a late period (see Fig. 460, *l*, from a bas-relief on an earthen lamp). The Greeks greatly perfected the battering-ram by introducing, instead of

Fig. 526.

the short beam, a mast composed of several pieces, the whole from 60 to 100 feet long (that invented by Hegetor, of Byzantium, measured 180 feet), which was suspended from a horizontal beam, and put in motion by means of ropes fastened to the beams. Another large battering-ram stood on a sort of bank, and could be pushed backwards and forwards by means of rollers.

To protect the battering-ram, and the soldiers working it, against the enemy's missiles, another engine, the so-called *testudo arietaria* (χελώνη κριοφόρος), was erected—a wooden frame or house (Fig. 527) with a slanting roof, to which frequently a smaller structure of the same kind, with a ram's head

Fig. 527.

protruding from its gable, was appended. Wall-sickles (*falx muralis*) to tear the stones out of the wall, and the wall-drill (*terebra, τρύπανον*), consisting of a battering-ram with a sharp point, were protected by similar roofs. The besieged threw pots of fire, torches of pitch, melted lead, burning arrows, and stones on the storming columns (Fig. 525). They interrupted the work of the besiegers in various manners, tried to set fire to their engines or to crush them. Large stones, suspended by ropes, slings, and

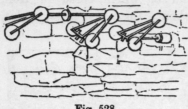

Fig. 528.

large pincers, were used to catch hold of and divert the ram; sand-bags or mats of reed were let down from the battlements to neutralise its force. An engine of defence difficult to explain appears on the Columna Traiana (Fig. 528). We have already mentioned the *musculus* (χελώνη διορυκτίς), a wooden structure covered with a roof, which, with its straight long side was pushed against the wall, to protect the sappers employed in undermining the foundation of the wall; an engine of this kind, resting on wheels (perhaps a *musculus*), appears on the Columna Antoniniana, pulled and pushed along by horses and soldiers on their march.

It is difficult to give a distinct idea of the working and moving of the large walking towers (*turris ambulatoria, mobilis,* πύργος), although their construction is sufficiently described by ancient authors. According to Diades, a Greek military authority, the smallest tower of this kind had a height of at least 90 feet by a base of 25½ square, and contained ten different stories, connected with each other by steps (*tabulata* or *tecta,* whence *turris contabulata,* στέγη). The beams protruding from the outer surface by several yards supported galleries with wooden battlements, surrounding the whole tower. The highest story, or, in other terms, the upper platform, covered with a roof, was the place for the light artillery, while the water and various contrivances for extinguishing flames were kept in the bottom story. On a level with the wall of the beleaguered city a drawbridge (*pons,* ἐπιβάθρα, σαμβύκη) was constructed to open the way to the top of the enemy's fortifications. About the way of moving the towers nothing appears in ancient writers.

To cross unfordable rivers light boats were used, consisting of wooden frames, timbered on the spot, the sides consisting of hides and osiers. In imperial times each legion carried ready-made pontoons with it. The bridges made of these boats were constructed by first placing the pontoons in their right position, which was done by means of light skiffs. They were anchored by means of pyramidally shaped baskets filled with stones. Beams with boards laid across them connected the boats with each other; wooden rails added to the firmness of the structure, and prevented accidents through falling over the edge of the bridge. Sometimes walking-towers were placed on one end of the bridge to protect it against the enemy. Fig. 529 illustrates the crossing of the Danube by the Roman army on a bridge constructed by the Emperor Trajan.

Fig. 529.

We add a representation of an *allocutio*, or speech of the general to his army (Fig. 530), a subject frequently treated on coins, and occurring on the columns of Trajan and Antoninus. Surrounded by his officers, standard-bearers, &c., the emperor used to address the army from a raised standpoint, praising, blaming, or encouraging to new deeds of valour, according to circumstances; from here he pronounced the punishment of cowardice, which was at once executed by his lictors*; from here

---

* We add a few remarks about the *fasces*, seen in the hands of the lictors, Fig. 530 (compare Fig. 540). The fasces were bundles of rods (*virgæ*) of elm or birch-wood, tied together round the handle of an axe (*securis*) with (most likely red) straps. The iron of the axe, which was the executioner's tool, protruded from the sticks. The fasces were carried on their left shoulders by the lictors, who walked in front of certain magistrates, making room for them, and compelling all people to move out of the way (*summovere*), barring Vestals and Roman matrons. To about

he divided the prizes awarded by him, or the army itself, to the
bravest among them.

108. Military decorations and rewards of valour (*dona, præmia
militaria*) occur in many forms amongst the Romans. We pass
over such *dona* as a share of the booty, advancement, or the
honourable mentioning of a soldier's name before the assembled

Fig. 530.

legion. The highest military decoration was the crown of grass
(*corona graminea*), awarded, according to Pliny ("Hist. Nat.,"
XXII. 3, 4), only after a desperate deed of valour, and by
common consent of the whole army. "All other rewards were
given by the general to the soldiers, but this the soldiers gave to
their leader. It was also called crown of siege (*corona obsidionalis*)

the end of the Republic, when a special executioner was appointed, the lictors
inflicted capital punishment. The king was entitled to twelve fasces, the same
number being granted to the consuls (after the passing of P. Valerius Publicola's
law "de provocatione ad populum," only one of the two consuls within the walls of
Rome was allowed to have the axe carried in front of him), or the officials endowed
with *consularis potestas*, also to *decemviri*, war-tribunes, and proconsuls outside Rome.
The dictator was entitled to twenty-four lictors, the magister equitum appointed by
him to six, the Roman prætor to two, the provincial prætor to six, an equal
number being allowed to proprætors. Since 42 B.C., the Flamen Dialis and the
Vestals also were entitled to one lictor each. In case a higher official met his inferior
in the street, he was saluted by the lictors of the latter withdrawing the axe and
lowering the fasces (*fasces submittere*).

in case a whole camp had been delivered from a siege or dishonourable terms. It was composed of green herbs picked on the spot where the besieged had been delivered." This honour was conferred only in very rare cases.

The *corona triumphalis,* a laurel crown, was given to generals returning in triumph from a victorious campaign. Originally it was made of real leaves, afterwards imitated in gold ; after Cæsar's dictatorship it became the diadem of the emperors, worn by them in the theatre and circus. The radiated crown (*corona radiata*), at first a decoration of the images of the dead, occurs after Nero's time on senatorial coins, but did not become the imperial crown till the third century. The myrtle crown (*corona myrtea*), worn by the generals at the so-called *ovatio* (small triumph, whence its other name *ovalis*), resembles the triumphal crown. The rescue of a citizen from the throng of battle was rewarded with the *corona civica,* made of oak-leaves. The heads of Augustus and Galba are crowned with it on several coins ; still more frequently we see it on the reverses of imperial coins, with the surrounding motto : OB CIVES SERVATOS. He who first mounted the walls of a besieged city or camp received the golden *corona muralis,* also called *castrensis* or *vallaris.* The *corona rostrata, navalis,* or *classica* was the reward of him who first boarded the enemy's vessel. It was awarded on rare occasions, and only to commanders. Agrippa received it after the double victory of Actium. We see it, on a gold coin, adorning the head of Agrippa, a mural crown being placed on the top of the *corona navalis ;* the latter, in the form of a laurel-wreath studded with rostra, also appears on a bronze coin of the city of Nikopolis, founded by Augustus after the battle of Actium.

Another class of decorations adorned the chest of the brave soldier. We first mention the chain of honour (*torques*), originally worn by barbarian leaders (we remind the reader of the single combat of T. Manlius with a Gallic warrior, to which he owed his surname Torquatus), but afterwards adopted by the Romans, who distinguished a heavy kind (*torques* proper) and a lighter kind (*catellæ*), wound several times round the neck and hanging down over the chest. To these we add the decorations in our modern sense, *i.e.* small round silver tablets (*phaleræ*) adorned with bas-reliefs, resembling the tablets found on the standard of the cohortes.

Since Caracalla they consisted of large gold medals, frequently adorned with jewels, and fastened by means of straps across the cuirass, as is proved by the *phaleræ* found on the Lauersfort estate, near Crefeld. We finally name amongst signs of honour, armrings (*armillæ*), the *hasta pura* (a lance of precious metal with a button instead of a point), and the different kinds of

Fig. 531.

vexilla, named according to their colours *pura, argentea, cærulea,* or *bicolora*. The tombstones of the centurio Q. Sertorius, at Verona, of the standard-bearer, Cn. Musius, at Mayence, and of the *legatus* Manius Cælius, killed in the battle lost by Varus (Fig. 531), show the profusion with which emperors and generals rewarded military merit. Cælius is adorned with one or even two civic crowns, his neck is encircled with a massive torques; two heavy rings, held by a ribbon laid across the shoulders, hang down on his chest, which is adorned besides with five medals attached to straps; he also wears bracelets round his knuckles. L. Siccius Denatus, the tribune of the people, was rewarded for his valour, proved in one hundred and twenty battles, with 22 *hastæ puræ*, 25 *phaleræ*, 83 *torques*, 160 *armillæ*, and 26 *coronæ*, viz. 14 *civicæ*, 8 *aureæ*, 3 *murales*, and one *obsidionalis*.

109. The highest reward of the commander was the triumphal entrance. At first it was awarded by senate and people to real merit in the field, and its arrangement was simple and dignified; but soon it became an opportunity of displaying the results of insatiable Roman rapacity and love of conquest. Only the dictators, consuls, prætors, and, in late republican times, occasionally legates, were permitted by the senate to enter Rome in triumph, the permission to the legate being granted only in case he had commanded independently (*suis auspiciis*), and conducted the army to Rome from a victorious campaign *in sua provincia*. As in later times it was impossible to conduct the whole army from distant provinces to Rome, the last-mentioned condition was dispensed with, the claim of the commander to a triumph being

acknowledged in case in one of the battles gained by him 5,000 enemies had been killed. The senate granted the expenses necessary for the procession after the quæstor urbanus had examined and confirmed the commander's claims. Streets and squares through which the procession had to pass were festively adorned. The temples were opened, and incense burnt on the altars. Improvised stands were erected in the street, filled with festive crowds shouting "Io triumphe!" The commander, in the meantime, collected his troops near the temples of Bellona and Apollo, outside the gates of Rome; the *imperium* within the walls being exceptionally granted him during the triumph. The victor was met at the *porta triumphalis* by the senate, the city magistrates, and numerous citizens, who took the lead of the procession, while lictors opened a way through the crowd. After the city dignitaries followed tibicines, after them the booty, consisting of armour, standards arranged as trophies, also models of the cities or ships taken from the enemy, and pictures of battles, tablets with the deeds of the victor inscribed on them, statues personifying the rivers and towns of the subjected country—all these being carried by crowned soldiers at the points of long lances or on portable stands (*furculæ*) ; we further mention treasures of art, valuable plate and vases, silver and gold coins, and products of the conquered soil. Fettered kings, princes, and nobles followed, doomed to detention in the Mamertine prison. Next came sacrificial oxen with gilt horns, accompanied by priests ; and finally, preceded by singers, musicians, and jesters, the triumphal chariot drawn by four horses. Clad in a toga picta and the tunica palmata, temporarily taken from the statue of the Capitoline Jupiter, the triumphator stood in his chariot holding the eagle-crowned ivory sceptre* in his hand, while a servus publicus standing behind him held the corona triumphalis over his head. The army brought up the rear of the procession, which moved from the Campus Martius through the circus of Flaminius to the Porta Carmentalis, and thence, by way of the Velabrum and the Circus Maximus, the Via Sacra and the Forum,

---

* According to a custom introduced by Augustus, the emperors wore a crown and held a branch of laurel taken from a grove which that emperor had planted at the ninth milestone of the Via Flaminia, near the Villa of Livia. After the triumph, the laurel-branch was planted again.

to the Capitol.   Here the triumphator deposited his golden crown
in the lap of the Capitoline Jupiter, and sacrificed the usual
suovetaurilia.   A festive meal concluded the day.   In the last
centuries of the Republic, when the art-treasures of Greece and
the wealth of the East were paraded in these processions, one day

Fig. 534.   Fig. 533.   Fig. 532.

was found insufficient.   The triumph of Sulla, for instance, lasted
two; that of Æmilius Paullus, after his victory over Perseus,
three days.   The last triumph of a Roman general was that
granted to Octavianus, after his victory over Antonius.   After this
the emperors reserved the right of the triumphal entrance to

Fig. 535.

themselves, the *ornamenta triumphalia*, consisting of the toga
picta, the tunica palmata, the Scipio eburneus, the sella curulis, the
currus triumphalis, and the corona laurea being granted to the
generals instead.   The emperors immortalised their feats by the

erection of triumphal arches. Our illustrations of the triumphs
are taken from the bas-reliefs of several imperial monuments, being
arranged in the order indicated above. The buglers opening the
procession (Fig. 532) are taken from the arch of Constantine, as

Fig. 536.

are also the soldiers following them, who carry Victories and other
statuettes (Fig. 533).   The next following figure of a warrior and
his tropæum (Fig. 534) we have had to compose from various statues
for want of an original suiting our purpose; the soldier himself is

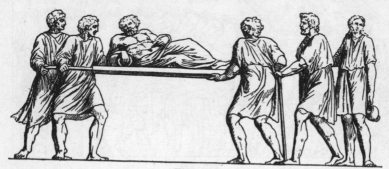

Fig. 537.

from the arch of Severus, the trophy from the theatre of Orange.
Fig. 534, soldiers with carts containing stores, is taken from the
column of Severus: we add it for the sake of completeness.
Fig. 536, from the arch of Titus, shows soldiers carrying the

treasure of the temple of Jerusalem: in front the golden table of
sacrifice, the chalice, the *tubæ* used at the Jewish service, and
further back the seven-branched candlestick. Magistrates clad in
the toga accompany these valuable pieces of booty. Fig. 537,

Fig. 538.   Fig. 539.

from the same arch, shows the river-god Jordan in a similar
position to those of Rhenus and Nilus in the Vatican. The group
of fettered Parthian princes (Fig. 538) is taken from the arch of
the Goldsmiths. Fig. 539, from the arch of Titus, shows an ox

Fig. 540.

led by a butcher and accompanied by priests. Fig. 540, lastly,
shows the emperor, with the sceptre in his right, in his triumphal
chariot. The corona triumphalis is held over his head by the
Goddess of Victory, while Roma leads the horses of the quadriga.

Lictors and senators surround the chariot. Sometimes the chariot was drawn by four elephants, as is proved by monumental (coins) and written evidence. Fig. 541, from the arch of Constantine, shows the sacrifice performed by Trajan in the presence of his army.

Fig. 541.

The *ovatio* was granted for less important conquests, or to a general for victories not won *suis auspiciis.* The victor, adorned with the toga prætexta and the myrtle crown, originally used to walk ; in later times he rode on horseback.

110. *Justa facere* or *ferre* was the expression used for doing the last honour to the dead (compare the Greek expressions τὰ δίκαια and τὰ νόμιμα, § 60). The nearest relative used to receive the last breath of the dying person in a kiss (*extremum spiritum ore excipere*) ; his hand also closed the eyes and the mouth of the deceased, so as to produce a peaceful impression of death. After this, the name of the deceased or a wail was uttered several times by those present, so as to make sure of his death, after which the last farewell (*extremum vale*) was said (*conclamatio*).

The preparation for the burial naturally varied according to the wealth of the owner. The body of a poor person was, after the usual ablutions, put on a bier (*sandapila*) and carried at night by the *vespillones* (carriers of corpses) to the common burial-ground outside the Esquiline gate—a quarter chosen by Horace for the scene of Canidia's conjurings, but transformed by Mæcenas into a park (*horti Mæcenatiani*). Burial-clubs (*collegia tenuiorum*) were formed by the poorer classes, from whose funds, supplied by annual contributions, a certain sum was paid to the surviving families of the members. The burials of the wealthy classes were conducted on a more splendid scale. The death was first announced to the *libitinarius* (an official of the temple of Venus Libitina), who inserted the name in the register of deaths (a

register of births was kept at the temple of Venus Lucina). The
libitinarius furnished for payment the utensils and slaves necessary for the preparation and burial of the corpse. The corpse was
taken from the death-bed and laid on the ground (*deponere*), where
it was washed with hot water and anointed by the *pollinctor*,
partly in order to take away from the terror of death, partly to
stop the decomposition, because amongst well-to-do people it was
kept for seven days. Clad in a toga and adorned with the richest
garments, the body was placed on the *lectus funebris*, a bed entirely
made of ivory, or at least resting on ivory legs, over which purple
blankets embroidered with gold were spread. Flowers and foliage
adorned the bed, but not the body itself, as was the custom
amongst the Greeks; only crowns of honour, earned during their
lifetime, were deposited in the graves of dead persons, and have
repeatedly been discovered there, being made of very thin gold
leaf. The lectus funebris was put in the atrium of the house,
with the foot end turned towards the door, and a pan with
incense was placed by its side. Branches of cypress and fir-trees
were fastened in front of the house as signs of mourning.

After having been exhibited for seven days, the body was buried
in the forenoon, when the streets were filled with the bustle of life,
and when the largest attendance of invited guests and spectators
might be expected. In case the funeral was connected with public
games, a herald solicited the attendance of the people. A public
burial of this kind was called *funus indictivum* or *funus publicum*.
The following is the formula used by the public crier in inviting
the spectators: " *Ollus Quiris leto datus est. Exsequias (L. Titio.
L. filio) ire cui commodum est, iam tempus est. Ollus ex œdibus
effertur.*" The procession was arranged in front of the house of
the deceased by the *dissignator*, with the aid of an *accensus* and of
one or several lictors to keep order. Ten tibicines (this was the
highest number permitted by the law of the twelve tablets)
opened the procession, followed, at least in older times, by female
mourners (*præficæ*) singing plaintive songs (*næniæ, mortualia*) in
honour of the deceased. A band of actors following served to
attract and entertain the crowd; they recited passages from tragic
poets with reference to the deceased, or they acted comic scenes,
one amongst their number sometimes mimicking the peculiarities
of the dead person. In front of the deceased, the wax masks of

his ancestors were worn by persons appointed for the purpose; the historic costume of the dead person, including even his insignia, had to be rendered exactly. The collateral lines of old families used to send their ancestors to the funeral of a relative, while *parvenus* frequently paraded images of fictitious persons. The bier was carried by the nearest relatives, or by the slaves liberated by the last will of the deceased. Other relatives, friends, and freedmen surrounded the bier in black garments without gold ornaments. In imperial times, when the wearing of colours had become customary, white was considered mourning, at least for women. The procession went to the Forum, where the bier was set down in front of the rostra, whereat the wearers of the ancestral masks sat down on the sellæ curules, and one of the relatives mounted the tribune to deliver an oration (*laudatio funebris*) in honour of the deceased and of his ancestors, whose images were present. The expression of Cicero as to the earlier Greek funeral eulogiums, "*nam mentiri nefas habebatur,*" was not strictly acted upon by the Romans, their orators refraining at least from all censure. After the speech was over, the procession proceeded to the burial-place in the order described.

The corpse was either placed in a sarcophagus (*arca, capulus*) and deposited in a grave made of brick or stone, according to the older custom* retained by some patrician families, for instance, by the Cornelii, up to a late period, or it was burnt, and the ashes, collected in an urn, deposited in the grave-chamber (see § 77). Cremation is said to have been introduced by Sulla, who feared that his body would be defiled by the people. Inhumation in coffins (*humatio*), however, by no means ceased; both kinds of burial existed together, no law being made on the subject. Each burial-place had a separate enclosure for burning the bodies (*ustrinum*), private ustrina being attached to large family-graves where there was no law to prevent it. In the ustrinum the pyre (*pyra, rogus*) was erected, the height and decorations of which again depended upon the wealth of the family. It consisted of pieces of wood and other combustible materials, piled up in the shape of an altar, on which the bier with the body was placed, after having

---

* According to Pliny (" Hist. Nat.," II. 98 ; compare XXXVI. 27), there existed near Assos, in Troas, a kind of stone which, made into coffins, destroyed the corpse in forty days, excepting the teeth, and which therefore was called flesh-eater (*sarcophagos*).

been covered with balsam, incense, utensils, ornaments, or weapons. The pile was ignited by one of the nearest relatives or friends, with face averted, the bystanders raising a *conclamatio.*

After the pile was consumed (*bustum*) the hot ashes were extinguished with wine, and the bones collected by the relatives (amidst acclamations to the manes of the deceased) in the folds of their mourning robes (*ossilegium*) ; a previous washing of the hands was, of course, not forgotten. The remains were sprinkled with milk and wine, then dried with linen, and mixed with scents, after which preparations they were enclosed in an urn (*ossa condere*), to be afterwards deposited in the grave-chamber. The last farewell was spoken by those present in the words : "*Have anima candida,*" or "*Terra tibi levis sit,*" or "*Molliter cubent ossa ;*" and after the usual lustrations had been performed the mourners separated. Urns (*urna, olla ossuaria*), frequently in the form of hydriæ, or (in Etruscan graves) of cinerary boxes with covers to them, are found in most of the grave-chambers described in § 77 *et seq.*, as also in the columbaria (Fig. 401 *et seq.*) and sarcophagi : they are generally made of burnt clay, travertine, marble, alabaster, porphyry, or bronze. We also meet with glass urns, mostly protected by leaden cases of a shape similar to that of the urn : three urns of this kind have been found in the abovementioned grave of Nævoleia Tyche at Pompeii.

The second offering to the manes, and a meal connected with it, took place on the ninth day after the burial (*novemdialia, feriæ novemdiales*), in accordance with the Greek custom. On the steps of the grave-monument a simple meal (*epulæ funebres*), consisting of milk, honey, oil, and blood of the sacrificed animals, was prepared ; larger tombs had a separate *triclinium funebre* attached to them, where the meal was taken. The limited space of the necropolis did not admit of numerous guests, for which reason wealthy people (particularly in cases where games were connected with the funeral) used to distribute meat (*viscerationes*), in later times money, amongst the people. The sacrifices to the manes were repeated by the relatives on the anniversary of the birth or death of the deceased (*parentalia*) : the 21st of February of each year was the day of the dead celebrated by the whole people by sacrifices to the manes (*feralia*).

The funeral of the emperor was arranged in the grandest way, particularly if his *consecratio* by the senate was connected with it. Cæsar was the first Roman received amongst the gods as Divus Julius by decree of the senate : Octavianus instituted a permanent worship of this divinity. The same honour after death was awarded to Augustus himself, and after him to many emperors and empresses down to Constantine the Great ; their names appear on coins marked as consecration-medals by the word CONSECRATIO inscribed on them. Herodian (IV. 3) gives a full account of the ceremony of consecration. " It is the Roman custom," he says, " to consecrate the emperors who leave heirs. The mortal remains are buried, according to custom, in a splendid manner ; but the wax image of the emperor is placed on an ivory bed covered with gold-embroidered carpets in front of the palace. The expression of the face is that of one dangerously ill. To the left side of the bed stand, during greater part of the day, the members of the senate ; to the right the ladies entitled by birth or marriage to appear at court, in the usual simple white mourning dresses, without gold ornaments or necklaces. This ceremony lasts seven days, during which time the imperial physicians daily approach the bed as if to examine the patient, who, of course, is declining rapidly. At last they declare the emperor dead ; after which the bier is carried by the highest-born knights and the younger senators through the Via Sacra to the old Forum, and there deposited on a scaffolding built in the manner of a terrace. On one side stand young patricians, on the other noble ladies, intoning hymns and pæans in honour of the deceased to a solemn, sad tune ; after which the bier is taken up again and carried to the Campus Martius. A wooden structure in the form of a house has been erected on large blocks of wood on a square base ; the inside has been filled with dry sticks ; the outside is adorned with gold - embroidered carpets, ivory statues, and various sculptures. The bottom story, a little lower than the second, shows the same form and ornamentation as this ; it has open doors and windows : above these two stories rise others, growing narrow towards the top like a pyramid (Fig. 542). The whole

Fig. 542.

structure might be compared to the lighthouses (φάροι) erected in harbours. The bier is placed in the second story, spices, incense, odoriferous fruits, and herbs being heaped round it. After the whole room has been filled with incense, the knights move in procession round the whole structure, and perform some military evolutions; they are followed by chariots filled with persons wearing masks, and clad in purple robes, who represent historic characters, such as celebrated generals and kings. After these ceremonies are over the heir to the throne throws a torch into the house, into which, at the same time, flames are dashed from all sides, which, fed by the combustible materials and the incense, soon begin to devour the whole building. At this juncture an eagle rises into the air from the highest story as from a lofty battlement, and carries, according to the idea of the Romans, the soul of the dead emperor to heaven (Fig. 543); from that moment he partakes of the honours of the gods."

Fig. 543.

LIST OF ILLUSTRATIONS.